D0444502

Success with Rhododendrons and Azaleas

Revised Edition

Reiley, H. Edward.
Success with
rhododendrons and azalea
c2004.
33305213476504
la   03/18/08

Success with Rhododendrons and Azaleas

Revised Edition

H. Edward Reiley

TIMBER PRESS

Portland ■ Cambridge

Text copyright © 2004 by H. Edward Reiley
Photographs copyright © 2004 by H. Edward Reiley unless otherwise noted
All rights reserved

Published in 2004 by
Timber Press, Inc.
The Haseltine Building
133 S.W. Second Avenue, Suite 450
Portland, Oregon 97204-3527, U.S.A.

Timber Press
2 Station Road
Swavesey
Cambridge CB4 5QJ, U.K.

www.timberpress.com

Printed in China

Library of Congress Cataloging-in-Publication Data
Reiley, H. Edward.
   Success with rhododendrons and azaleas / H. Edward Reiley.– Rev. ed.
      p. cm.
Includes bibliographical references and indexes.
   ISBN 0-88192-637-X (pbk.)
  1. Rhododendrons. 2. Azaleas. I. Title.
SB413.R47R35 2004
635.9'3366–dc22
                      2003022816

A catalogue record for this book is also available from the British Library.

To my mother, whose love of flowers
inspired me to spend a lifetime gardening
and enjoying nature and its beauty,
and to my wife, Mary,
whose support over the years
has made it all possible.

Contents

Color plates follow page 80

Preface

Rhododendrons and azaleas are more exacting in their cultural require-ments than many commonly grown plants and so will not readily grow in every garden. The genus *Rhododendron* is so diverse, however, that with some modification of site and the correct selection of cultivar, most garden sites can be modified to meet the plants' requirements.

Wherever successfully grown, rhododendrons and azaleas are without equal as landscape plants. The evergreen forms are beautiful year-round. The deciduous azaleas have beautiful fall foliage and offer some of the brightest colors of yellow and orange, not often found in flowers of hardy rhododen-drons or in evergreen azaleas. As a group, they surpass any other plant in the landscape in their beauty.

This book is written out of years of practical knowledge of propagating and growing rhododendrons and azaleas in the garden, nursery, and landscape. It will not simply advise the reader on what needs to be done to successfully grow these plants, but gives specific details on how this can be accomplished. This book represents my personal experience and successful techniques used over many years of growing these beautiful plants. Technical information is derived from a number of state university experimental stations and the U.S. Department of Agriculture (USDA).

I believe that the information presented here is sufficient to lead the begin-ner to success in growing these plants and will assist current growers to grow rhododendrons and azaleas more successfully. A word of caution is in order, however. By becoming a successful grower, the reader will be exposed to a contagion for which there is no cure. Once infected with an appreciation of rhododendrons and azaleas most gardeners spend a lifetime collecting these most beautiful of all plants.

Acknowledgments

I thank my wife Mary for the many hours at the computer; Don Hyatt, Don Voss, and Sandra McDonald for their assistance; Lisa DiDonato for her patience and editorial skill; and all those listed below who provided pictures, information, and encouragement:

Mrs. Melvin Allen, Santa Cruz, California
Frank Arsen, Lindenhurst, New York
Mrs. George Beasley Sr., Lavonia, Georgia
William Bedwell, Richmond, Virginia
Walter Behrendt, St. Louis, Missouri
Werner Brack, St. James, New York
Richard Brooks, Concord, Massachusetts
Dr. Henry Cathey, Washington, D.C.
Dr. Richard Chaiken, Palm Beach Gardens, Florida
Dee Daneri, Fortuna, California
Robert Dickhout, Niagara Falls, Ontario, Canada
Dr. Ethyle Dutki, University of Maryland
Russell Dyer, Southampton, Hampshire, U.K.
Mr. and Mrs. Eaton, Lesley, Australia
Stephen and Anne Fox, Manchester, U.K.
John Golab, Barrington, Illinois
Dr. Francis R.Gouin, College Park, Maryland
Harold Greer, Eugene, Oregon
John Hammond, Lancashire, England
Virginia Heller, Detroit, Michigan
John Hixson, Watsonville, California

Dr. H. A. J. Hoitink, Ohio State University
Don Hyatt, McLean, Virginia
Paul S. James, Boones Mill, Virginia
Adele Jones, Lake Oswego, Oregon
Michael Jurgens, Berkshire, U.K.
Clive L. Justice, Vancouver, British Columbia
Kenneth McDonald Jr., Hampton, Virginia
Dr. Sandra McDonald, Hampton, Virginia
Pete McNees, Tuscumbia, Alabama
Wayne Mezitt, Hopkinton, Massachusetts
Joe B. Parks, Dover, New Hampshire
Eugene Paschall, Palos Heights, Illinois
Eleanor Philp, Fort Bragg, California
Dr. Thomas L. Ring, Bellaire, Ohio
C. E. Robinson, Auburn, Alabama
Mrs. J. J. Sandifur, Aberdeen, Washington
Brian Schram, Fenwick, Ontario, Canada
Tom Schuetz, Mechanicsburg, Pennsylvania
Dr. Paula M. Shreusbury, University of Maryland
Clarence Smith, Gaston, Oregon
Hugh B. Sproul Jr., Staunton, Virginia
Mike Stewart, Sandy, Oregon
Dr. John T. Thornton, Franklinton, Louisiana
Robert B. Trumble, College Park, Maryland
Donald H. Voss, Vienna, Virginia
Dr. Sara Wright, USDA, Beltsville, Maryland

1

Taxonomy and History

The genus Rhododendron belongs to the family Ericaceae, commonly called the heath family. The genus is one of the largest in the plant kingdom, made up of approximately 850 species. Members of the genus range in size from alpines that may be 2 in. (5 cm) tall to tree size plants up to 80 ft. (24 m) tall. They bear flowers in nearly every color other than true blue, and some, especially those producing lighter colored flowers, are fragrant.

There is no need to overwhelm the novice rhododendron grower with classification and listing of all of the *Rhododendron* species. For present purposes we need only note that all *Rhododendron* species can be assigned to one of two divisions: elepidote and lepidote. The rhododendrons commonly classified as azaleas will be discussed later. The major difference between azaleas and rhododendrons are:

▶ Azalea flowers usually have five stamens; other rhododendrons have ten or more stamens.
▶ Azalea leaves and stems never have scales, as do the lepidote rhododendrons.
▶ Azalea leaves have simple hairs, unlike the branched hairs that form the indumentum on some other rhododendrons.

The elepidote rhododendrons are nonscaly, large-leaved forms that generally grow to be large plants at maturity. The lepidote species are scaly-leaved forms that generally mature at a smaller size. (*Scaly* refers to the presence or absence of small, almost microscopic scales on the underside of the plant leaves.) The two groups differ sufficiently in their genetic makeup that hybridizing between them is virtually impossible. Most growers' catalogs, as well as other materials describing rhododendrons, maintain the elepidote-lepidote differentiation.

The many species in the genus *Rhododendron* are not only diverse in size, shape, and color but also in the growing conditions they require. Up and down Asian mountain slopes, they are found growing as epiphytes in the tops of trees in rainforests and as terrestrials under trees, along river beds, on rocks on bare cliffs, on crumbled rocky sites, on ledges, in ravines, and in open grassland. Light conditions vary from full sun to complete shade. They so dominate the terrain in some areas that entire mountain slopes are completely covered, yet in other cases they may appear as single trees. Very few plant groups show as much variability as the genus *Rhododendron*.

In *Plant Hunters' Paradise* (1938), Kingdon-Ward observed that rhododendrons simply change their growth form as they adapt to different altitudes, a characteristic shared by no other genus. He found them growing from sea level to 15,000 ft. (4572 m) in the Himalayas, in what he described as "three broad belts." The first belt, from sea level to 5000 ft. (1524 m), was dominated by small, often epiphytic shrubs; the second belt, from 5000 to 10,000 ft. (1524 to 3048 m), as trees and shrubs; and the third belt, from 10,000 to 15,000 ft. (3048 to 4572 m), with shrubs becoming increasingly more dwarf at the higher elevations.

Rhododendrons at first were believed to have originated in Asia, for it is here that the greatest number of species exists in the wild. The center of origin seems to be at about where Burma, Yunnan, and Tibet meet because the widest range of species is found in this area. The region is marked by high humidity, the atmosphere is always wet and misty because the rains persist all summer, and deep snow covers the ground in winter. From this area they continued to spread around the world to wherever soil and climate allowed growth. Figures 1.1 and 1.2 show the distribution in the wild in North America and in Europe and Asia, respectively. With a few minor exceptions, their distribution is confined to the Northern Hemisphere. Dr. David G. Leach, in his *Rhododendrons of the World* (1961, p. 19), wrote, "They reach their southernmost limit in northern Australia, which has one species, possibly an immigrant from a secondary concentration of about 200 species in New Guinea." Recent evidence shows that rhododendrons existed more than 50 million years ago over much of North America and Europe, and perhaps other areas, in the same form as found in Asia today. Climatic change or other natural catastrophe appears to have eliminated them from much of their previous habitat. A look at their native habitat indicates that *Rhododendron* generally inhabit mountains.

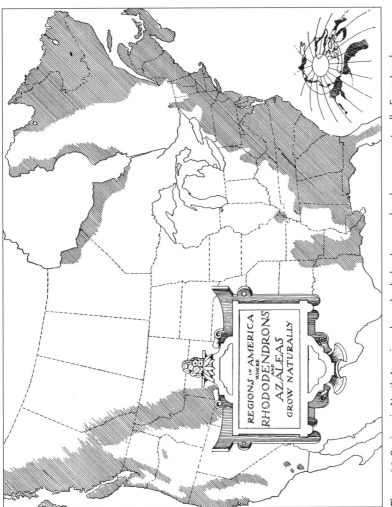

Figure 1.1. Regions in North America where rhododendrons and azaleas grow naturally. From Leach, *Rhododendrons of the World* (1961, 20). Reprinted by permission.

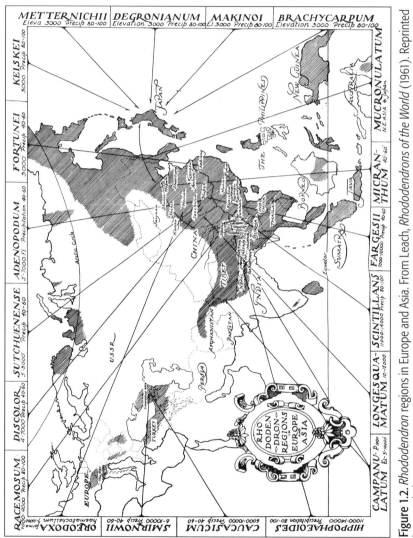

Figure 1.2. *Rhododendron* regions in Europe and Asia. From Leach, *Rhododendrons of the World* (1961). Reprinted by permission.

The climatic and soil conditions of mountainous areas appear most congenial to their growth and can be characterized by cooler temperatures and more precipitation. These same climatic conditions readily evolve acidic soil and a buildup of organic matter on top of the soil. Furthermore, mountain soils are largely formed by erosion of bedrock, resulting in a coarse, well-drained soil. Cooler summer temperatures, continued high humidity, and good snow cover in winter found in most mountain areas round out the environment in which rhododendrons evolved and to which they are adapted.

In all situations in which soil, site, and climatic conditions are favorable, rhododendrons are capable of dominating the landscape. The huge numbers of seeds produced each year, some of which are winged for better distribution by the wind, often result in solid masses of seedlings that quickly cover the ground and smother out all competition. Being plants capable of growing in dense clumps, they successfully crowd out other species and in effect produce their own wind protection and shade. Plant collector Kingdon-Ward described, in *RHS-Rhododendron Yearbook 1947*, "The rocks glowing with a bright red crest of *R. simsii* as the entire surface was covered with and dominated by rhododendron."

Plant Introductions

It is difficult to convey the anticipation and eagerness with which the introduction of a new species or hybrid from the wild is greeted by *Rhododendron* collectors and hybridizers. They become inextricably bound up in the excitement of a find offering a new color, disease resistance, outstanding foliage, compact plant habit, or any one of a number of new and potentially outstanding characteristics. Being among the first to grow a new introduction or use it in a breeding program bestows a definite prestige on the grower. This kind of excitement filled the minds and hearts of the early plant explorers, motivating them to risk life and limb in inhospitable settings to discover and return to the gardening world yet another example of the superb plants found in the genus *Rhododendron*.

The new species were collected and sent in increasing numbers primarily to Britain as well as to Germany, Holland, or wherever discerning horticulturists were prepared to spend the money to support the collectors in the field. Only in the twentieth century were North Americans prepared to join the ranks of their European counterparts. One can imagine the excitement these new, heretofore unheard of, species provoked and the extraordinary competition among collectors to be among the first to own each new treasure.

One of the first explorers was Sir Charles Hooker, who in 1850 introduced forty-five species from Sikkim in the Himalayas. Introductions included the luminous, yellow-flowered *Rhododendron campylocarpum* and *R. wightii*, the red *R. thomsonii*, the epiphytes *R. dalhousiae*, and the treelike *R. falconeri*, *R. grande*, and *R. hodgsonii*.

Robert Fortune sent seeds of *R. fortunei* from China to England in 1850. This species proves to be one of the most valuable parents in breeding large-flowered, fragrant hybrids that are also widely adaptable and cold hardy. Also in the nineteenth century Dr. Augustine Henny introduced the blue-flowering *R. augustinii*. One can only imagine the breathtaking sights unfolding before the early plant explorers as they encountered entire mountainsides radiating in full color or their anticipation of what lay over the next hill or hidden in the valley below.

Twentieth-Century Explorers

By the beginning of the twentieth century, 300 *Rhododendron* species were known to botanists and about 35 were in cultivation. Meanwhile, enthusiasm for the genus was growing and led to increasing support among plant collectors eager to send explorers into the wilderness to search out new and exciting plants. Some of the most notable of these twentieth-century explorers are discussed below.

E. H. Wilson, 1900—Wilson sent back forty new species of *Rhododendron* among hundreds of other plants during his first two years in China. Many of his finds are cold hardy and widely adaptable. They include *Rhododendron discolor* with large, fragrant, white blossoms and *R. williamsianum*, a low-growing, dense species with nodding, pink bells. Both these species contributed to the interest and enthusiasm for *Rhododendron*, encouraging others to join the race of discovery and return to Europe and North American gardens a seemingly inexhaustible array of exotic wonders.

George Forrest, 1904—Forrest was sent to China to explore south of the area E. H. Wilson explored. He introduced 260 species ranging from the 3 in. (7.5 cm) tall, scarlet-flowered *Rhododendron forrestii* to the treelike *R. sinogrande*, which is 30 ft. (9 m) tall with leaves 1 ft. (30 cm) wide by 3 ft. (90 cm) long. Wilson's introductions were hardier than those made by Forrest, but Forrest sent back more species.

F. Kingdon-Ward, 1911—Kingdon-Ward introduced nearly 100 species from China, Tibet, Burma, and Assam. Most notable among his introductions is

Rhododendron wardii, the classic yellow. Other introductions include *R. macabeanum*, *R. elliottii*, *R. pemakoense*, and *R. leucaspis*.

Joseph F. Rock, 1920—The USDA sent Joseph Rock to Burma, Assam, and Siam in 1920. He led other expeditions for the National Geographic Society of the United States and for the Arnold Arboretum of Harvard University, under the direction of Charles Sargent. Rock lived in Tibetan areas in China from the 1920s to 1949. He introduced many superior forms of the species including rock garden plants such as *R. racemosum*. I am quite familiar with two excellent *R. vernicosum* selections Joseph Gable made from seed brought back by Rock. He collected seed of nearly 500 taxa of rhododendrons of the region, with his largest number of collections being from the Likiang area in the border region between China and Tibet.

While far from complete, this brief account of the major plant explorers and their collections does give some sense of the fascination rhododendrons have held for gardeners for nearly 200 years. The search continues as explorers from the United States, England, Scotland, Japan, New Zealand, and other countries carry on the quest for new and better forms of known species.

Species and Hybrids in the Wild

Species rhododendrons are plants that have essentially evolved in isolation. Plants in isolated groups tend to become more alike and each such group evolves uniform characteristics. Such uniformity of character is the result of inbreeding within the species over great lengths of time. Plants inheriting characteristics unsuited to local growing conditions do not survive. Consequently, a uniform race of plants adapted to a specific area is the result, and movement of plants into areas widely divergent gives a less than favorable plant response. Species tend to propagate "true" from seed with a range of variability among seedlings, some species exhibiting a wider variability than others.

Hybrids in the wild result from the cross-pollination between individuals of two different species. The resulting seedlings are genetically more heterogeneous than their parents, exhibiting more variation among themselves and differing from either parent. Hybrids are often more vigorous and adapt more readily to a wider variety of growing conditions than their parents. It is initially difficult to determine whether a plant newly discovered in the wild is a species or a natural hybrid. Hybridization spontaneously occurs whenever populations of species come together; this can lead to much debate regarding whether such plants are species or hybrid. The significant thing to most gardeners fortunate enough to own one of the best selections of these natural gems is that they can be beautiful, exciting plants and a great addition to the garden regardless of whether they are species or hybrid.

Hybridizing

In 1810 the Englishman Michael Waterer made an artificial cross of rhododendron species using the North American *Rhododendron maximum* and *R. catawbiense*. His success led to further hybridizing activity using the newly discovered Asian species to improve flower size and color. The first hybrids introduced into commerce were those of Anthony Waterer, of Knap Hill Nursery, in the 1860s. Some of these hybrids are so outstanding that they remain standard commercial hybrids in the eastern United States and in other areas of extreme cold. They are commonly known as the "Ironclads" due to their cold hardiness and ease of cultivation.

Hybridizing is an ongoing activity pursued by horticulturists and professional geneticists as well as hobbyists. Numerous new hybrids—and a handful of very exciting hybrids—are released to the world each year. A few of these introductions are genuine improvement upon previous cultivars.

Azaleas

Azaleas are members of the genus *Rhododendron*, and the binomial system for identifying azaleas uses, for example, *Rhododendron* (genus) *kaempferi* (species). But because most gardeners and nurseries continue to separate azaleas from the rest of the genus, I refer to them as "azaleas" in this book, using "*Rhododendron*" for the balance of the genus. There are two distinct groups of azaleas: the deciduous azaleas, which lose their leaves in winter, and the evergreen azaleas, which hold some of their leaves year-round. These two groups are not sufficiently related genetically to readily crossbreed, although there are a few cases where a viable hybrid has resulted.

Azaleas prefer the same soil and climatic conditions as other rhododendrons—namely a cool, moist atmosphere, an acid soil with good internal drainage, and some protection from strong winds. They tolerate more sun and wind than the larger-leaved rhododendrons. The natural distribution of azaleas is generally in mountainous regions providing these conditions. To date, no yellow-flowered or deep blue–flowered evergreen azaleas have been discovered. However, the deciduous azaleas present some beautiful yellows and oranges as well as white, pink, red, but no blue.

Azaleas are not as widely distributed throughout the world as are the other rhododendrons. Wild deciduous azalea species are found in North America and eastern Asia, China, Taiwan, Japan, Korea, the Philippines, and central Vietnam. The Pontic azalea (*R. flavum*) is found in the Caucasus Mountains, parts of Eastern Europe, the island Lesbos, and along the Pontic Mountains of Northern Turkey, whereas *R. occidentale* is native to the Pacific Northwest. The largest number of the deciduous species is found in North America. The evergreen azaleas grow naturally in Japan, Taiwan, the Philippines, Korea, southeastern China, and central Vietnam.

Because of the reorganization of the genus *Rhododendron* based on various taxonomic studies, the revision submitted by Chamberlain and Rae (1990) included the evergreen azaleas in a subgenus that also includes some deciduous azalea forms. That subgenus is called *Tsutsusi* and it has two sections, *R. Tsutsusi* and *R. Brachycalyx*. Subgenus *Tsutsusi* section *Tsutsusi* contains sixty-six species and is equivalent to the classification formerly know as the azalea subseries *Obtusum*. This section contains all the evergreen azaleas. It includes a number of new species identified by P. X. Tan in a 1983 survey of rhododendrons in China as well as a new species (*R. arunachalense*) identified in northeast India by Chamberlain and Rae. This species natural range is the farthest west of any know evergreen azalea species. The following lists identify known evergreen azalea species and their native regions.

CHINA
   R. microphyton
   R. simsii

JAPAN
   R. eriocarpum (includes *R. tamurae*)
   R. indicum (formerly *R. macranthum*)
   R. kaempferi
   R. kiusianum
   R. ripense var. *mucronatum*
   R. scabrum
   R. serpyllifolium
   R. stenopetalum (includes *R. macrosepalum*)
   R. tashiroi
   R. tosaense
   R. tschonoskii
   R. tsusiophyllum

NOTE: The former species *R. obtusum* has been dropped. Most azaleas under that species name are now considered hybrids or selections of *R. kaempferi* and *R. kiusianum*.

KOREA
  R. yedoense
  R. yedoense var. *poukhanense*

TAIWAN
  R. nakaharae
  R. oldhamii
  R. rubropilosum

Geographic distribution of evergreen azalea species in the section *R. Tsutsusi* are: China (39), Japan (13), Korea (1),

The deciduous azalea species are native to China, Japan, Korea, Europe, and North America and include plants from two subgenera. One group belongs to the subgenus *R. Tsutsusi* section *Brachycalyx* mentioned previously that includes a number of Asian deciduous azaleas with leaves in pseudo-whorls of two to three. The other is the subgenus *Pentanthera* that includes all of the North American native azaleas as well as a few other species from Asia and Europe.

Because of the reorganization within *Rhododendron*, some previously used names from subgenus *Pentanthera* have been changed. The former species known as *R. molle* from China and the species formerly known as *R. japonicum* from Japan are now considered to be regional variants of the same species, *R. molle*. However, they do maintain a subspecies distinction. Also the widespread and highly variable species known as *R. viscosum* from North America now includes species formerly known as *R. coryi*, *R. oblongifolium*, and *R. serrulatum*. Some familiar names have also been changed to follow rules of nomenclature. In addition, a new deciduous azalea species from South Carolina, *R. eastmanii*, was identified in 1999. Deciduous azalea species are listed here by their native regions.

CHINA
  R. farrerae
  R. mariesii
  R. molle

EUROPE
  R. luteum

JAPAN
  R. albrechtii
  R. amogianum
  R. dilatatum
  R. kiyosumense
  R. molle subsp. *japonicum*
    (formerly *R. japonicum*)
  R. nipponicum
  R. nudipes
  R. pentaphyllum
  R. quinquefolium
  R. reticulatum
  R. sanctum
  R. wadanum
  R. weyrichii

KOREA
  R. schlippenbachii

NORTH AMERICA
R. *alabamense*
R. *arborescens*
R. *atlanticum*
R. *austrinum*
R. *calendulaceum*
R. *canadense*
R. *canescens*
R. *cumberlandense*
(formerly R. *bakeri*)
R. *eastmanii*

R. *flammeum*
(formerly R. *speciosum*)
R. *occidentale*
R. *periclymenoides*
(formerly R. *nudiflorum*)
R. *prinophyllum* (formerly R. *roseum*)
R. *prunifolium*
R. *vaseyi*
R. *viscosum*
(including R. *coryi*, R. *oblongifolium*,
and R. *serrulatum*)

2

Site Selection and Growing Requirements

Site selection and modification, if necessary, are the most important elements in successfully growing rhododendrons and azaleas. Because they prefer an acid soil, their requirements differ markedly from most landscape plants. Rhododendron growers having a naturally satisfactory site are fortunate because these plants can be grown with very little effort. As with most plants, a poor site yields poor growth; it is in these cases that modification of the site becomes necessary. Fortunately, a few minor adjustments can often transform a poor site into one very satisfactory for rhododendrons and azaleas.

As noted in chapter 1, rhododendrons generally grow most luxuriously and in greater numbers and variety of species in mountainous areas. Success is dependent upon duplicating these conditions as nearly as possible. Some of the specific conditions rhododendrons and azaleas need to flourish are:

▶ an acid soil (pH 4.5–6.0);
▶ good soil drainage (especially refers to the structural drainage of the soil);
▶ cool soil temperature;
▶ high percentage of organic matter in the soil, especially near the surface;
▶ loose, porous mulch;
▶ light shade (the larger the plant's leaves, the more shade is required);
▶ adequate light for flower bud formation;
▶ protection from wind and air drainage with no frost pockets; and
▶ air temperature to match cold hardiness and heat tolerance of the plant.

Regardless of which landscape use is intended, the above conditions must be met for rhododendrons to flourish. If most of these conditions are present in the garden, little or no modification will be needed. But as existing conditions diverge from these characteristics, an increasing number of modifications are required.

Soil pH

A pH above 7 indicates an alkaline (or sweet) soil, whereas a pH below 7 indicates an acid (or sour) soil (Figure 2.1). Measurements of pH are logarithmic, meaning that each pH unit is 10 times as acidic or alkaline as the unit before or after it. A soil pH of 5.5 is 10 times more acid than a soil pH of 6.5 and 100 times more acid than a pH of 7.5.

Azaleas and rhododendrons grow best in soil with a pH range of 4.5–6.0 (pH 5.5 is ideal) because the soil minerals most needed by these plants for good growth are in soluble form in this pH range. Soil pH also affects the pH of plant cell sap. Departures from proper acidity cause elements of plant food to become insoluble in the cell sap and thus unavailable to the plant. As soil pH changes, the availability of various plant food elements in the soil solution

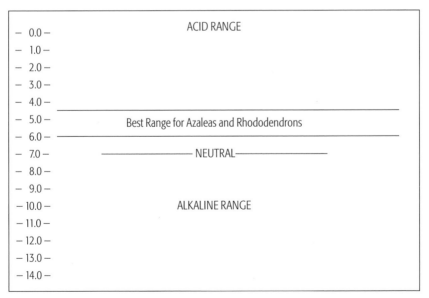

Figure 2.1. pH scale. A pH of 1.0 is extremely acidic, pH 7.0 is neutral, and pH 14.0 represents the most alkaline soil. Each unit on the scale is ten times more acidic or alkaline than the one next to it. Thus, a pH of 4.5 is ten times as acidic as a pH of 5.5 and 100 times as acidic as pH 6.5.

changes. Figure 2.2 shows the availability of plant nutrients at various pH levels. Iron availability, for example, which is essential to *Rhododendron* for the manufacture of chlorophyll, decreases dramatically above pH 6.0. Conversely, at a pH range of 5.5–6.5 available calcium and magnesium begin to increase. Rhododendrons and azaleas are adversely affected by high soil levels of free calcium. Thus, not only are necessary elements unavailable above pH 6.0, but other elements are available at toxic levels.

The only way to accurately determine soil pH is by taking a soil test. The do-it-yourself pH tests are very simple and can be done by the gardener with equipment such as a pH meter or with chemicals available in soil test kits. If you suspect a problem, however, it is best to resort to the more accurate tests made by local soil testing laboratories, including those at state agricultural

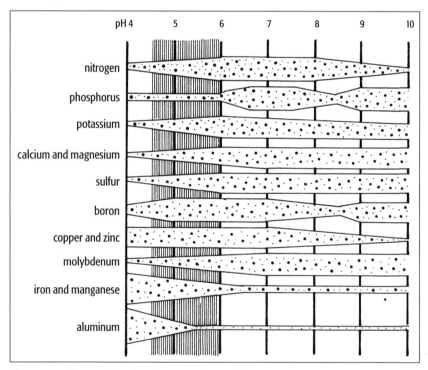

Figure 2.2. Different mineral nutrients vary in availability to plants by soil pH. In this illustration, the wider the bar the more available is that particular element. *Rhododendron* grow best in soils between pH 4.5 and 6.0. Notice how much more iron and manganese are available in acid (below 7.0) soils. Also of note is how aluminum, which is toxic to some plants, increases at pH below 5.0. From Truog, *USDA Yearbook of Agriculture*, 1943–47.

colleges. If soil pH is not within the proper range, the following guidelines can be used to correct it.

Soil too acid—If the soil tests indicate a pH below 4.5, some correction is necessary. The most effective material to use in raising soil pH is dolomitic limestone, which contains more of the essential plant food element magnesium than do other forms of lime. Lime moves through the soil very slowly and should be incorporated into the soil before planting. Surface applications to landscape plants are effective, however, because rhododendrons have feeder roots near the soil surface and lime does move down into the soil at about 1 in. (2.5 cm) per year. To raise pH one unit, approximately 7–8 lb. (2.6–3.0 kg) of ground limestone per 100 sq. ft. (9.3 m²) is required for loam soils. Heavy soils, those with high clay content, need slightly more, 9–10 lb. (3.3–3.7 kg); sandy soils require only 6 lb. (2.2 kg) to change the pH one unit. These differences are due to the higher cation exchange capacity of clay that allows it to hold more hydrogen ions (pH is a measure of hydrogen ions). These must be replaced by calcium ions and by a reaction of hydrogen with the carbonate in lime to form carbonic acid, which quickly breaks down into water and carbon dioxide to change soil pH. The soil should be retested a month after the lime application to determine the amended pH. If additional lime is needed, it can be broadcast on the soil surface after planting and will move down through the soil at the rate of about 0.5–1.0 in. (1.3–2.5 cm) per year. Because limestone is finely ground stone, there is no danger of root burning in mixing limestone in the soil at planting time. Applying too much calcium by an overly heavy lime application, however, can produce toxic levels of calcium.

Acidity in the proper range—If soil pH tests between 4.5 and 6.0, which fortunately is the case in many soils, no modification is necessary. The pH of any acidic soil amendments used, such as sphagnum peat moss, should be checked if the soil pH is near 4.5 because their addition may lower soil pH below the satisfactory range. To cancel out this effect, 1.5 lb. (0.6 kg) of dolomitic limestone per 3.8 cu. ft. (0.1 m³) bag of sphagnum peat moss raises the pH of the moss from 3.5 to 5.8. This matter is discussed in greater detail under soil amendments.

Soil not acid enough—In some areas the soil is too alkaline for the best growth of rhododendrons. High pH readings are usually the outcome of one of two processes. One is that calcium and/or sodium ions build up in the soil in regions of low rainfall. These ions replace hydrogen ions, which are the acidifiers, and soil pH goes up. The other common cause is soil formed from limestone, which results in excess calcium ions in the soil. In either case a soil pH above 6.0 requires modification.

Two materials are recommended to lower soil pH, or acidify the soil. The first is iron or ferrous sulfate, a fast-acting material that changes pH immediately upon watering the soil. The sulfate portion combines with calcium to form soluble calcium sulfate, which leaches from the soil and removes the calcium. The treatment of soil of limestone origin is only a temporary measure because further weathering of the limestone causes the pH to rise again. Additional soil tests, about every six months, are advised to monitor the condition. Because iron sulfate is a salt, if too much is applied at once it can severely damage plant roots to the point of toxicity, even in wet soils. Reverse osmosis occurs when the soil salt content is higher than the salt content of the root cells; that is, water moves out of the plant cells and into the surrounding soil, leading to dehydration of the roots. To avoid a salt buildup, use several light applications of ferrous sulfate at 1 lb. per 100 sq. ft. (0.4 kg per 9.3 m^2) of area at one-week intervals. Wet the soil thoroughly with about 1 in. (2.5 cm) of water. Each application will change soil pH about 0.2 pH units. When preparing new beds, the entire quantity of ferrous sulfate needed to bring about the desired pH change can be applied in a single application (see Table 2.1 for amount to use). Wait at least one week after treatment before planting. Use of ammonium sulfate when applying nitrogen fertilizer also lowers pH.

The other material used to lower soil pH is sulfur. It is much slower in its action, but the acidifying effect lasts much longer. It is slower because elemental sulfur first forms sulfuric acid. Sulfates then develop; these combine with calcium and remove calcium ions from the soil. The more finely ground the sulfur, the faster it will react to remove calcium. Sulfur must be physically incorporated into the soil because it is not water-soluble. The change in pH caused by sulfur begins slowly, gradually gathering speed as the soil becomes more acid. The soil microorganisms that break down elemental sulfur and convert it to sulfate are not active above soil pH 6.0. Iron sulfate should be used to lower pH to 6.0 before sulfur is applied. A retest of soil pH should be delayed for a year to best determine the effect of the sulfur application.

Aluminum sulfate is often recommended as a soil acidifier and, although very effective, it is not generally recommended for rhododendrons. Plants in the genus *Rhododendron* are rather tolerant of aluminum, but can be damaged by excess aluminum in the soil. Aluminum sulfate should therefore be used

Table 2.1. Amounts of ferrous sulfate and sulfur required to adjust soil pH

To change pH from	Pounds of ferrous sulfate needed per 100 sq. ft.	Kilograms of ferrous sulfate needed per 9.3 m²	Pounds of sulfur needed per 100 sq. ft.	Kilograms of sulfur needed per 9.3 m²
7.5 to 7.0	8.2	3.7	1.6	0.7
7.5 to 6.5	9.4	4.3	1.9	0.9
7.5 to 6.0	16.5	7.2	3.3	1.4
7.5 to 5.5	23.5	10.5	4.7	2.1
7.5 to 5.0	30.6	13.7	6.1	2.7
7.0 to 6.5	7.1	3.2	1.4	0.6
7.0 to 6.0	9.4	4.3	1.9	0.9
7.0 to 5.5	16.5	7.2	3.3	1.4
7.0 to 5.0	23.5	10.5	4.7	2.1
6.5 to 6.0	7.1	3.2	1.4	0.6
6.5 to 5.5	11.8	5.4	2.4	1.1
6.5 to 5.0	18.8	8.6	3.8	1.7
6.0 to 5.5	7.1	3.2	1.4	0.6
6.0 to 5.0	14.1	6.2	2.8	1.2
5.5 to 5.0	7.1	3.2	1.4	0.6

Adapted from Leach (1961, p. 281)

sparingly, if at all. As soil pH drops below 5.0, more aluminum ions become available in increasing numbers.

Rhododendrons do not grow well in alkaline soils, including those of limestone parent material. This need not be cause for despair, however, because plantings can still be very successful. To assure success, the gardener need only incorporate large amounts of organic matter into the soil, place acid soil atop existing soil, or employ a combination of these two methods. The important point is to raise the plant roots above the native alkaline soil and allow them to grow into an amended or replaced medium of a proper pH. More detail on this alternative is given in chapter 6.

Proper soil pH is especially important when plants are heavily fertilized to promote maximum growth. The higher the concentration of soluble salts in the soil, a result of heavy fertilization, the more sensitive the plant will be to soil pH. Rhododendrons grow much more satisfactorily, and over a wider range of pH, in woodland soils that are very low in soluble plant food elements than in the well-fertilized landscape or nursery. This difference may reflect an imbalance of minor plant food elements such as iron or magnesium in relation to the major elements of nitrogen, phosphorus, and potassium available to the plant. This idea is supported by research, which shows that when sphagnum peat moss is used along with heavy applications of fertilizer, pH tolerance is widened. It is thought that the peat moss supplies minor elements responsible for the difference. Similar effects result from the addition of minor elements to major-element fertilizers in the absence of peat moss. Peat moss also has a high ion exchange capacity and thus can buffer the effect of excess calcium.

Rhododendron pH tolerance varies among cultivars. For example, the cultivar 'Cunningham's White' tolerates a higher soil pH than most other rhododendrons. This is one of the reasons 'Cunningham's White' is commonly used as a rootstock in grafting plants for the alkaline regions of Europe. The new rootstock Inkarho® is tolerant of high pH, as well as being vigorous. It was developed in Europe and is in use there. Inkarho® rootstock performs better than most conventional rhododendrons, is lime tolerant, and grows well up to pH 6.5. Strong healthy roots are essential to optimum performance of any plant.

Soil Drainage and Moisture

Rhododendrons and azaleas, being mostly represented as broad-leaved evergreens, require ample moisture year-round. In addition, they require high levels of oxygen around their roots. Thus, they need to be grown in a well-drained yet moisture-retentive soil. Such a medium may seem a contradiction but is not: moist is quite different from wet.

Soils are made up of a collection of solid particles with pore spaces between them. These pore spaces are largest in sandy soils, with their characteristic large soil particles, and smallest in clay soils, which are composed of small, tightly packed soil particles. The pore space in soils fills with water and air in different percentages; these percentages constantly vary. The pore spaces of a poorly drained soil contain a much higher percentage of water than air. The heavier water simply replaces the air in the pore space and thereby excludes soil oxygen. In a well-drained soil, water moves through the pores and down into the subsoil and oxygen-rich air is pulled in behind the water. Well-drained soil, except for sandy soils, retains enough moisture and plant food elements in a film around the soil particles to allow plant roots to grow rapidly. Optimum growing conditions exist when soil pore space is filled with approximately 50 percent air and 50 percent water. Plants grow over a wide range of soil moisture and air conditions, but rhododendrons and azaleas require more oxygen around the roots than do most.

Soils are classified according to texture or size of soil particles. Sandy soils have large soil particles and are classified as light, whereas clay soils have small soil particles and are classified as heavy. Soil texture determines to a large extent how much water a soil will retain. Small particles collectively present a greater soil surface area. Because each particle holds a thin film of water around it by the forces of adhesion and cohesion, much more water can then be held than in soils composed of large particles. Smaller pore spaces also better act as capillary tubes to pull up and hold water. Light or sandy soils with larger soil particles and less surface area thus hold less water than silt and clay soils.

Adding organic matter can increase soil water holding capacity. Compost is the most active and beneficial form of organic material to use as a soil amendment. If composted properly, it contains many beneficial microorganisms and nutrients, which improve soil texture, plant growth, and insect and disease resistance. Composted pine bark is also an excellent soil amendment.

The growing medium for rhododendrons should consist of 25 to 50 percent organic matter. Sphagnum peat moss holds more water than most organic amendments, and if coarse sphagnum moss is used, it will last a reasonable length of time. Pine bark will last even longer in the soil, but it will not retain as much moisture. Hardwood barks have high cellulose content and will decompose quickly in the soil, so they are not recommended as amendments.

Sandy soils lose water and soluble fertilizer elements rapidly. The best way to improve a sandy soil is to add organic matter such as coarse sphagnum peat moss, bark, sawdust, compost, or other materials that will remain in the soil as long as possible before total decay. Although sandy soils benefit greatly from the moisture-retentive qualities of sphagnum moss, the moss rots quickly in oxygen-rich sandy soils. I recommend using 25 percent coarse, light-colored sphagnum peat moss and 75 percent pine bark or other slow-decaying, moisture-retaining material to make up the organic amendments incorporated into sandy soils. Sandy soils also benefit from an organic mulch. Not only does its cooling effect conserve moisture, but as the mulch decays organic matter moves into the soil.

Clay soils, in contrast, tend to be too wet. Incorporating organic amendments will always result in improved soil drainage. Bark or sawdust may be more effective than peat moss in clay soils because they do not hold as much moisture. In my opinion, however, there is no substitute for the advantages of coarse sphagnum peat moss. Even for clay soils it should comprise at least 25 percent of the total organic amendment. Research has shown that peat moss acts quicker in amending clay soils. A few months after adding organic materials, clay soil particles start to stick together like breadcrumbs. In effect, larger soil particles form and the increasing pore size improves internal (structural) drainage.

The texture and drainage of loam soils is intermediate between that of sandy and clay soils, and it is the best soil texture for rhododendrons and azaleas. Loams are classified as sandy loam, silt loam, and clay loam depending on the percent of sand, silt, and clay present. Requirements of organic soil amendments for loam soils are essentially the same as mentioned above, except that smaller amounts of organic matter are needed to improve soil structure and moisture content. With regard to drainage, loam soils tend to perform more uniformly than soils of extreme diversity in particle size and texture.

It is easy to check soil drainage. Dig a 12-in. (30-cm) deep hole and fill it with water. If water remains in the hole for more than two hours, there is a drainage problem, which can be corrected by amending the soil as outlined above. If water remains for twenty-four hours or more, there is a serious drainage problem that cannot ordinarily be corrected simply by adding organic matter. In this situation all plantings need to be made on top of the soil in raised beds about 18 in. (45 cm) above the existing soil level. Rainwater remaining on top of the soil for more than a few hours after the rain stops also indicates poor drainage and a need to grow in raised beds. A well-drained soil is essential for rhododendrons and azaleas. If the native soil in the planting site drains poorly, the planting site must be modified.

Rhododendrons and azaleas grow best if their roots have a cool, moist environment. Soil moisture will not be lost as quickly from a cool soil and will be available longer to the plant. Moreover, the major root-rot diseases need high soil temperatures as well as wet conditions to become pathogenic. When plants have an adequate supply of moisture and healthy roots, good plant growth will not be interrupted. The most effective way to keep the soil cool is by shading the soil surface. Shade can be provided naturally by trees or smaller plants or with a loose organic mulch. Lath houses or planting in the shade cast by buildings is equally effective, especially for smaller plants in nursery beds.

Organic Matter and Soil Structure

Organic matter plays an important role in good soil tilth and health of the microbial population, which in turn are extremely important to plant health. It also encourages root extension in the soil. I must impress upon the reader the importance of organic matter both dug into the soil and placed on top of the soil as mulch. Even in sandy soils where drainage and aeration are not a problem, organic matter used as a mulch continues to add organic matter to the soil, thus insuring the many advantages of its presence to soil microflora and to plants. Soil structure starts improving within three months of incorporating organic matter.

Healthy soil communities have diverse fungal and bacterial species. Organic matter supports life in the soil by providing an environment favorable to the growth of beneficial organisms including mycorrhizal fungi and rhizosphere bacteria. The mycorrhizal fungi form a very intimate, symbiotic relationship with plant roots, greatly increasing root surface area and thus efficiency in extracting water and nutrients from the soil. A mycorrhizal symbiosis is rather persistent and not likely to be lost due to ordinary environmental stresses. However, spread of the mycorrhizal fungi to roots is dependent on the spread of new roots.

If soil conditions are stressed, such as drought or compacted soil, spread of mycorrhizal fungi will be limited. After such stress, mycorrhizal fungi can be added to the soil for trees and many other plants. According to Dr. Donald Marx, chief scientist of Plant Health Care, Inc., however, there is currently no commercially available mycorrhizal fungi for ericaceous plants. It is rather safe to say that ericaceous plants grown in containers are not inoculated with this fungus. A symbiotic relationship between mycorrhizal fungus and rhododendron roots will probably occur once plants are placed in the landscape. This is more likely to occur if ericaceous plants such as native mountain laurel, blueberries, rhododendrons, and azaleas grow nearby. The spores of mycorrhizae are formed in puffballs and spread by the wind. The relationship between plant roots and mycorrhiza will be encouraged by amending soils with organic material over a wide area around the plant root ball to encourage active root growth.

Rhizosphere bacteria are free-living and do not form a true symbiotic relationship with plants. Unlike mycorrhiza, they do *not* colonize plant tissue. The bacteria live in the root zone, or rhizosphere, where they thrive on root exudates such as sugars and vitamins and on dead root cells. These bacteria can fix atmospheric nitrogen and convert insoluble minerals such as phosphorous into soluble phosphates that plants can absorb. They also improve soil tilth. Rhizosphere bacteria are sold in many commercial products for use when plants are transplanted or under stress.

Beneficial fungi and bacteria can outcompete pathogens if soils are aerated and otherwise conducive to root growth. Conversely, compacted soils result in plant susceptibility to pathogenic microbes, which are generally present in the soil. Some beneficial organisms produce plant hormones that stimulate growth, others produce natural chelators that keep iron available even at pH 7.6, and some provide antibiotics to control pathogens. Plants grown in association with beneficial organisms are more resistant to plant diseases.

Compost is a mixture that consists largely of decayed organic matter and is used for fertilizing and conditioning land. Most beneficial effects induced by compost are due to the activity of microorganisms. Composted organic matter, either incorporated into the soil or used as a mulch, is the best way to encourage beneficial soil organisms. Soil structure and microbial activity begins to improve soon after adding composted organic matter, and the benefits last from two to five years. An Ohio State University study found that compost used as a mulch in field plantings gave the best results. Peat moss is generally not as effective in supporting high populations of beneficial microorganisms because it is too decomposed. Three to four inches (7.5 to 10 cm) of composted pine bark dug into the soils assists in development of healthy root systems.

Harry A. J. Hoitink et al. (1977) showed that some microorganisms colonizing roots in compost mixes activate plant biochemical pathways that lead to resistance to root *and* foliar diseases. Composts do not provide total disease control, but when conditions are favorable they may reduce many diseases including phytophthora root rot. Earthworm castings contain organic matter, beneficial organisms, carbon, and enzymes, all of which enhance plant growth, prevent disease and improve soil tilth. Reduced soil tillage encourages an increase in soil organic matter and earthworm populations.

The only practical method for improving soil structure is by adding organic amendments to the soil. Adding sand is not a practical solution because of the large amount of sand necessary to create pore space. To form pore spaces, and thus improve soil structure, sand particles must touch each other. Addition of sand does not result in soil particle aggregation as occurs with organic matter. According to Dr. Francis R. Gouin, professor emeritus from the University of Maryland, enough sand to make up at least 60 percent of the soil by weight is required to make any difference in aeration and drainage.

Mycorrhizal fungi play an important role in improving soil structure. Humic acid, formed as organic matter breaks down, and glomalin, formed by mycorrhizae, are the glues that stick soil particles together and improve soil tilth. Research by USDA scientist Dr. Sara F. Wright resulted in the discovery of a new glue formed by the arbuscular mycorrhizal fungi, a substance called glomalin (pronounced glo-may-lin). In 1996 Wright discovered a soil "superglue" that "was mistaken for an unidentifiable constituent of soil organic matter. . . . Rather, it permeates organic matter, binding it to silt, sand, and clay particles" (Comis 2002). Glomalin forms aggregates of soil granules that add structure to soil. Organic matter accelerates root growth and subsequent production of glomalin. Ericaceous plant roots are colonized by ericoid mycorrhizae; this fungus has not been studied for formation of glomalin, but it is possible that the same process exists.

Glomalin is causing a complete reexamination of what makes up soil organic matter. It accounts for 27 percent of the carbon in soil and is a major component of soil organic matter. Humic acid, once thought to be the main contributor of soil carbon, accounts for only 8 percent of the carbon in soils. It is glomalin that gives soil its tilth. The mycorrhizal fungi use carbon from the plant to grow and make glomalin. In return the fungi's hairlike filaments, called hyphae, extend the reach of plant roots. As roots extend, the mycorrhizal fungi moves down the root to colonize the growing root tip. On older sections of root the fungal hyphae stop transporting nutrients and the protective glomalin sloughs off into the soil, where it attaches to soil particles and organic matter, forming aggregates and thus improving soil structure or tilth.

A higher carbon dioxide level in the atmosphere stimulates the mycorrhizal fungus to produce more glomalin. Levels of glomalin, which is a very stable compound, are higher in untilled soils. In addition to the soil stability, nutrient accessibility, and nutrient cycling provided by glomalin, it is also possible that the large amounts of iron found in glomalin could be protecting plants from pathogens.

When amending the soil, I advise incorporating only composted organic material into the soil. The decomposition of the organic material requires nitrogen, and the microorganisms responsible for decomposition are more efficient at using soil nitrogen than are plants. Nitrogen is later released and made available to plants as the soil organisms die and their bodies decompose. Therefore, when incorporating fresh bark, sawdust, and similar materials into the soil, a nitrogen fertilizer, preferably a slow-release form such as urea formaldehyde (38 percent nitrogen) or Osmocote®, should be dug in with the material prior to planting. Sphagnum peat moss and composted organic materials withdraw very little nitrogen from the soil.

Composted organic material of high lignin content, such as pine bark and coniferous sawdust, are recommended for digging into the soil. Other materials may also be dug into the soil to add organic matter, but nothing is as safe and uniform in results as sphagnum peat moss or composted bark. Leaves, leaf mold, wood chips, and sawdust may be used but leaves and leaf mold do not persist in a landscape planting. Chips and hardwood sawdust adversely affect nitrogen availability unless nitrogen is added and the material composted before digging into the soil. Nitrogen reduction is not as severe with pine, fir, or redwood sawdust. Hardwood bark should not be used as a soil amendment because of its high cellulose content. Severe nitrogen withdrawal occurs because the cellulose is quickly broken down by soil organisms. The net effects of adding hardwood bark are that it disappears rapidly while creating a critical nitrogen deficiency.

To maintain soil organic matter, loose organic mulch should be added each year, late in the season, just after the soil freezes or growth has hardened off. This late application of mulch will also help control stem bark split. As the organic mulch rots over the years, earthworm activity carries it down through the soil to maintain a higher level of soil organic matter. The rotting mulch also builds a layer of humus on top of the soil that benefits the plant roots and is much like the conditions many *Rhododendron* species enjoyed in their native regions. This buildup of a humus layer on top of the soil is very important for larger plants in the landscape over the long term. Rhododendrons and azaleas in nature grow in soils with most of the organic matter in the top 2–3 in. (5–7.5 cm) of soil. Woodland soils, the habitat of many ericaceous plants, have a layer of humus on top of the soil surface. A mulch that slowly rots down over the years and is replenished each year duplicates natural conditions and is very beneficial.

Mulch also provides good weed control and, by keeping the soil cooler, conserves moisture and helps prevent root rot. Maintaining an organic mulch provides plant food as it rots or is broken down by soil organisms and maintains organic matter in the proper stage of decomposition to support biocontrol organisms, which suppress plant diseases. In winter, mulches can prevent soil from freezing deeply, thus permitting at least some plant roots to pick up moisture. By keeping moisture available to the plant, mulch goes a long way in offering winter protection. In the woodland, leaves from deciduous trees and needles from conifers serve to mulch plants growing nearby. This loose, airy mulch is ideal, providing shade and insulating the soil against freezing while allowing air movement to the roots. Woodland soils freeze less deeply in winter, if at all, while open grass areas freeze much more deeply. When selecting a mulch, look for coarse, light materials that will not pack tightly and exclude air from the roots.

Light

The amount of sun a particular species or hybrid of rhododendron can tolerate is often difficult to learn in advance, whereas azaleas seem to be better understood in this regard. The various species and hybrids of rhododendron and azalea display a rather wide tolerance to sunlight, illustrating their strong ability to adapt. Most rhododendron species evolved in a wet, misty atmosphere under a canopy of trees or in the open in the cool temperatures and high humidity of mountaintops. Others evolved in sunnier and drier conditions. The amount of sunlight will have pronounced effects on a variety of plant responses, including the profusion of flowers, the compactness of plant growth, cold hardiness, and color quality of foliage.

So how can the grower determine the amount of sun or shade a particular cultivar requires? Several criteria can be used to answer this question. The first general rule of thumb is that the larger the leaves, the more shade required. Species that evolved in full sun such as *R. catawbiense*, which grows on the mountaintops of the Blue Ridge Mountains in North America, tolerate more sun but not necessarily more heat.

Other factors that influence sun tolerance are humidity, amount and seasonal distribution of precipitation, summer high temperatures, and number of cloudy days. Full exposure on cooler mountaintops where humidity is high is not nearly as harsh as full exposure in a dry, low-humidity site. The west coast of North America has about 65 percent more cloudy days than the east coast, so full sun in these locations is not the same in terms of heat and subsequent drying of foliage. Misty, cloudy conditions, such as those prevalent in England, will permit the use of a wider selection of species and hybrids.

It is probably best to plant in as much sun as a specimen can tolerate without adverse effects. Plants will grow more compactly in sun; their stems seem to be tougher and more cold hardy, and they certainly set more flower buds. Conversely, plants in too much shade bloom sparingly and tend to grow tall and produce leggy flushes of growth with fewer branches.

The foliage of a plant getting too much sun will turn lighter green to yellow. The color change becomes more pronounced as sun damage progresses until edges or spots brown from completely dead tissue. The yellowing is a result of the rapid destruction of chlorophyll due to heat buildup. The same heat buildup also causes the leaf to transpire faster and thus lose moisture more rapidly. When moisture is lost from the leaves faster than the roots can replenish it, the leaf tissue dries out and the tissue dies, turning brown. This problem is often worse in the winter because roots in frozen soil are unable to absorb moisture to replace that lost from the leaves.

Remember that sun tolerance and heat tolerance are not the same. Plants can flourish in full sun under lower temperatures, but in temperatures above 90°F (32°C) more shade is required. Many of the small-leaved rhododendron and azaleas grow very well in full sun except in climates where temperatures stay above 90°F (32°C) week after week and the humidity is low. Temperatures above 95°F (35°C) and a relative humidity of 40 percent or lower can grievously injure virtually every *Rhododendron* species. To reduce or eliminate damage, site plants so they receive shade from other plants or buildings during the afternoon hours of greatest heat. Planting under trees is particularly recommended because the moisture transpired from the tree leaves raises humidity and lowers the temperature in the immediate vicinity. Buildings may offer enough shade, particularly on their northern and eastern sides. If other plants or buildings are not available, lath houses may be constructed to provide shade.

Most rhododendrons growing in unmanaged woodlands do not receive enough sunlight to form compact plants or to flower at their maximum. When rhododendrons and azaleas are planted as a primary landscape feature, many trees may have to be removed and others trimmed up to allow the best results. In my experience enough trees had to be removed prior to planting to provide open areas of sunlight at least two times the width of the crowns of the remaining trees—a spacing of 75–100 ft. (23–30 m)—and all lower branches had to be removed up to at least 30 ft. (9 m) above the ground level. The trees had to be removed before any planting was done to prevent possible damage to plants from falling limbs. Figure 2.3 illustrates this forest area clearing for rhododendrons.

A plant will display its need for more light or shade by how compactly it grows, whether the foliage is green or yellow and brown, and whether it sets flower buds profusely. It is not always necessary to learn this through trial and error; contact experienced growers in the local gardening area for suggestions.

Minerals

The only way to positively determine the need for fertilizer in a new planting area is to test the soil and then apply the amounts of nutrient elements recommended. Phosphorus and potassium can be dug in prior to planting because these elements remain for long periods in the soil. If these elements are

Figure 2.3. Notice the wide spacing of large oak trees to allow sufficient light for good growth of rhododendrons. Large evergreens in the background provide a windbreak. Author's garden, Woodsboro, Maryland. Photograph by H. Edward Reiley

supplied by chemical fertilizers such as superphosphate or muriate of potash, they should be dug in at least a month before planting. Organic sources of the same elements, such as rock phosphate, may be dug in at time of planting. Sandy soils with their low nutrient-holding capacity need more of these fertilizers applied more often than is needed for heavier soils. Organic forms of phosphorus and potassium remain in sandy soils longer than chemical forms.

Because nitrogen is lost from all soils rather quickly, it is necessary not only to dig this element in at the time the site is prepared but also to add it as a top dressing from time to time after planting. Nitrogen will leach down through the soil and thus is effective as a top dressing. Urea formaldehyde and ammonium sulfate are excellent forms of nitrogen. Because urea formaldehyde is an organic material containing 38 percent nitrogen, the nitrogen is released slowly (as urea and ammonium ions) over a period of six to eight months and will not burn or damage roots. Dig urea formaldehyde in at the rate of 15 lb. per 1000 sq. ft. (5.6 kg per 93 m²). Nitrogen release from urea formaldehyde is slow to nonexistent in cold soils and speeds up as soils warm in the spring, which provides the nitrogen when plants are actively growing and need it. The slow-release nature of this form is also significant because nitrogen can leach from soil rapidly. Nitrogen in the nitrate form, such as nitrate of soda, can damage ericaceous plants and it leaches rapidly. Therefore, I do not recommend its use. Ammonium sulfate leaches slowly, and ammonium is a preferred form of nitrogen for rhododendron

There are many other organic forms of fertilizer that are entirely safe to use. I recommend them for small plantings because they may be too expensive in large plantings. Materials such as cottonseed meal (7 percent nitrogen, 3 percent phosphorus, and 2 percent potassium) and soybean meal are excellent organic sources when used at the rate of 4–5 lb. per 100 sq. ft. (1.5–1.9 kg per 9.3 m²). These meals are complete fertilizers containing all three of the major plant food elements as well as trace elements. Rock phosphate, a very safe form of phosphorus, and granite meal, a safe source of potassium, can be used as organic sources for these two elements.

Rhododendrons require a number of secondary and micronutrients, yet these are seldom in short supply in the average soil. Sandy soils may have shortages severe enough to slow plant growth, but if organic soil amendments are used and a good organic mulch is maintained, enough minor elements are usually added to insure satisfactory growth. Nurserymen pushing plants for maximum growth rate and using large amounts of fertilizers need to test for minor elements from time to time. A soil-testing laboratory can advise on the specific tests needed to define the amount needed.

Rhododendrons and azaleas do not require much fertilizer but do respond well to appropriate application. When properly mulched, large landscape plants, may never need fertilizer. Again, organic matter in and on top of the soil releases plant food as it decomposes.

Wind Damage and Air Drainage

Rhododendrons and azaleas cannot tolerate strong winds and on windy sites would benefit greatly from a good windbreak. Reduced wind speed reduces both moisture loss from leaves and leaf damage. Preventing moisture loss is important in the summer and perhaps even more important in below-freezing temperatures. Because most rhododendrons have broad leaves, moisture loss is high. If moisture is lost through the leaves faster than the roots can absorb it, plant leaves wilt and burn on the margins and may eventually die if the situation is not corrected. Deciduous azaleas are able to survive windy winter locations better because they lose their leaves in winter and thus do not have moisture needs as great as their evergreen relatives.

A windbreak is generally considered to affect an area to a horizontal distance of about seven to ten times its height. Whenever possible, I think living windbreaks, such as hedges, shrubs, or trees, should be used because their beauty can add to the overall landscape effect. Evergreen trees or evergreen shrubs tall enough to break the wind are ideal. Even deciduous trees in large numbers will reduce wind velocity considerably. Use deep-rooted trees for windbreaks as they do not compete so vigorously with plantings for nutrients and moisture; definitely do not use maples because their roots are very competitive. If possible, plant *Rhododendron* far enough away from windbreaks to eliminate root competition. (An advantage of structural windbreaks, such as picket fences, is that plantings may be made close to them with no concern about root competition.) A needled evergreen such as pine or an upright yew provides an excellent windbreak at building corners, which experience especially high wind velocity, and will greatly benefit plants on the lee side. Small microclimate alterations such as creating a windbreak often make the difference between a successful or failed planting and can be created quite easily.

Air drainage refers to the downward movement of heavier cold air and the rising of lighter warm air. It is not the same thing as wind movement but is rather the slow, steady movement of cold air into low-lying areas or into physical barriers, which dam air movement. The accumulation of cold air reduces the temperature in these areas and is usually observed on still nights with little or no wind to mix the cold and warm air. Such cold air pockets should be avoided when planting rhododendrons for two reasons. First, temperatures fall below freezing earlier in the fall, damaging plants that have not yet hardened off. Second, frost occurs later in the spring, resulting in damage to early-flowering plants.

Air Temperature

As mentioned earlier, azaleas and rhododendrons grow best in moderate temperatures. This moderate range encompasses USDA plant hardiness zones 5 through 8. When temperatures drop below −15°F (−26°C) the flower buds of many rhododendron and azalea species and cultivars are blasted. Prolonged temperatures above 90°F (32°C) damage virtually all rhododendrons and azaleas planted in full sun. Chapter 3 presents lists of species and cultivars adapted to specific geographic areas. Tables in appendix A provide cold-hardiness information, and appendix B lists species and cultivars that are heat tolerant.

In summary, it is important when growing rhododendrons and azaleas to select or modify the planting site so that it provides an acid soil pH (4.5–6.0) and good internal soil drainage. Sufficient light is also important: sun or bright indirect light 50 percent or more of the day induces good flower bud formation. A porous mulch should be regularly replenished to keep the soil cool and provide organic matter to the soil. Soil must be high in organic matter (25–50 percent) and have adequate fertility. The site should also provide protection from wind and good air drainage. Finally, plants adapted to the site must be selected with both cold and heat tolerance in mind.

3

Selection of Rhododendrons

After selecting and preparing the planting site (chapter 2), proper plant selection is the next most important thing in insuring success. Selecting the
best performing plants for a given geographic area is difficult. If you have been
part of a group selecting good doer or proven performer rhododendrons you
know the controversy that arises. How can a group of experienced gardeners
disagree on the top performing plants for a specific area? There are some obvious factors that result in different performance of the same cultivar from garden to garden in the same geographic area. The strongest determining factor
is site selection and the degree of site preparation.

In the early 1980s I started planting the same cultivars under different conditions of exposure. The primary goal was to evaluate sun and heat tolerance
measured by leaf damage. Over the years, I noticed other physical damage to
plants in varying degrees at the different sites. A good example was noted while
evaluating the cultivar 'Janet Blair'.

Three plants of 'Janet Blair' were planted under the same soil conditions
but under different exposure and competition from other plants. At the first
site 'Janet Blair' was planted in high filtered shade cast by four large oak trees
growing within 20–40 ft. (6–12 m) of the rhododendron and completely surrounding it. Other rhododendrons at this site restrict air movement. The rhododendron was exposed to full sun from 8:00 until 10:30 A.M. and to root
competition for moisture from all four trees. Resulting dry soil conditions
causes severe stress every year, lowering the plants resistance to branch
dieback (*Botryosphaeria*). Diligent disease control through pruning as well as
watering five or six times each summer, when needed, maintained the plant
in good condition. In this situation intensive care was necessary to maintain

a satisfactory plant, and 'Janet Blair' in this site would not be considered a good doer.

The second site has one large oak tree located about 10 ft. (3 m) east of 'Janet Blair'. Most tree feeder roots are farther from the tree than 10 ft., and this oak offers little competition for moisture. The plant is exposed to sun from 1:00 to 5:00 P.M., and air movement is restricted by other rhododendrons. There is no visible damage to this plant except for an occasional twig dying back. It is seldom if ever watered. This plant would be rated a good doer.

The third 'Janet Blair' is fully exposed to sun and has good air circulation around it. A tall windbreak located about 80 ft. (24 m) away provides protection from strong wind. This plant, with no competition for moisture, does not suffer from branch dieback or any other problems and it does not require watering. This plant would be high on the good doer list.

It becomes obvious that the conditions under which a plant is grown must be considered in plant evaluation and in selecting the proper plant for a given site. Cultivars differ in tolerance to drought, heat, cold, soil drainage and disease resistance. The cultivars 'Caroline' and 'Mist Maiden', growing at the same site as the first-mentioned 'Janet Blair' in my garden, tolerate the dry conditions from root competition with no visible damage and no watering. 'Caroline' has a superior root system and is thus better able to compete for moisture. I could speculate as to why 'Mist Maiden' is drought tolerant, but I am not positive.

Selecting the best plant for a particular region and site is at the heart of creating a fine garden. When one sees a huge, beautiful, old rhododendron thriving without help, one can be certain that is a plant well adapted to local conditions and clearly a form for the local gardener to consider. A poorly adapted plant, however, will require continual attention and never become a magnificent specimen. Proper selection can greatly reduce the number and extent of cultural problems encountered. Only after developing some expertise can the gardener risk planting marginally adapted plants (or new, untested cultivars) with any hope for success.

The surest and safest way to select plants suitable to a particular region is to choose from those included in the Good Doer Lists at the end of this chapter. Thousands of rhododendrons have been tested in an expensive, time-consuming process of elimination, resulting in these lists. The lists specify those plants that have survived the test of time in a particular garden and have performed well in the region.

Another useful criterion in selecting rhododendrons is the quality of the plant as established by the American Rhododendron Society's (ARS) quality rating system. This rating system evaluates the quality of both the flower and the plant. The rating scale ranges from 1 to 5, with 1 the poorest and 5 the best. The quality rating is written 5/4, the first number referring to flower quality and the second to plant quality. The rating 5/4 designates a species or hybrid with a superb flower and above average plant. Sometimes an evaluation of the entire plant in terms of how it performs in the garden is added. This performance character is designated using a third number, based on the 1–5 scale as used for the flower and plant, and, for example, would be written 5/4/4.

A wide variety of sources for further assistance in plant selection are available, some of course more reliable than others. I recommend the books *Guide to Choosing Rhododendrons* by Cox, *Rhododendron Species*, Vols. I–IV by Davidian, *Azaleas* by Galle, *Greer's Guidebook to Available Rhododendrons*, *Rhododendron Hybrids* by Salley and Greer, and *Rhododendrons in America* by Van Veen. Local gardeners and nurseries can be good sources of information, as can the ARS Proven Performer Lists. If you join the local chapter of the ARS or the Azalea Society of America, enthusiastic, willing help can always be found among its members.

Following the general discussion of major factors involved in the selection of rhododendrons, the bulk of this chapter is devoted to the Good Doer Lists. These were compiled with the generous help of a number of leading rhododendron gardeners in this country and abroad, including members of various chapters of the ARS. I offer my deep appreciation to them for their contribution. The criteria used for inclusion as a good doer rhododendron or azalea adapted to a particular area is that the plant has performed well for at least five years in the garden. Good performance is based on disease resistance, cold hardiness, heat tolerance, production of a vigorous root system, drought tolerance, insect resistance, consistently heavy blooms, and good plant form.

Climate

Climate must be considered prior to the purchase of any rhododendron or azalea. In addition to moisture availability, the gardener must determine the temperature range plants will encounter. There is much recorded cold hardiness information, especially for rhododendrons. This information usually refers to the lowest temperature at which a plant will flower suffering no or minimal cold damage to flower buds. The vegetative part of the plant is usually more cold hardy than flower buds.

Heat tolerance is often overlooked as a limiting factor to plant growth when, in fact, heat and drought probably result in damage and death of more rhododendrons than cold. Heat tolerance is overlooked because accurate information concerning heat tolerance of plants is rarely available, and until very recently heat zones were not established.

Selection of Rhododendrons

In 1997 Dr. H. Marc Cathey, president emeritus of the American Horticultural Society, created a heat zone map (Plate 1). This U.S. map is divided into twelve heat zones, according to the average number of days per year that temperature exceeds 86°F (30°C). This is the temperature at which plants begin to experience damage to cellular proteins, which, according to Dr. Cathey permanently inactivates hormonal control of growth. Heat zones on the map range from zone 1, with no heat days, to zone 12, with 210 heat days. As plants are rated for heat tolerance, their zone designation assumes that adequate water is supplied to plants. (Heat damage is usually linked to an insufficient supply of water, which prevents effective evaporative cooling.) The nursery industry will soon be able to recommend plants not only for cold hardiness zones but also for heat zones.

Average cold temperatures are outlined on the USDA Plant Hardiness Zone Map of North America (Figure 3.1, Table 3.1). This is a primary reference tool for every gardener, who must then only consider microclimate effects—the

Table 3.1. U.S. Department of Agriculture hardiness zone designations based on average annual minimum temperatures

HARDINESS ZONE	°F	°C
1	below −50	−45.6 and below
2a	−45 to −50	−42.8 to −45.5
2b	−40 to −45	−40.0 to −42.7
3a	−35 to −40	−37.3 to −40.0
3b	−30 to −35	−34.5 to −37.2
4a	−25 to −30	−31.7 to −34.4
4b	−20 to −25	−28.9 to −31.6
5a	−15 to −20	−26.2 to −28.8
5b	−10 to −15	−23.4 to −26.1
6a	−5 to −10	−20.6 to −23.3
6b	0 to −5	−17.8 to −20.5
7a	5 to 0	−15.0 to −17.7
7b	10 to 5	−12.3 to −15.0
8a	15 to 10	−9.5 to −12.2
8b	20 to 15	−6.7 to −9.4
9a	25 to 20	−3.9 to −6.6
9b	30 to 25	−1.2 to −3.8
10a	35 to 30	1.6 to −1.1
10b	40 to 35	4.4 to 1.7
11	40 and above	4.5 and above

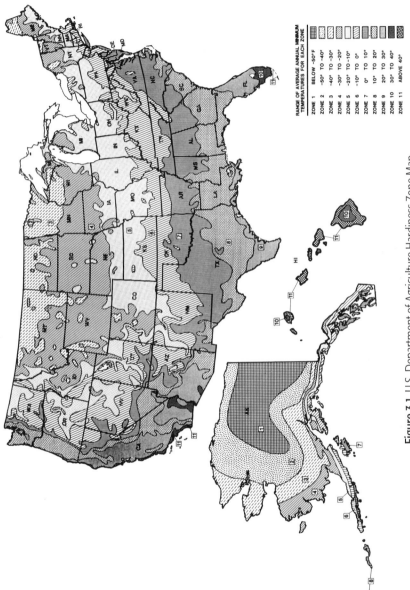

Figure 3.1. U.S. Department of Agriculture Hardiness Zone Map

RANGE OF AVERAGE ANNUAL MINIMUM
TEMPERATURES FOR EACH ZONE

ZONE 1	BELOW -50°F
ZONE 2	-50° TO -40°
ZONE 3	-40° TO -30°
ZONE 4	-30° TO -20°
ZONE 5	-20° TO -10°
ZONE 6	-10° TO 0°
ZONE 7	0° TO 10°
ZONE 8	10° TO 20°
ZONE 9	20° TO 30°
ZONE 10	30° TO 40°
ZONE 11	ABOVE 40°

specific situations of higher or lower temperatures always found within the larger zones. For example, USDA zone 6 represents regions in which the average annual minimum temperature is 0 to −10°F (−18 to −23°C). This indicates that only plants known to be cold hardy to this temperature should be selected for planting in USDA zone 6. The reader must keep in mind that both the hardiness and heat zone maps give average temperatures and that temperatures will fluctuate above and below these averages.

The hardiness zone map is helpful in determining the lowest temperature a plant can survive without injury. It does not help with other survival factors necessary to the adaptability of a plant. Factors such as heat tolerance, root system tolerance to pH and poor drainage, inherent plant vigor, disease and insect resistance, and sun tolerance must be considered in addition to cold hardiness. For this reason the Good Doer Lists are very important: the only way to determine adaptability of a plant is to evaluate it in your geographic area, and others have done this for you.

In addition to minimum temperatures, rapid temperature changes must be taken into account. Sudden temperature drops, especially in the fall or early winter before plants have hardened off, can be devastating. In these areas use plants known to harden off early. Cultural practices during the growing season will also affect fall plant hardiness. If moisture is readily available and nitrogen fertilizer is applied late in the summer, plants may remain in active growth. They will then be subject to damage by sudden drops in temperatures to below freezing in the early fall. Some cultivars are more sensitive to these cultural practices than others. During the cold of winter damage can occur to flower buds of some cultivars if buds are warmed too quickly by direct sun in the morning. Some hybrids of 'Cunningham's White' seem to suffer such damage. In this case the flower buds are cold hardy enough to withstand the low temperatures, but suffer from rapid warming. Placing such hybrids in morning shade may help solve this problem. Late spring frosts represent a different kind of temperature hazard; obviously early-flowering plants need to be avoided in regions experiencing such frosts with any regularity.

Maximum temperatures affect the selection of plants as surely as do minimum temperatures. Heat-tolerant forms are those able to endure temperatures above 86°F (30°C) and up to 100°F (38°C) for short periods of time. At high temperatures, afternoon shade is required even for heat-tolerant rhododendrons and azaleas. All rhododendrons and azaleas will suffer severely from prolonged periods of 100°F (38°C) temperatures in full sun. Extreme heat is especially harmful to flowers and tender new growth, both of which can be severely damaged in one such afternoon. Additional problems associated with high temperature appear in the forms of increased insect damage and disease attacks, particularly the fungus causing root rot. Rhododendrons and azaleas grow better at maximum temperatures of 80°F (27°C) or less.

Another kind of temperature problem is encountered in regions in which warm periods regularly occur during late winter and early spring and are interrupted by days of freezing temperatures. Some cultivars lose dormancy quickly after 7 to 10 consecutive days of temperatures above 50°F (10°C) and are easily damaged by temperatures that they readily tolerate when completely dormant. Rhododendrons typically complete dormancy following a period of approximately 320 hours spent at temperatures above 28°F (–2°C) but below 43°F (6°C) and day length reaches 10 hours.

Information on the average rainfall of the various regions is also important and is readily available from local weather stations. Even if a review of rainfall data for a region indicates a fairly uniform annual distribution, the heat of summer results in faster moisture loss from the soil and so creates a relatively drier condition than found in spring, fall, or winter. While some rhododendrons and azaleas are more drought tolerant than others, none does well in dry conditions. The early-flowering forms adapt better to areas with dry summers because flowering and active vegetative growth, both of which require a good supply of moisture, occur early in the season ahead of such droughts.

Factors other than annual rainfall also contribute to the amount of soil moisture available to the plant: the amount of rainfall during the growing season, the capacity of the soil to absorb and retain moisture, soil temperatures, and the presence or absence of competitive plants. Of course, the gardener can do nothing about the total amount of rainfall but can affect all other factors determining the amount of water available to plants.

An open, porous soil absorbs more water faster than a compacted soil; the former readily absorbs a greater quantity of water from rain or irrigation. A loam soil fortified with organic matter will store more water for a longer period of time than a sandy soil or a compacted, clay soil. Furthermore, a loose mulch on top of the soil not only prevents soil compaction, allowing more water to enter the soil, but also lowers soil temperatures, resulting in less moisture loss. Thus, an open, porous, loam soil fortified with organic matter and properly mulched provides better use of available water.

Any plant species grows best in the area in which it evolved or in other parts of the world having similar growing conditions. Most Rhododendron species are from mountain ranges, where higher elevations and cool mountain mists greatly reduce maximum summer temperature and provide high humidity. For example, Japanese azaleas do well along the eastern seaboard of North America, where the climate is similar to Japan's. For the same reason the natives of temperate Asia do well in England and the Pacific Northwest because these areas have climates similar to that in which the plants evolved. Species native to the tropics succeed in warm climates. Thus, the origin of a species, or in the case of a hybrid, the origin of its parents, has much to do with growing success in a particular region. There are of course exceptions to this rule of thumb, as a few *Rhododendron* are suitable to a wide range of conditions.

What Plants to Buy and Where to Purchase Them

Only nursery-grown plants should be purchased, not plants collected in the wild. This recommendation is given for several reasons. Collected plants are seedlings that will exhibit all the variation in plant characteristics associated with sexual reproduction. They seldom have the compact form of top or root system associated with well-grown nursery plants and so do not transplant and grow as well. Finally, plants should not be dug from the wild in the interest of plant conservation. I do not believe gardeners should encourage this practice by purchasing collected plants.

In addition to the matter of selecting plants based on particulars of a given region and site, the gardener must also consider the size of the selected plant to be purchased and planted. For example, one gardener may wish to have an instant landscape and will need to buy good-sized plants. Another gardener with an established landscape may prefer a small plant that will be grown along to ultimately replace a plant no longer wanted. Plants in the 2- to 3-ft. (0.6- to 1.0-m) size probably best survive transplanting into the landscape. Mature size must also be a selection factor. Where growing space is limited, as in small lots or foundation plantings, dwarf or low-growing forms are most suitable.

There is also the question of species versus hybrid that is endlessly argued by rhododendron fanciers. Hybrids are typically larger and easier to grow and bear larger, more spectacular flowers. A majority of gardeners seem to prefer hybrids, yet there is a growing body of collectors dedicated to growing species. The latter may argue that the plant habit is more satisfying and that the plant and its flowers are more proportionate. Each gardener is urged to develop his or her opinion on this matter based on personal landscape aesthetics.

The gardener is well advised to purchase only named cultivars that are asexually propagated. Such plants are consistent in their characteristics because each is a clone of a parent plant of known character and will be identical to the parent. This will eliminate future surprises or disappointments in the landscape.

It cannot be assumed that a local retailer sells only locally adapted plants. Plant availability from growers or wholesalers, who may be located hundreds of miles away, often determines which cultivars are offered for sale. Genetic makeup of the plant will determine performance to a large extent, and buying a plant not adapted to the local area cannot be rectified through good cultural practices. Another essential matter is to consider only fresh material. Plants that exhibit wilting due to improper care should be avoided, regardless of price.

Local growers who sell retail are excellent plant sources because they grow locally adapted plants, understand cultural requirements, and are better able to advise the gardener on proper plant care. Additionally, if the local nurseryperson grows plants in the field, in local soil, there could be a further advantage. Plants transplanted into a medium of similar texture will extend roots into the surrounding soil faster after transplanting than plants growing in a medium of different texture.

Reputable mail order nurseries are another source of healthy plants, but it might be wise to determine which cultivars are adapted to your area before opening the catalogs. The beautiful pictures and poetic descriptions can redirect purchases to plants not locally adapted.

Acclimation is a factor often considered in purchasing plants with the assumption that northern-grown plants are more cold hardy. The area the plants are grown in does *not* affect genetic cold hardiness; thus a 'Nova Zembla' rhododendron purchased in Maine, for example, has no more hardiness potential than one purchased in North Carolina or Oregon. The maturity or dormancy of the plant, however, does affect survival of a fall-planted rhododendron but is not a consideration in spring planting. In the fall, plants grown in southern areas (with longer growing seasons) and not yet dormant and hardened off will be damaged if moved north and planted where temperatures below freezing are encountered prior to hardening off. The southern-grown plant is thus more tender because of differences it has experienced in the current growing season between the two geographic locations. An exception is a species that grows naturally over a wide temperature range. Over many years the same species may evolve to develop more or less cold hardiness as a result of exposure to different temperature conditions.

Selection of a specific cultivar adapted to the local area—a good doer—is vital to the successful culture of rhododendrons and azaleas. There are many outstanding *Rhododendrons* available that have been tested by experienced growers in specific regions and under specific conditions of climate. The local gardener is wise to take advantage of this extensive testing and selection process.

The Good Doer Lists

The remainder of this chapter is devoted to the Good Doer Lists. (Detailed information, arranged alphabetically by species and hybrids, can be found in appendix A for most plants on the lists.) The lists are presented as guides and should not be construed to include all the cultivars that can be grown in a region. Rather, the lists represent plants that are widely grown in and well adapted to that particular geographic area.

The letters following rhododendron species plant names refer to elepidote (E) and lepidote (L). Elepidote species are nonscaly, large-leaved forms; lepidote species are scaly-leaved forms. Rhododendron hybrid listings (cultivars) have been separated by elepidote and lepidote. Azaleas follow in order by deciduous species, deciduous hybrid, evergreen species, and evergreen hybrid. Color photographs of each type are presented in Plates 2–55.

Alabama, Zone 7a

Afternoon shade, attention to good drainage, pine bark dug into the soil, and a pine bark or pine needle mulch are needed. This list is provided by Pete McNees of Tuscumbia, Alabama.

RHODODENDRON SPECIES
R. catawbiense E
R. degronianum ssp. *yakushimanum* E
   ('K. Wada')
R. maximum E
R. minus L

RHODODENDRON HYBRIDS—ELEPIDOTE
'Catawbiense Boursault'
'Champaign'
'County of York'
'Cynthia'
'Gigi'
'Gomer Waterer'
'Janet Blair'
'Kate Waterer'
'Maximum Roseum'

RHODODENDRON HYBRIDS—LEPIDOTE
'Blue Ridge'
'Early Bird'
'Lanny's Pride'
'Mary Fleming'
'Pioneer'
'Windbeam'

DECIDUOUS AZALEA SPECIES
R. alabamense
R. arborescens
R. atlanticum
R. austrinum
R. cumberlandense (formerly *bakeri*)
R. prunifolium
R. flammeum (formerly *speciosum*)
R. viscosum

EVERGREEN AZALEA HYBRIDS
'Ben Morrison'
'Delaware Valley White'
'Dorothy Clark'
'Fascination'
'George L. Tabor'
'H. H. Hume'
'Margaret Douglas'
'Mrs. G. G. Gerbing'
'Pink Ruffles'
'Sherwood Red'

Montgomery, Zone 8a

This list is provided by C. E. Robinson of Auburn, Alabama.

RHODODENDRON SPECIES
R. fortunei E
R. maximum E
R. minus L

RHODODENDRON HYBRIDS—ELEPIDOTE
'A. Bedford'
'America'
'Anah Kruschke'
'Anna Rose Whitney'
'Belle Heller'
'Caroline'
'Gomer Waterer'
'Grierosplendour'
'Nova Zembla'
'Scintillation'

'Trude Webster'
'Vulcan'

DECIDUOUS AZALEA SPECIES
R. alabamense
R. arborescens
R. austrinum
R. calendulaceum
R. prunifolium
R. flammeum (formerly *speciosum*)
R. vaseyi

DECIDUOUS AZALEA HYBRIDS
'Gibraltar'
'Ilam Red Letter'
'Klondyke'
'Orangeade'

EVERGREEN AZALEA HYBRIDS
'Azuma Kagami' (syn. 'Pink Pearl')
'Fashion'
'Festive'
'George L. Tabor'
'Hinode giri'

'Kirin' (syn. 'Coral Bells')
'Margaret Douglas'
'Pink Ruffles'
'Red Ruffles'
'Snow'

California: Zones 7–10

Santa Cruz, Zone 10

List is provided by Mrs. Melvin C. Allen of Santa Cruz, California.

RHODODENDRON SPECIES
R. arboreum ssp. zeylanicum E
R. augustinii L
R. burmanicum L
R. davidsonianum L
R. degronianum ssp. yakushimanum E
R. dichroanthum ssp. scyphocalyx E
R. hyperythrum E
R. irroratum ssp. aberconwayi E
R. ponticum E
R. racemosum L

RHODODENDRON HYBRIDS—ELEPIDOTE
'Anah Kruschke'
'Jean Marie de Montague'
'Lem's Cameo'
'Loder's White'
'Markeeta's Flame'
'Mrs. G. W. Leak'
'Pink Pearl'
'Purple Splendor'
'Trilby'
'Trude Webster'
'Unique'

RHODODENDRON HYBRIDS—LEPIDOTE
'California Blue'
'Fragrantissimum'
'Lemon Mist'
'Mi Amor'

'Myrtifolium'
'Pink Snowflakes'
'P.J.M.'
'Ramapo'
'Saffron Queen'

DECIDUOUS AZALEA HYBRIDS
'Betty Oliver'
'Cecile'
'Corringe'
'Gibraltar'
'Homebush'
'Klondyke'
'Princess Royal'
'Renne'
'Sun Chariot'

EVERGREEN AZALEA SPECIES
R. kiusianum

EVERGREEN AZALEA HYBRIDS
'Cloud Nine'
'Glamour'
'Gumpo'
'Iveryana'
'Jean Haerens'
'Kirin' (syn. 'Coral Bells')
'Refrain'
'Sherwood Orchid'
'Sherwood Red'
'Starlight' (Kerrigan Hybrid)

Monterey Bay, Zone 11

List is provided by John Hixson of Watsonville, California.

RHODODENDRON SPECIES
R. *augustinii* L
R. *bureavii* E
R. *burmanicum* L
R. *davidsonianum* L
R. *moupinense* L
R. *ponticum* E
R. *smithii* E
R. *veitchianum* L
R. *yunnanense* L

RHODODENDRON HYBRIDS—ELEPIDOTE
'Anah Kruschke'
'Antoon van Welie'
'Gomer Waterer'
'Halfdan Lem'

'Jean Marie de Montague'
'Markeeta's Flame'
'Markeeta's Prize'
'Pink Walloper'
'Queen Nefertite'
'Ruby Bowman'

RHODODENDRON HYBRIDS—LEPIDOTE
'Bric-a-brac'
'Elsie Frye'
'Forsterianum'
'Frangrantissimum'
'Lemon Mist'
'Ramapo'
'Snow Lady'

Northern California, Zone 9b

This list furnished by Dee Denari and the Eureka Chapter ARS.

RHODODENDRON SPECIES
R. *calophytum* E
R. *campylogynum* E
R. *williamsianum* E

RHODODENDRON HYBRIDS—ELEPIDOTE
'Alice'
'Anah Kruschke'
'Bibiani'
'Bruce Brechtbill'
'Christmas Cheer'
'Cornubia'
'Cupcake'
'Fastuosum Flore Pleno'
'Grace Seabrook'
'Halfdan Lem'
'Hallelujah'
'Horizon Monarch'
'Jean Marie de Montague'
'Lem's Cameo'
'Loderi King George'
'Loderi Venus'

'Manda Sue'
'May Day'
'Mrs. Charles E. Pearson'
'Mrs. E. C. Stirling'
'Mrs. G. W. Leak'
'Nancy Evans'
'Naselle'
'Noyo Brave'
'Noyo Chief'
'Noyo Dream'
Olympic Lady Group
'Peter Faulk'

RHODODENDRON HYBRIDS—LEPIDOTE
'Blaney's Blue'
'Bodega Crystal Pink'
'Dora Amateis'
'Frangrantissimum'
'Ginny Gee'
'Goldilocks'
'Mi Amor'

Georgia: Zones 7–8

This list is provided by Mrs. George Beasley Sr. of Lavonia, Georgia.

RHODODENDRON SPECIES
R. adenopodum E
R. catawbiense E
R. degronianum ssp. *yakushimanum* E
R. fortunei E
R. makinoi E
R. minus L (Carolinianum Group)
R. mucronulatum L

RHODODENDRON HYBRIDS–ELEPIDOTE
'A. Bedford'
'Anna Rose Whitney'
'Caroline'
'Chionoides' (syn. 'Lemon Ice')
'County of York'
'Cynthia'
'Jean Marie de Montague'
'Ken Janeck'
'Mr. W. R. Coe'
'Nova Zembla'
'Old Copper'
'Sappho'
'Scintillation'
'Taurus'
'Tom Everett'
'Vulcan'
'Wheatley'

RHODODENDRON HYBRIDS–LEPIDOTE
'Olga Mezitt'

DECIDUOUS AZALEA SPECIES
R. alabamense
R. austrinum
R. calendulaceum

R. canescens
R. flammeum (formerly *speciosum*)
R. periclymenoides (formerly *nudiflorum*)
R. prinophyllum (formerly *roseum*)
R. prunifolium
R. viscosum

DECIDUOUS AZALEA HYBRIDS
'Gibraltar'
'Girard's Yellow Pom Pom'
'Klondyke'
'My Mary'
'Peachy Keen'
'Windsor Buttercup'

EVERGREEN AZALEA SPECIES
R. nakaharae
R. oldhamii
R. serpyllifolium
R. stenopetalum (includes *macrosepalum*)

EVERGREEN AZALEA HYBRIDS
'Adelaide Pope'
'Anna Kehr'
'Ben Morrison'
'Dayspring'
'Debonnaire'
'Delos'
'Easter Parade'
'Glacier'
'Nancy of Robinhill'
'Parfait'
'Refrain'
'Sunglow'

The Great Lakes Chapter Western Pennsylvania, New York, Ohio, Eastern Michigan, Zone 6

This region experiences broad temperature swings from –25°F (–32°C) to 100°F (38°C). Evergreen azaleas do not do well in this area. This list is provided by Dr. Thomas L. Ring, Bellaire, Ohio, Great Lakes Chapter ARS.

RHODODENDRON SPECIES
R. catawbiense E
R. degronianum ssp. *yakushimanum* E

R. fortunei E
R. maximum E
R. minus L (Carolinianum Group)

RHODODENDRON HYBRIDS–ELEPIDOTE
'Albert Close'
'Ben Moseley'
'Besse Howells'
'Calsap'
'Capistrano'
'Catawbiense Album'
'English Roseum'
'Ice Cube'
'Ken Janeck'
'Lee's Dark Purple'
'Merley Cream'
'Newburyport Belle'
'Parker's Pink'

RHODODENDRON HYBRIDS–LEPIDOTE
'Carolina Rose'
    Early bloomers are frequently caught by frost.

DECIDUOUS AZALEA SPECIES
R. calendulaceum
R. cumberlandense (formerly *bakeri*)
R. prunifolium
R. vaseyi

DECIDUOUS AZALEA HYBRIDS
'Girard's Crimson Tide'
'Girard's Yellow Pom Pom'
'Rufus'

EVERGREEN AZALEA SPECIES
R. kiusianum 'Komo Kulshan'

EVERGREEN AZALEA HYBRIDS
'Boudoir'
'Carrie Amanda'
'Delaware Valley White'
'Elsie Lee'
'Fedora'
Pride Hybrids

Illinois: Zones 5–6

This list is provided by Eugene Paschall of Palos Heights, Illinois, Midwest Chapter ARS, and Roger Dunlap, past president of the Midwest Chapter.

RHODODENDRON SPECIES
R. brachycarpum ssp. *tigerstedtii* E
R. degronianum ssp. *yakushimanum* E
    ('Mist Maiden', 'Pink Parasol')
R. minus L
R. smirnowii E

RHODODENDRON HYBRIDS–ELEPIDOTE
'Barrington Rose'
'Belrose'
'Calsap'
'Mrs. Charles S. Sargent'
'County of York' (syn. 'Catalode')
'Dexter-Bosley 1020'
'Edmund Amateis'
'Henry's Red'
'High Summit'
'Janet Blair'
'Joe Paterno'
'July Hope'
'Ken Janeck'
'Late Arrival'
'Lavender Princess'
'Mary Kittel'

'Newburyport Belle'
'Pearce's American Beauty'
'Persia'
'Peter Vermuelin'
'Pink Scallop'
'Red River'
'Scintillation' (Mehlquist form)
'Trinidad'
'White Peter'
'Wojnar's Purple'
'Wyandanch Pink'
'Years of Peace'

RHODODENDRON HYBRIDS–LEPIDOTE
'Aglo'
'Fasia'
'Ivory Coast'
'Llenroc'
'Milestone'
'Pioneer Silvery Pink'

DECIDUOUS AZALEA SPECIES
R. atlanticum
R. calendulaceum ('Carlson's Coral Queen')

R. schlippenbachii
R. viscosum

DECIDUOUS AZALEA HYBRIDS
'Cannon's Double'
'Daviesii'
'Fireball'
'George Beasley'

'Girard's Crimson Tide'
'Mt. St. Helens'

EVERGREEN AZALEA SPECIES
R. yedoense var. *poukhanense*

EVERGREEN AZALEA HYBRIDS
'Herbert'
'Hino Red'

Illinois, Zone 5

This list supplied is by John Golab, Barrington, Illinois.

RHODODENDRON SPECIES
R. brachycarpum E
R. brachycarpum var. *tigerstedtii* E
R. catawbiense E
R. degronianum ssp. *yakushimanum* E
   ('Angel', 'Mist Maiden', 'Pink Parasol')
R. maximum E
R. smirnowii E

RHODODENDRON HYBRIDS–ELEPIDOTE
'America'
'Anna H. Hall'
'Ballad'
'Barrington Rose'
'Besse Howells'
'Calsap'
'Caroline'
'Catawbiense Album'
'County of York'
'Dexter-Bosley 1020'
'Red River'
'Joe Paterno'
'Ken Janeck'
'Today and Tomorrow'

RHODODENDRON HYBRIDS–LEPIDOTE
'Aglo'
'Alice Swift'
'April Rose'
'Carolina Rose'
'Fasia'
'Hudson Bay'
'Llenroc'
'Milestone'
'Molly Fordham'
'Mrs. J. A. Withington'
'New Patriot'
'Olga Mezitt'

DECIDUOUS AZALEA SPECIES
R. arborescens
R. atlanticum
R. calendulaceum
R. cumberlandense (formerly *bakeri*)
R. kiusianum 'Komo Kulshan'
R. prinophyllum (formerly *roseum*)
R. prunifolium
R. vaseyi 'White Find'
R. viscosum

DECIDUOUS AZALEA HYBRIDS
'Cannon's Double'
'Cecile'
'Gibraltar'
'Lemon Drop'
'My Mary'
Northern Lights Series (all)
'Old Gold'
'Oxydol'
'Parade'

EVERGREEN AZALEA SPECIES
R. yedoense var. *poukhanense*

EVERGREEN AZALEA HYBRIDS
'Elsie Lee'
'Girard's Hot Shot'
'Gordon'
'Helen Curtis'
'Herbert'
'Hino Red'
'Louise Gable'
'Mildred Mae'
'Pride's Joe Gable'
'Rosebud'
'Schroeder Sunray'

Maryland: Zone 6

This list is provided by the author.

RHODODENDRON SPECIES
- *R. catawbiense* E
- *R. dauricum* L
- *R. degronianum* E (formerly *metternichii*)
- *R. degronianum* ssp. *yakushimanum* E ('Mist Maiden')
- *R. keiskei* L
- *R. maximum* E
- *R. minus* L (Carolinianum Group)
- *R. minus* var. *chapmanii* L

RHODODENDRON HYBRIDS–ELEPIDOTE
- 'Acclaim'
- 'Albert Close'
- 'Anita Gehnrich'
- 'Anna H. Hall'
- 'Brown Eyes'
- 'Caroline'
- 'Catawbiense Album'
- 'Chionoides'
- 'County of York'
- 'David Gable'
- 'English Roseum'
- 'Fantastica'
- 'Great Eastern'
- 'Ice Cube'
- 'Janet Blair'
- 'Lodestar'
- 'Nepal'
- 'Red Companion'
- 'Roseum Pink'
- 'Spring Parade'
- 'Wynterset White'

RHODODENDRON HYBRIDS–LEPIDOTE
- 'Alice Swift'
- 'Conewago'
- 'Dora Amateis'
- 'Malta'
- 'Mary Fleming'
- 'Molly Fordham'
- 'Olga Mezitt'
- 'P.J.M.'
- 'Windbeam'

DECIDUOUS AZALEA SPECIES
- *R. calendulaceum*
- *R. cumberlandense* (formerly *bakeri*)
- *R. periclymenoides* (formerly *nudiflorum*)
- *R. prunifolium*
- *R. schlippenbachii*

DECIDUOUS AZALEA HYBRIDS
- 'Brazil'
- 'Gibraltar'
- 'Girard's Crimson Tide'
- 'Girard's Yellow Pom Pom'
- 'Homebush'
- 'Kathleen'
- 'Klondyke'
- 'Narcissiflorum'
- 'Old Gold'
- 'Strawberry Ice'
- 'Toucan'

EVERGREEN AZALEA SPECIES
- *R. kaempferi*
- *R. kiusianum*
- *R. yedoense* var. *poukhanense*

EVERGREEN AZALEA HYBRIDS
- 'Delaware Valley White'
- 'Elsie Lee'
- 'Girard's Border Gem'
- 'Girard's Chiara'
- 'Girard's Fuchsia'
- 'Helen Curtis'
- 'Herbert'
- 'Hino Red'
- 'James Gable'
- 'Louise Gable'
- 'May Belle'
- 'Rose Greeley'
- 'Rosebud'
- 'Springtime'
- 'Stewartstonian'

Massachusetts: Zones 5–6

This list, from a 1980 survey by the Massachusetts Chapter ARS, is provided by A. Richard Brooks of Concord, Massachusetts. An asterisk indicates a record updated by Wayne Mezitt.

RHODODENDRON SPECIES
R. brachycarpum E
R. dauricum L
R. degronianum ssp. yakushimanum E
  ('K. Wada')
R. ferrugineum L
R. fortunei E
R. hippophaeoides L
R. impeditum L
*R. maximum E
R. minus L (Carolinianum Group)
*R. minus ssp. minus L
R. mucronulatum L ('Cornell Pink')
R. racemosum L
R. russatum L

RHODODENDRON HYBRIDS—ELEPIDOTE
'Anna H. Hall'
'Besse Howells'
*'Big Deal'
'Boule de Neige'
'Cadis'
'Catawbiense Album'
*'Catawbiense Boursault'
'English Roseum'
'Janet Blair'
'Jean Marie de Montague'
'Ken Janeck'
'Mary Belle'
'Mrs. Charles S. Sargent'
'Mrs. Furnivall'
'Nova Zembla'
'Scintillation'
*'Trojan Warrior'
'Wheatley'

RHODODENDRON HYBRIDS—LEPIDOTE
*'April Snow'
'Balta'
'Dora Amateis'
*'Landmark'
'Laurie'
'Llenroc'
'Mary Fleming'

'Olga Mezitt'
'Pioneer'
'P.J.M.'
'Ramapo'
*'Weston's Aglo'
*'Weston's Pink Diamond'
'Windbeam'

DECIDUOUS AZALEA SPECIES
R. calendulaceum
R. molle ssp. japonicum
R. prinophyllum (formerly roseum)
R. schlippenbachii
R. vaseyi
R. viscosum

DECIDUOUS AZALEA HYBRIDS
'Cecile'
'Daviesii'
'Gibraltar'
'Golden Oriole'
'Homebush'
Jane Abbott Hybrids
'Klondyke'

EVERGREEN AZALEA SPECIES
R. kaempferi
R. kiusianum (including var. album)
R. nakaharae
R. yedoense var. poukhanense

EVERGREEN AZALEA HYBRIDS
'Boudoir'
'Buccaneer'
'Delaware Valley White'
'Fedora'
'Guy Yerkes'
'Herbert'
'Hino Crimson'
'Lorna'
'Mother's Day'
'Palestrina' (syn. 'Wilhelmina Vuyk')
'Rosebud'
'Springtime'
'Stewartstonian'

Cape Cod, Zone 7a

This list is provided by Dr. Richard Chaiken of Falmount, Massachusetts, Cape Cod and Islands Chapter ARS.

RHODODENDRON SPECIES
R. bureavii E
R. calophytum E.
R. degronianum E
R. degronianum ssp. *yakushimanum* E
R. fastigiatum L
R. ferrugineum L
R. fortunei E
R. impeditum L
R. keiskei L ('Yaku Fairy')
R. makinoi E
R. minus L (Carolinianum Group)
R. pachysanthum E
R. pseudochrysanthum E
R. racemosum L
R. russatum L
R. smirnowii E

RHODODENDRON HYBRIDS—ELEPIDOTE
'Anna H. Hall'
'Atroflo'
'Baden Baden'
'Bonnie Maid'
'Buttermint'
'Catawbiense Album'
'Chikor'
'Chionoides'
'Crest' (syn. 'Hawk Crest')
'David Gable'
Dexter's Hybrids
'Golden Star'
'Gomer Waterer'
'Hello Dolly'
'Janet Blair'
'Jean Marie de Montague'
'Mary Belle'
'Melanie Shaw'
'Olin O. Dobbs'
'Parker's Pink'
'Platinum Pearl'
'Purple Splendor'
'Scintillation'
'Taurus'
'Unique'
'Vulcan'
'Vulcan's Flame'

RHODODENDRON HYBRIDS—LEPIDOTE
'April Gem'
'Conewago'
'Dora Amateis'
'Laurie'
'Llenroc'
'Mary Fleming'
'Molly Fordham'
'Olga Mezitt'
'Patty Bee'
'Pioneer'
'P.J.M.'
'Purple Gem'
'Rose Marie'
'Tiffany'
'Weston's Pink Diamond'

DECIDUOUS AZALEA SPECIES
R. arborescens
R. calendulaceum
R. cumberlandense (formerly *bakeri*)
R. prunifolium
R. schlippenbachii
R. vaseyi
R. vaseyi var. *alba*

DECIDUOUS AZALEA HYBRIDS
'George Reynolds'
'Mt. St. Helens'
'My Mary'
'Persian Melon'
'Windsor Appleblossom'
'Windsor Buttercup'

EVERGREEN AZALEA SPECIES
R. kiusianum
R. kiusianum 'SH-RBF'

EVERGREEN AZALEA HYBRIDS
'Conversation Piece'
'Desiree'
'Eureka'
'Girard's Hot Shot'
'Girard's Rose'
'Louise Gable'
'Mary Dalton'
'Nancy of Robinhill'
'Surprise'

Michigan: Zones 5–6

This list is provided by Mrs. Virginia L. Heller of Detroit, Michigan.

RHODODENDRON HYBRIDS–ELEPIDOTE
'Album Elegans'
'Calsap'
'Hong Kong'
'Janet Blair'
'Lemon Ice' (syn. 'Chionoides')
'Mrs. Tom Lowinsky'
'Sham's Candy'
'Spring Parade'
'Summer Summit'
'Yaku Queen'

RHODODENDRON HYBRIDS–LEPIDOTE
'Ambie'
'Dora Amateis'
'Mary Fleming'
'Molly Fordham'
'Towhead'

DECIDUOUS AZALEA HYBRIDS
'Brazil'
'Gibraltar'
'Ginger'
'Golden Eagle'
'Klondyke'
'Mt. St. Helens'

Missouri: Zones 5–6

This list is provided by Walter Behrendt Jr., Missouri Botanical Garden.

RHODODENDRON SPECIES
R. degronianum ssp. yakushimanum E
  ('Mist Maiden')

RHODODENDRON HYBRIDS–ELEPIDOTE
'Brown Eyes'
'Burma'
'English Roseum'
'Henry's Red'
'Janet Blair'
'Ken Janeck'
'Madrid'
'Nova Zembla'
'Roseum Superbrum'
'Scintillation'
'Solidarity'
'Yaku Prince'
'Yaku Queen'

RHODODENDRON HYBRIDS–LEPIDOTE
'Alice Swift'
'Carita'
'Creeping Jenny'
'Dora Amateis'
'Ginny Gee'
'Mary Fleming'
'P.J.M.'
'Tom Koenig'

'Tow Head'
'Weston's Pink Diamond'

DECIDUOUS AZALEA SPECIES
R. calendulaceum
R. prinophyllum (formerly roseum)

DECIDUOUS AZALEA HYBRIDS
'Camp's Red'
'Fanny'
'George Reynolds'
'Gibraltar'
'Ginger'
'Mt. St. Helens'
'My Mary'
'Narcissiflorum'
Northern Light Series (all)

EVERGREEN AZALEA SPECIES
R. yedoense var. poukhanense

EVERGREEN AZALEA HYBRIDS
'Amoenum'
'Atlanta'
'Boudoir'
'Cascade' (Shammarello Hybrid)
'Corsage'
'Fedora'
'Girard's Hot Shot'

'Girard's Rose'
'Hino Crimson'
'Mrs. Henry Schroeder'
'Palestrina'
'Purple Splendor'

'Schroeder's Lavender Rose'
'Sherwood Orchid'
'Stewartstonian'
'Susan Camille'

This list is provided by Ed Wood, of the Great Rivers Chapter ARS.

RHODODENDRON SPECIES
R. degronianum ssp. *yakushimanum*
('Mist Maiden')

RHODODENDRON HYBRIDS–ELEPIDOTE
'Album Elegans'
'Apple Blossom'
'Blue Ensign'
'Bosley-Dexter 1009'
'Boule de Neige'
'Catawbiense Album'
'Francesca'
'Great Eastern'
'Ice Cube'
'Janet Blair'
'Ken Janeck'

'Lodestar'
'Maximum Roseum'
'Parson's Gloriosum'
'Purpureum Elegans'
'Roseum Pink'
'Russell Harmon'
'Scintillation'
'Shawme Lake'

RHODODENDRON HYBRIDS–LEPIDOTE
'Conewago Improved'
'Olga Mezitt'
'P.J.M.'
'Windbeam'
'Wyanoki'

New Hampshire: Zones 4–5

This list is provided by Joe B. Parks of Dover, New Hampshire.

RHODODENDRON SPECIES
R. catawbiense E
R. dauricum L
R. degronianum ssp. *yakushimanum* E
(Exbury Form, 'Mist Maiden')
R. impeditum L
R. keiskei L
R. maximum E
R. minus L
R. minus L (Carolinianum Group)
R. smirnowii E

RHODODENDRON HYBRIDS–ELEPIDOTE
'America'
'Anna H. Hall'
'Besse Howells'
'Boule de Neige'
'Dolly Madison'
'Henry's Red'
'Ice Cube'
'Ken Janeck'

'Lodestar'
'Mrs. Charles S. Sargent'
'Tony'
'Vernus'

RHODODENDRON HYBRIDS–LEPIDOTE
'Aglo'
'April Snow'
'Balta'
'Llenroc'
'Olga Mezitt'
'P.J.M.'
'Ramapo'
'Wally'
'Waltham'
'Weston's Pink Diamond'
'Windbeam'

DECIDUOUS AZALEA SPECIES
R. arborescens
R. canadense

Selection of Rhododendrons

R. mucronulatum 'Cornell Pink'
R. prinophyllum (formerly *roseum*)
R. prunifolium
R. vaseyi
R. viscosum

DECIDUOUS AZALEA HYBRIDS
'Brazil'
'Gibraltar'
'Golden Oriole'
'Golden Sunset'
'Homebush'

'Lemon Drop'
'Queen Emma'
'Satan'
'Toucan'

EVERGREEN AZALEA SPECIES
R. kaempferi
R. yedoense var. *poukhanense*

EVERGREEN AZALEA HYBRIDS
Not adapted, act as deciduous plants. Two that
flower are 'Pride's Pride' and 'Pride's White'.

——————————————— New York: Zone 7 ———————————————

This list is provided by Frank Arsen, Lindenhurst, New York.

RHODODENDRON SPECIES
R. bureavii E
R. degronianum E (formerly *metternichii*)
R. degronianum ssp. *yakushimanum* E
R. fortunei E
R. keiskei L
R. makinoi E
R. pseudochrysanthum E
R. racemosum L
R. roxieanum E

RHODODENDRON HYBRIDS–ELEPIDOTE
'Boule de Neige'
'Dexter 974'
'Everestianum'
'Gigi'
'Janet Blair'
'Old Port'
'Parker's Pink'
'Scintillation'
'Tom Everett'
'Vulcan'

RHODODENDRON HYBRIDS–LEPIDOTE
'Fairy Mary'
'Ginny Gee'
'Mary Fleming'
'Patty Bee'
'P.J.M.'
'Spring Song'
'Windbeam'

DECIDUOUS AZALEA SPECIES
R. albrechtii
R. arborescens

R. calendulaceum
R. luteum
R. pentaphyllum
R. periclymenoides (formerly *nudiflorum*)
R. prunifolium
R. schlippenbachii
R. vaseyi

DECIDUOUS AZALEA HYBRIDS
'Coccinea Speciosa'
'Copper Cloud'
'Corneille'
'Fireball'
'Gibraltar'
'Homebush'
'Narcissiflorum'

EVERGREEN AZALEA SPECIES
R. kaempferi
R. kiusianum
R. nakaharae
R. serpyllifolium
R. stenopetalum (includes *macrosepalum*)

EVERGREEN AZALEA HYBRIDS
'Ben Morrison'
'Dayspring'
'Delaware Valley White'
'Forest Fire'
'Margaret Douglas'
'Nancy of Robinhill'
'Orange Beauty'
'Stewartstonian'
'Surprise'

─── North Carolina, Northern South Carolina, Northern Georgia, ─── and Eastern Tennessee: Zones 6–8

The list is submitted by Ed Collins of the Southeastern Chapter ARS with members in North Carolina, northern South Carolina, northern Georgia, and eastern Tennessee.

RHODODENDRON SPECIES
R. keiskei L
R. maximum E
R. minus L

RHODODENDRON HYBRIDS–ELEPIDOTE
'A. Bedford'
'Acclaim'
'Anah Kruschke'
'Ben Moseley'
'Blue Ensign'
'David Gable'
'Dexter's Giant Red'
'Dexter's Purple'
'English Roseum'
'Francesca'
'Gigi'
'Grace Seabrook'
'Great Smokey'
'Janet Blair'
'Jean Marie de Montague'
'Ken Janeck'
'Mardi Gras'
'Parker's Pink'
'Roseum Elegans'
'Scintillation'
'Solidarity'
'Taurus'
'Todmorden'
'Tom Everett'
'Trude Webster'
'Vulcan'
'Wheatly'
'Wyandanch Pink'

RHODODENDRON HYBRIDS–LEPIDOTE
'Anna Baldsiefen'
'Donna Totten'
'Dora Amateis'
'Ginny Gee'
'Manitou'
'Mary Fleming'
'Olga Mezitt'
'Patty Bee'

'P.J.M.'
'Ramapo'
'Southland'
'Windbeam'
'Yellow Eye'

DECIDUOUS AZALEA SPECIES
R. alabamense
R. arborescens
R. atlanticum
R. austrinum
R. calendulaceum
R. canescens
R. cumberlandense (formerly *bakeri*)
R. eastmanii
R. flammeum (formerly *speciosum*)
R. periclymenoides (formerly *nudiflorum*)
R. prinophyllum (formerly *roseum*)
R. prunifolium
R. vaseyi
R. viscosum

DECIDUOUS AZALEA HYBRIDS
'Evening Glow'
'Gibraltar'
'Homebush'
'Klondyke'
'Mt. St. Helens'

EVERGREEN AZALEA SPECIES
R. kiusianum ('Komo Kulshan')
R. yedoense var. *poukhanense*

EVERGREEN AZALEA HYBRIDS
'Ben Morrison'
'Conversation Piece'
'Daphne'
'Delaware Valley White'
'Easter Parade'
'Elsie Lee'
'George Lindley Tabor'
'Gillie'
'Girard's Hot Shot'
'Gumpo'
'Hardy Gardenia'

Selection of Rhododendrons

'Helen Curtis'
'Hilda Niblett'
'Kehr's White Rosebud'
'Koromo Shikibu'
'Marion Lee'
'Martha Hitchcock'

'Midnight Flair'
'Nancy of Robinhill'
'Purple Splendor'
'Renee Michelle'
'Wintergreen'

Oklahoma: Zone 6

Rhododendrons in this area require irrigation, shade, raised plantings in clay soil areas, lots of pine bark dug into the soil to help control phytophthora root rot, and a good mulch of pine bark, pine needles, or oak leaves. This list is provided by Dr. Leonard Miller of Grove, Oklahoma.

RHODODENDRON HYBRIDS–ELEPIDOTE
'Blue Peter'
'Bravo'
'Edmond Amateis'
'Fantastica'
'Nova Zembla'
'Percy Wiseman'
'Polaris'
'Roseum Elegans'

RHODODENDRON HYBRIDS–LEPIDOTE
'Ginny Gee'
'Jericho'
'Northern Starburst'
'Olga Mezitt'
'P.J.M.'
'Weston's Aglo'

DECIDUOUS AZALEA SPECIES
R. austrinum
R. prunifolium
R. schlippenbachii

DECIDUOUS AZALEA HYBRIDS
'Gibraltar'
'Golden Flare'
'Golden Lights'
'Jolie Madam'
'King's Red'
'Rosy Lights'
'White Lights'

EVERGREEN AZALEA SPECIES
R. kiusianum

EVERGREEN AZALEA HYBRIDS
'Delaware Valley White'
'Girard's Crimson'
'Girard's Fuchsia'
'Girard's Hot Shot'
'Girard's Pleasant White'
'Hino Crimson'
'Kirin' (syn 'Coral Bells')
'Margaret Douglas'

Oregon: Zones 5–9

In the western half of Washington and Oregon the zones range from 7 through 8. The eastern part of Washington and Oregon is much drier and has more extremes of both hot and cold. Zones in that region range from 5 through 7. The conditions in eastern Oregon require choices of plants much like those used on the east coast of the United States. This list is provided by Harold Greer of Greer Gardens, Eugene, Oregon, Zone 8.

RHODODENDRON SPECIES
R. augustinii L
R. calophytum E
R. calostrotum ssp. keleticum
R. davidsonianum L

R. decorum E
R. degronianum E (formerly metternichii)
R. degronianum ssp. yakushimanum E
R. fortunei E
R. haematodes E

R. hippophaeoides L
R. impeditum L
R. keiskei L
R. litangense L (syn. *R. impeditum*)
R. mucronulatum L
R. pseudochrysanthum E
R. racemosum L
R. roxieanum E
R. sutchuenense E
R. williamsianum E
R. yungningense L

RHODODENDRON HYBRIDS–ELEPIDOTE
'Anah Kruschke'
'Autumn Gold'
'Grace Seabrook'
'Hallelujah'
'Jean Marie de Montague'
'Ring of Fire'
'September Song'
'Trude Webster'
'Unique'
'Van'

RHODODENDRON HYBRIDS–LEPIDOTE
'Blaney's Blue'
'Crater Lake'
'Dora Amateis'
'Ginny Gee'
'Mother Greer'
'Patty Bee'
'P.J.M.'
'Ramapo'
'Senora Meldon'
'Wigeon'

DECIDUOUS AZALEA SPECIES
R. atlanticum
R. canadense
R. luteum
R. molle ssp. *japonicum*
R. occidentale
R. periclymenoides (formerly *nudiflorum*)
R. schlippenbachii

DECIDUOUS AZALEA HYBRIDS
'Cecile'
'Gibraltar'
'Ginger'
'Homebush'
'Kathleen'
'Chetco'
'Tangelo'
'Washington State Centennial'
'White Lights'

EVERGREEN AZALEA SPECIES
R. indicum (formerly *macranthum*)
R. kiusianum
R. nakaharae
R. yedoense

EVERGREEN AZALEA HYBRIDS
'Alexander'
'Gaiety'
'Glamour'
'Hershey's Red'
'Hino Crimson'
'Polypetalum'
'Purple Splendor'
'Sherwood Orchid'
'Stewartstonian'
'Vuyk's Scarlet'

Portland, Zones 7–8

This list is provided by Clarence Smith, past president of the Tualatin Valley Chapter ARS; compiled by the chapter membership.

RHODODENDRON SPECIES
R. augustinii L
R. decorum E
R. degronianum ssp. *yakushimanum* E
R. fortunei E
R. mucronulatum L

R. oreodoxa L
R. oreodoxa var. *fargesii*
R. oreotrephes L
R. racemosum L
R. russatum L
R. williamsianum E

Selection of Rhododendrons

RHODODENDRON HYBRIDS–ELEPIDOTE
'Anna Rose Whitney'
'Golfer'
'Halfdan Lem'
'Helene Schiffner'
'Medusa'
'Mrs. Betty Robertson'
'Pink Walloper'
'Purple Splendor'
'Taurus'
'Unique'

RHODODENDRON HYBRIDS–LEPIDOTE
'Barto Alpine'
'Cilpinense'
'Dora Amateis'
'Olive'
'P.J.M.'
'Ramapo'
'Rose Elf'
'Sapphire'
'Seta'
'Small Gem'

DECIDUOUS AZALEA SPECIES
R. albrechtii
R. arborescens
R. atlanticum
R. canadense
R. cumberlandense (formerly bakeri)
R. luteum
R. occidentale
R. periclymenoides (formerly nudiflorum)

R. schlippenbachii
R. vaseyi

DECIDUOUS AZALEA HYBRIDS
'Chetco'
Exbury Hybrids
Ghent Hybrids
'Gibraltar'
'Homebush'
Knap Hill Hybrids
'Marina'
Mollis Hybrids
'Princess Royal'
'Renne'

EVERGREEN AZALEA SPECIES
R. indicum (formerly macranthum)
R. kaempferi
R. kiusianum
R. nakaharae
R. oldhamii
R. simsii

EVERGREEN AZALEA HYBRIDS
'Blue Danube'
'Conversation Piece'
'Everest'
'Hino Crimson'
'Mildred Mae' (Gable Hybrid)
'Mother's Day'
'Purple Splendor'
'Rosebud'
'Stewartstonian'
'Twenty Grand'

Pennsylvania: Zones 6a

This list is provided by Tom Schuetz, Mechanicsburg, Pennsylvania.

RHODODENDRON SPECIES
R. degronianum ssp. yakushimanum E

RHODODENDRON HYBRIDS–ELEPIDOTE
'Blue Peter'
'Caroline'
'County of York'
'English Roseum'
'Janet Blair'
'Ken Janeck'

'Nova Zembla'
'Scintillation' (requires shade)
'Tom Everett'
'Yaku Prince'

RHODODENDRON HYBRIDS–LEPIDOTE
'Hudson Bay'
'Mary Fleming'
'Olga Mezitt'
'P.J.M.'

'Princess Anne
'Rhein's Luna'
'Tiffany'
'Weston's Pink Diamond'
'Windbeam'
'Wyanoki'

DECIDUOUS AZALEA SPECIES
R. periclymenoides (formerly *nudiflorum*)
R. schlippenbachii

DECIDUOUS AZALEA HYBRIDS
'Cecile'
'Gibraltar'
'Golden Lights'
'Homebush'

'Klondyke'
'Lemon Drop'
Lights Series
'Mt. St. Helen'

EVERGREEN AZALEA HYBRIDS
'Delaware Valley White'
'Elsie Lee'
'Gable's Rosebud'
'Hardy Gardenia'
'Herbert'
'Madam Butterfly'
'Martha Hitchcock'
'Mother's Day'
'Pleasant White'
'Red Red'

Texas (North-Central): Zone 7

In this area plants must be grown in raised beds of coarse, well-drained pine bark and watered often. This list is from Keith G. Johansson of Arlington, Texas.

RHODODENDRON SPECIES
R. adenopodum E
R. arboreum E
R. degronianum E
R. degronianum ssp. *yakushimanum* E
R. hyperythrum E
R. makinoi E
R. ponticum E
R. pseudochrysanthum E

RHODODENDRON HYBRIDS–ELEPIDOTE
'Anah Kruschke'
'Anna Rose Whitney'
'Bibiani'
'Blue Ensign'
'Nova Zembla'
'Peppermint Twist'
'Pink Pearl'
'Roseum Elegans'
'Very Berry'
'Wheatley'

RHODODENDRON HYBRIDS–LEPIDOTE
'Emasculum'
'Olga Mezitt'
'P.J.M.'

DECIDUOUS AZALEA SPECIES
R. alabamense
R. arborescens
R. austrinum

DECIDUOUS AZALEA HYBRIDS
Crosses with *R. austrinum*

EVERGREEN AZALEA SPECIES
R. indicum (formerly *macranthum*)
R. kaempferi
R. kiusianum
R. nakaharae
R. obtusum

EVERGREEN AZALEA HYBRIDS
'Germanique'
'Hershey's Red'
'H. H. Hume'
'Matsuyo'
'Olga Niblett'
'Pink Ruffles'
'Sakura kagami'
'Shugetsu'
'Tradition'
'Ward's Ruby'
'Yomo no haru'

Virginia

Roanoke, Zones 6a–b

This list is from a survey by Hugh B. Sproul Jr., of Staunton, Virginia, Middle Atlantic Chapter ARS.

RHODODENDRON SPECIES
R. catawbiense E
R. degronianum E (formerly metternichii)
R. degronianum ssp. yakushimanum E
R. fortunei E
R. keiskei L
R. makinoi E
R. maximum E
R. minus L (Carolinianum Group)
R. minus var. chapmanii L
R. racemosum L

RHODODENDRON HYBRIDS–ELEPIDOTE
'A. Bedford'
'Caroline'
'Catawbiense Boursault'
'County of York'
'David Gable'
'Dr. H. C. Dresselhuys'
'English Roseum'
'Gomer Waterer'
'Jean Marie de Montague'
'Nova Zembla'
'Roseum Elegans'
'Scintillation'

RHODODENDRON HYBRIDS–LEPIDOTE
'Mary Fleming'

'P.J.M.'
'Windbeam'

DECIDUOUS AZALEA SPECIES
R. calendulaceum
R. cumberlandense (formerly bakeri)
R. periclymenoides (formerly nudiflorum)
R. prinophyllum (formerly roseum)
R. vaseyi

DECIDUOUS AZALEA HYBRIDS
'Cecile'
'Gibraltar'
'Goldflakes'
'Klondyke'
'Toucan'

EVERGREEN AZALEA HYBRIDS
'Corsage'
'Delaware Valley White'
'Elsie Lee'
'Glacier'
'Herbert'
'Hershey's Red'
'Hino Crimson'
'Kirin' (syn. 'Coral Bells')
'Rosebud'
'Stewartstonian'

Norfolk, Zone 8a

This list is provided by Sandra McDonald of Hampton, Virginia, and based on a survey by Kenneth McDonald Jr., of Hampton, Virginia.

RHODODENDRON SPECIES
R. degronianum ssp. heptamerum E
R. hyperythrum E
R. maximum E
R. minus L
R. mucronulatum L

RHODODENDRON HYBRIDS–ELEPIDOTE
'A. Bedford'
'Bellringer'
'Daphnoides'
'English Roseum'

'Gable's Little Bonnie'
'Janet Blair'
'Judy Spillane'
'Lodestar'
'Moser's Maroon'
'Scintillation'
'Tom Everett'

RHODODENDRON HYBRIDS–LEPIDOTE
'April Pink'
'Mary Fleming'
'Olga Mezitt'

'P.J.M.'
'Windbeam'

DECIDUOUS AZALEA SPECIES
R. alabamense
R. atlanticum
R. arborescens
R. austrinum
R. canescens
R. cumberlandense (formerly bakeri)
R. periclymenoides (formerly nudiflorum)
R. prunifolium
R. vaseyi
R. viscosum

ORIENTAL DECIDUOUS AZALEAS
R. mariesii
R. reticulatum
R. wadanum

DECIDUOUS AZALEA HYBRIDS
'Brazil'
'Kilauea'
'Klondyke'
'Toucan'

EVERGREEN AZALEA SPECIES
R. indicum (formerly macranthum)
R. kaempferi
R. nakaharae
R. oldhamii
R. serpyllifolium

R. simsii
R. tashiroi
R. yedoense var. poukhanense

EVERGREEN AZALEA HYBRIDS
'Ambrosia'
'Cavalier'
'Dawn'
'Dayspring'
'Dream'
'Elsie Lee'
'Festive'
'Girard's Hot Shot'
'Glacier'
'Hampton Beauty'
'Helen Curtis'
'Herbert'
'Hino Crimson'
'Hino Red'
'Kirin' (syn. 'Coral Bells')
'Marjorie Ann' (Pericat Hybrid)
'Martha Hitchcock'
'Misty Plum'
'Palestrina'
'Pure Perfection'
'Red Red'
'Rose Greeley'
'Stewartstonian'
'White Surprise'
'Williamsburg'

Richmond, Zone 7

This list is provided by Bill Bedwell of Dinwiddie, Virginia.

RHODODENDRON HYBRIDS—ELEPIDOTE
'Anah Kruschke'
'Aunt Martha'
'Betty Wormald'
'Blue Peter'
'Bonfire'
'Cadis'
'Caroline'
'Chionoides'
'Cynthia'
'Grierosplendour'
'Ice Cube'

'John C. White'
'Lodestar'
'Roseum Pink'
'Westbury'
'Wheatley'
'Willard'

DECIDUOUS AZALEA HYBRIDS
'Homebush'
'Marion Merriman'
'Old Gold'
'Queen Emma'
'Toucan'

—————————— Washington, D.C.: Zone 7 ——————————

This list is from Don Hyatt, Potomac Valley Chapter ARS.

RHODODENDRON SPECIES
R. adenopodum E
R. chapnanii L
R. dauricum L
R. degronianum E (formerly *metternichii*)
R. degronianum ssp. *yakushimanum* E
   ('Mist Maiden')
R. hyperythrum E
R. makinoi E
R. minus L (Carolinianum Group)

RHODODENDRON HYBRIDS–ELEPIDOTE
'A. Bedford'
'Anna Rose Whitney'
'Avondale'
'Bellringer'
'Betty Hume'
'Brown Eyes'
'Cadis'
'Capistrano'
'Caroline'
'Champaign'
'David Gable'
'Disca'
'Dr. Rock'
'Fantastica'
'Gigi'
'Great Smokey'
'Janet Blair'
'Katherine Dalton'
'Ken Janeck'
'Mt. Siga'
'Parker's Pink'
'Rochelle'
'Shaazam'
'Solidarity'
'Taurus'
'Trilby'
'Vulcan'
'Vulcan's Flame'

RHODODENDRON HYBRIDS–LEPIDOTE
'24 Karat'
'April White'
'Blue Ridge'

'Cornell Pink'
'Crater Lake'
'Dora Amateis'
'Ginny Gee'
'Mary Fleming'
'Olga Mezitt'
'Southland'
'Windbeam'

DECIDUOUS AZALEA SPECIES
R. arborescens
R. atlanticum
R. austrinum
R. calendulaceum
R. canescens
R. cumberlandense (formerly *bakeri*)
R. flammeum
R. molle ssp. *japonicum*
R. periclymenoides (formerly *nudiflorum*)
R. prunifolium
R. vaseyi

DECIDUOUS AZALEA HYBRIDS
'Admiral Sermmes'
'Balzac'
'Chetco'
'Choptank'
'Gibraltar'
'Golden Lights'
'Goldflakes'
'Homebush'
'King's Red'
'Klondyke'
'Marina'
'Mary Dell'
'Mt. St. Helens'
'Narcissiflorum'
'Old Gold'
'Oxydol'
'Sham's Yellow'
'Snow Bird'
'Sweet Christy'
'Weston's Innocence'
'White Lights'
'Yellow Cloud'

EVERGREEN AZALEA SPECIES
R. kiusianum
R. ripense var. *mucronatum*
R. nakaharae

EVERGREEN AZALEA HYBRIDS
Most evergreen azaleas grow well in this area.

Washington State: Zones 7–8

In the western half of Washington and Oregon the zones range from 7 through 8. The eastern part of Washington and Oregon is much drier and has more extremes of both hot and cold. Zones in that region range from 5 through 7. The conditions in eastern Washington require choices of plants much like those used on the east coast of the United States. This list is provided by Mike Stewart.

RHODODENDRON SPECIES
R. augustinii L
R. degronianum ssp. *yakushimanum* E

RHODODENDRON HYBRIDS–ELEPIDOTE
'Anah Kruschke'
'Daphnoides'
'Gomer Waterer'
'Jean Marie de Montague'
'Lem's Monarch'
'Mrs. Furnivall'
'Odee Wright'
'Taurus'
'Unique'

RHODODENDRON HYBRIDS–LEPIDOTE
'Alison Johnstone'
'Blaney's Blue'

'Crater Lake'
'Dora Amateis'
'Ocean Lake'
'P.J.M.'
'Ramapo'

DECIDUOUS AZALEA SPECIES
R. mucronulatum
R. occidentale
R. schlippenbachii

DECIDUOUS AZALEA HYBRIDS
'Arneson Gem'
'Cheerful Giant'
'Gibraltar'
'Jolie Madame'
'Red Sunset'

Aberdeen, Zone 8a

This list is provided by Mrs. J. J. Sandifur of Aberdeen, Washington, Lewis County Chapter ARS. An asterisk indicates a record added by the author.

RHODODENDRON SPECIES
R. augustinii L
R. campylogynum E
R. decorum E
R. degronianum E
R. degronianum ssp. *yakushimanum* E
R. discolor E
R. fortunei E
R. impeditum L
R. orbiculare E
R. wardii E

RHODODENDRON HYBRIDS–ELEPIDOTE
'Anna Rose Whitney'
'Autumn Gold'
'Blue Ensign'
'Blue Peter'
'Faggetter's Favorite'
'Gomer Waterer'
*'Hallelujah'
'Hello Dolly'
'Jean Marie de Montague'
*'Lem's Cameo'
'Virginia Richards'

Selection of Rhododendrons

RHODODENDRON HYBRIDS–LEPIDOTE
'Blue Diamond'
'P.J.M.'

DECIDUOUS AZALEA SPECIES
R. atlanticum
R. canescens
R. cumberlandense (formerly bakeri)
R. occidentale
R. schlippenbachii

DECIDUOUS AZALEA HYBRIDS
'Beaulieu'
'Brazil'
'Chief Joseph'
'Gibraltar'
'Ginger'
'Homebush'
'Inspiration'
'Kathleen'

EVERGREEN AZALEA SPECIES
R. indicum (formerly macranthum)
R. kiusianum
R. nakaharae

EVERGREEN AZALEA HYBRIDS
'Edna'
'Fedora'
'Glamour'
'Hino Crimson'
'James Gable'
'Louise Gable'
'Mother's Day'
'Pink Drift'
'Purple Splendor'
'Rosebud'

Australia

The Dandenong Ranges at Mount Dandenong, 20 miles (31 km) east of Melbourne (Victoria), is an ideal growing area for rhododendrons and they can be grown with a minimum of care. This includes both deciduous and evergreen azaleas, as well as the vireya rhododendrons. Azaleas, especially the indicas, grow better near Melbourne, Sydney (New South Wales), and Brisbane (Queensland). Some evergreen azaleas grow well into the tropical areas. The cooler mountain areas around Sydney and Toowoomba (Queensland), and the island state of Tasmania are very suitable for rhododendrons. Conditions in southern Australia are not favorable for rhododendron culture except in the Mount Lofty Ranges, where the most hardy hybrids will grow.

Melbourne, Zones 9–11

This list is provided by Mr. and Mrs. Lesley Eaton.

RHODODENDRON SPECIES
R. arboreum E
R. degronianum ssp. yakushimanum E

RHODODENDRON HYBRIDS–ELEPIDOTE
'Alice'
'Antoon Van Welie'

'Blue Peter'
'Britannia'
'Broughtonii'
'Fragrantissimum'
'Mrs. E. C. Sterling'
'Trude Webster'
'White Pearl'

British Isles: Zones 8–9

Soil conditions along the west coast of Britain, between the shore and the hills and mountains, are generally sandy and are good for rhododendron cultivation. Those areas that are unfortunately located on clay can still succeed with some relatively straightforward soil amendment.

Soil conditions in central England are also good as far south as the Chiltern escarpment near Oxford, southeast of which there is an increasing level of chalk that gives rise to the need for raised beds. There are pockets where good growing conditions can be found, mainly in Surrey, Sussex, and Kent, and some well-known gardens are located in these areas. Raised beds made with peat blocks, coupled with a regular soil amendment regime, is the only approach in many areas.

The terrain is somewhat less undulating on the east coast of Britain. There is a prevalence of flat, wet areas and the soil is heavy clay. Raised beds are often the only practical option, although there are some notable exceptions where rhododendron gardens have been established against all expectations. Harsh, prolonged windy weather along this coast is just as much of a problem as the soil.

Hardiness Zone ratings are a difficult topic because Britain uses the RHS zone ratings and North America uses the USDA ratings. Locating a meaningful comparator between the two is not particularly straightforward. I list in Table 3.2 what I have found to be a useful conversion chart that is based on the RHS ratings (John Hammond), against which are listed the areas of Britain. You may have access to other information.

Table 3.2. Comparison of Royal Horticultural Society and U.S. Department of Agriculture hardiness zones

RHS HARDINESS ZONE	USDA HARDINESS ZONE	MINIMUM ANNUAL TEMPERATURE	COMMENTS
H0	10	0°C (32°F)	frost-free environment required (greenhouse, conservatory)
H1	8b	−10 to −8°C (14 to 16°F)	hardy in the mildest gardens on Britain's west coast
H2	8a	−12°C (10°F)	hardy outdoors in the milder parts of Britain (Cornwall, South West Scotland, Argyll)
H3	7b	−15°C (5°F)	hardy in a sheltered site in Britain
H4	7a	−18°C (0°F)	hardy in all but the coldest parts of Britain
H5	6a	−23°C (−10°F)	hardy anywhere in Britain
H6	5a	−29°C (−20°F)	hardy anywhere in Britain

Hampshire County, England

This list is provided by Russell Dyer of Exbury Enterprises Ltd., near Southampton.

RHODODENDRON SPECIES
R. augustinii L
R. degronianum ssp. yakushimanum E
R. impeditum L
R. johnstoneanum L
R. keiskei L
R. lutescens L
R. ponticum E

R. pseudochrysanthum E
R. racemosum L
R. williamsianum E

RHODODENDRON HYBRIDS–ELEPIDOTE
'Bud Flanagan'
'Christmas Cheer'
'Hawk Crest' (syn. 'Crest')

Selection of Rhododendrons

'Hotei'
'Mrs. G. W. Leak'
'Pink Pearl'
'Vanessa'

RHODODENDRON HYBRIDS–LEPIDOTE
'Blue Bird'
'Blue Diamond'
'Blue Tit'
'Dora Amateis'
'Oudijk's Favourite'
'Pink Drift'
'P.J.M.'
'Praecox'
'Princess Anne'

DECIDUOUS AZALEA HYBRIDS
'Annabella'
'Beaulieu Manor' (syn. 'Beaulieu')

'Delicatissima'
'Ginger'
'Golden Oriole'
'Narcissiflorum'
'Old Gold'
'Royal Command'
'Sunte Nectarine'

EVERGREEN AZALEA HYBRIDS
'Blaauw's Pink'
'Blue Danube'
'Hinomayo'
'Irohayama'
'Kirin' (syn. 'Coral Bells')
'Mother's Day'
'Palestrina'
'Rosebud'
'Rose Greeley'
'Vuyk's Scarlet'

Scotland, Zone 8

This list is provided by Stephen and Anne Fox, 20 miles (33 km) southeast of Manchester with poor moorland soil (pH 4.5) and higher rainfall than Manchester.

RHODODENDRON SPECIES
R. adenophorum E
R. anthopogon L
R. bureavii E
R. calostrotum ssp. *keleticum* L (Radicans Group)
R. campanulatum E
R. cephalanthum L
R. ciliatum L
R. citriniflorum var. *horaeum* E
R. clementinae E
R. concinnum L
R. decorum E
R. degronianum ssp. *heptamerum* E
   ('Ho Emma', 'Wada')
R. degronianum ssp. *yakushimanum* E
R. elegantulum E
R. fastigiatum L
R. fortunei E
R. fulgens E
R. glaucophyllum L
R. haemotodes E
R. hyperythrum E
R. impeditum L

R. insigne E
R. lacteum E
R. lutescens L
R. makinoi E
R. minus L
R. morii E
R. moupinense L
R. oreodoxa var. *fargesii* E
R. oreotrephes L
R. pachysanthum E
R. pingianum E
R. pseudochrysanthum E
R. rigidum L
R. roxieanum E
R. rubiginosumi
R. saluenense L
R. strigillosum E
R. temenium E ('Cruachan')
R. thayerianum E
R. triflorum L
R. wardii E
R. wasonii E (pink and yellow)
R. yunnanense L

RHODODENDRON HYBRIDS–ELEPIDOTE
'Blewbury'
'Carmen'
'Crest'
'Etta Burrows'
'Golden Gate'
'Goldsworth Yellow'
'Gomer Waterer'
'Graziella'
'Gretsel'
'Grumpy'
'Hansel'
'Hotei'
'Jean Marie de Montague'
'Loder's White'
'Matador'
'May Day'
'Moser's Maroon'
'Mrs. G. W. Leak'
'Percy Wiseman'
'Polar Bear'
'Rothenburg'
'Shrimp Girl'
'Sir Robert Peel'
'Temple Belle'

'Vanessa Pastel'
'W.F.H.'
'Winsome'

RHODODENDRON HYBRIDS–LEPIDOTE
'Airy Fairy'
'Blue Diamond'
'Cilpinense'
'Penheale Blue'
'Pink Drift'
'Sapphire'
'Snow Lady'

DECIDUOUS AZALEA SPECIES
R. atlanticum
R. canadense
R. luteum
R. occidentale
R. vaseyi

DECIDUOUS AZALEA HYBRIDS
'Coccinea Speciosa'

EVERGREEN AZALEA SPECIES
R. kiusianum
R. nakaharae

Lancashire, England

This list provided by John Hammond.

RHODODENDRON SPECIES
R. augustinii L
R. bureavii E
R. calophytum E
R. calostrotum 'Gigha' L
R. campylocarpum E
R. campylogynum 'Bodnant Red' L
R. ciliatum L
R. cinnabarinum Roylei Group L
R. davidsonianum L
R. falconeri E
R. fletcherianum L
R. fortunei E
R. keiskei L
R. neriiflorum E
R. orbiculare E
R. oreodoxa E
R. oreotrephes L
R. racemosum L

R. roxieanum var. oreonastes E
R. thomsonii E

RHODODENDRON HYBRIDS–ELEPIDOTE
'Bruce Brechtbill'
'Cynthia'
'Fabia'
'Jean Marie de Montague'
'Loderi King George'
'Nancy Evans'
'Phyllis Korn'
'Ring of Fire'
'September Song'
'Taurus'

YAKUSHIMANUM HYBRIDS
'Caroline Allbrook'
'Centennial Celebration'
'Cupcake'
'Dopey'

Selection of Rhododendrons

'Fantastica'
'Hydon Dawn'
'Ken Janeck'
'Mardi Gras'
'Percy Wiseman'
'Titan Beauty'

RHODODENDRON HYBRIDS—LEPIDOTE
'Anna Baldsiefen'
'Blue Tit Magor'
'Creeping Jenny'
'Curlew'
'Gristede'
'Lady Chamberlain Apricot'
'P.J.M.'
'Princess Anne'
'St. Breward'
'Wee Bee'

DECIDUOUS AZALEA SPECIES
R. luteum
R. occidentale
R. vaseyi

DECIDUOUS AZALEA HYBRIDS
'Cecile'
'Christopher Wren'
'Coccinea Speciosa'
'Daviesii'
'Gibraltar'
'Golden Horn'
'Nancy Waterer'

EVERGREEN AZALEA HYBRIDS
'Blacuni's Pink'
'Blue Danube'
'Elsie Lee'
'Gaiety'
'Hino Crimson'
'H. H. Hume'
'Mother's Day'
'Orange King'
'Vuyk's Rosyred'
'White Lady'

Berks, England

This list is provided by Michael J. Jurgens, chairman of the International Board RHS Rhododendron, Camellia, and Magnolia Group, The Old House, Silchester, Reading.

RHODODENDRON SPECIES
R. ambiguum L
R. callimorphum E
R. concinnum L (formerly pseudoyanthinum)
R. davidsonianum L
R. degronianum E
R. elegantulum E
R. fulvum E
R. griersonianum E
R. insigne E
R. macabeanum E
R. oreotrephes E
R. souliei E
R. sutchuenense E
R. triflorum L

RHODODENDRON HYBRIDS—ELEPIDOTE
'Anita'
'Atroflo'
'Blewbury'
'Champaign'

'Christmas Cheer'
'Day Dream'
'Desert Gold'
'Elizabeth'
'Elspeth'
'Fastuosum Flore Pleno'
'Golden Splendour'
'Goldstork'
'Gomer Waterer'
'Healist'
'Leanore'
'Loderi King George'
"Loder's White'
Marcia'
'Marinum Koster'
'Matador'
'Nobleman'
'Polar Bear'
'Purple Splendor'
'Rubioso'
'Sir Charles Lemon'

'Susan'
'Taurus'
'Teddy Bear'
'Temple Bells'
'Thor'
'Tidbit'
'Tortoiseshell'
'Tortoiseshell Wonder'
'Vanessa'
'Vanessa Pastel'
'Vergan Bay'
'Winsome'

RHODODENDRON HYBRIDS–LEPIDOTE
'Bo-Peep'
'Chick'
'Cilpinense'
'Penheale Blue'
'Praecox'
'Yellow Hammer'

DECIDUOUS AZALEA SPECIES
R. albrechtii
R. arborescens
R. atlanticum
R. cumberlandense (formerly *bakeri*)
R molle ssp. *japonicum*
R. luteum

R. occidentale ('Leonard Frisbee')
R. reticulatum
R. schlippenbachii
R. vaseyi
R. viscosum

DECIDUOUS AZALEA HYBRIDS
'Cecile'
'Chicago'
'Coccinea Speciosa'
'Daviesii'
'Homebush'
'Magnifica'
'Narcissiflorum'
'Norma'
'Onyx'
'Oxydol'
'Viscosepalum'

EVERGREEN AZALEA SPECIES
R. ripense var. *mucronatum*

EVERGREEN AZALEA HYBRIDS
'Hino Crimson'
'Hinomayo'
'Mother's Day'
'Palestrina'
'Rosebud'
'Vuyk's Scarlet'

Canada: Zones 1–9

Southwestern British Columbia, the east and west coasts of Vancouver Island, suburban areas around Vancouver, in the delta and lower portions of the Fraser River Valley and surrounding mountain slopes up to 2500 ft. (750 m). Summer drought occurs in Victoria and the lower east coast of Vancouver Island, whereas the west coast of Vancouver Island has more rain and parts of it are zone 9a.

British Columbia, Zone 9

This list is provided by Clive L. Justice, Vancouver.

RHODODENDRON SPECIES
R. augustinii L
R. auriculatum E
R. calophytum E
R. dauricum L
R. davidsonianum L
R. degronianum ssp. *yakushimanum* E
R. fortunei E

R. lutescens L
R. oreotrephes L
R. williamsianum E

RHODODENDRON HYBRIDS–ELEPIDOTE
'A. Bedford'
'Albert Close'
'Anna Rose Whitney'
'Beauty of Littleworth'

Selection of Rhododendrons

'Blue Peter'
'Bow Bells'
'Britannia'
'Christmas Cheer'
'Countess of Athlone'
'Cynthia'
'Elizabeth'
'Jan Dekens'
'Jock'
'Lady Grey Egerton'
'Moonstone'
'Mrs. Betty Robertson'
'Mrs. G. W. Leak'
'Mrs. J. G. Millais'
'Olympic Lady'
'Pink Pearl'
'Purple Splendor'
'Sir Charles Lemon'
'Susan'
'Unique'
'Virginia Richards'

DECIDUOUS AZALEA SPECIES
R. arborescens
R. calendulaceum
R. canadense
R. molle ssp. japonicum
R. occidentale
R. pentaphyllum
R. periclymenoides (formerly nudiflorum)
R. schlippenbachii
R. vaseyi (white form)
R. viscosum

DECIDUOUS AZALEA HYBRIDS
'Apple Blossom'
'Bouquet de Flora'

'Coccinea Speciosa'
'Fraseri'
'Gibraltar'
'Irene Koster'
'Koster's Brilliant Red'
'Narcissiflorum'
'Oxydol'

EVERGREEN AZALEA SPECIES
R. kaempferi
R. ripense var. mucronatum
R. yedoense var. poukhanense

EVERGREEN AZALEA HYBRIDS
'Adonis'
'Aladdin'
'Amy'
'Cameo'
'Christmas Cheer' (syn. 'Ima-shojo')
'Corsage'
'Diana'
'Elizabeth Gable'
'Fedora'
'Hino Crimson'
'Hinode giri'
'Hinomayo'
'James Gable'
'John Cairns'
'Louise Gable'
'Orange Beauty'
'Palestrina' (white form)
'Purple Splendor'
'Rosebud'
'Sakata Red'
'Stewartstonian'
'Ward's Ruby'

Ontario, Zones 3a–5b

The climate of Ontario varies considerably, with the mildest conditions being near the lower Great Lakes (Erie and Ontario). This is the most suitable area for rhododendrons. This list is provided by Brian Schram of Fenwick, Ontario.

RHODODENDRON SPECIES
R. brachycarpum E
R. catawbiense E
R. dauricum L
R. dauricum var. album L

R. degronianum E (formerly metternechii)
R. degronianum ssp. yakushimanum E
   ('Mist Maiden')
R. ferrugineum L
R. hippophaeoides L

R. maximum E
R. minus L (Carolinianum Group)
R. mucronulatum L

RHODODENDRON HYBRIDS–ELEPIDOTE
'Blue Peter'
'Calsap'
'Caroline'
'County of York'
'Janet Blair'
'Ken Janeck'
'Lodestar'
'Scintillation'
'Sham's Ruby'
'Tony'
'Wyandanch Pink'

RHODODENDRON HYBRIDS–LEPIDOTE
'Fasia'
'Malta'
'Olga Mezitt'
'P.J.M.'
'Purple Gem'
'Ramapo'
'Wilsonii'
'Windbeam'

DECIDUOUS AZALEA SPECIES
R. arborescens
R. atlanticum
R. calendulaceum

R. canadense
R. cumberlandense (formerly *bakeri*)
R. luteum
R. molle ssp. *japonicum*
R. periclymenoides (formerly *nudiflorum*)
R. prinophyllum (formerly *roseum*)
R. schlippenbachii
R. vaseyi
R. viscosum

DECIDUOUS AZALEA HYBRIDS
Exbury Hybrids
Ghent Hybrids
Knap Hill Hybrids

EVERGREEN AZALEA SPECIES
R. kaempferi
R. kiusianum
R. yedoense var. *poukhanense*

EVERGREEN AZALEA HYBRIDS
'Boudoir'
'Cascade' (Shammarello Hybrid)
'Corsage'
'Elsie Lee'
'Herbert'
'Karens'
'Kathleen' (Gable Hybrid)
'Pride's Pink'
'Purple Splendor'
'Rosebud'

This list provided by Robert Dickhart of Niagara Falls, Canada.

RHODODENDRON SPECIES
R. minus L (Carolinianum Group)
R. mucronulatum L ('Cornell Pink')

RHODODENDRON HYBRIDS–ELEPIDOTE
'Besse Howells'
'Calsap'
'Casanova'
'Catawbiense Boursault'
'Harrisville'
'Janet Blair'
'Ken Janeck'
'Nova Zembla'
'Pana'
'Roseum Elegans'

'Scintillation'

RHODODENDRON HYBRIDS–LEPIDOTE
'Aglo'
'Fasia'
'Olga Mezitt'
'Pink Diamond'
'Pink Pom Pom'
'Pioneer Silvery Pink'
P.J.M. Group
'Ramapo'
'Windbeam'

DECIDUOUS AZALEA SPECIES
R. schlippenbachii

DECIDUOUS AZALEA HYBRIDS
'Buzzard'
'Chetco'
'Gibraltar'
'Homebush'
'Klondyke'
'Tunis'
'Vineland Duke'
'Vineland Gold'

EVERGREEN AZALEA HYBRIDS
'Al's Picotee'
'Bixby'
'Boudoir'
'Cascade'
'Corsage'
'Helen Curtis'
'Herbert'
'Karens'
'Phyllis Moore'

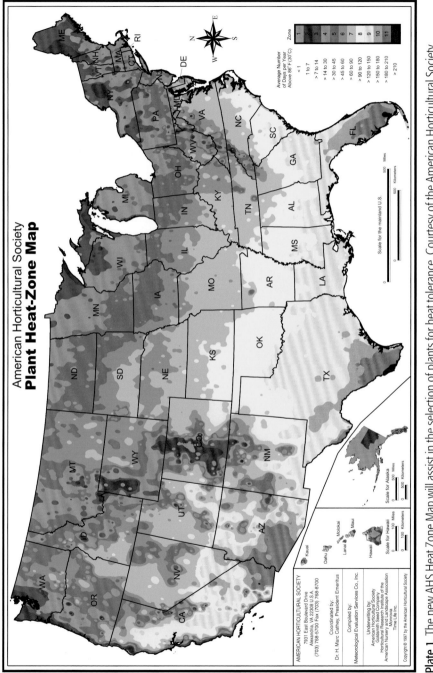

American Horticultural Society
Plant Heat-Zone Map

Average Number
of Days per Year
Above 86° F (30°C)

Zone	
1	< 1
2	1 to 7
3	> 7 to 14
4	> 14 to 30
5	> 30 to 45
6	> 45 to 60
7	> 60 to 90
8	> 90 to 120
9	> 120 to 150
10	> 150 to 180
11	> 180 to 210
	> 210

Scale for the mainland U.S.

0   500 Miles
0   500 Kilometers

AMERICAN HORTICULTURAL SOCIETY
7931 East Boulevard Drive
Alexandria, VA 22308 U.S.A.
(703) 768-5700 Fax (703) 768-8700

Coordinated by:
Dr. H. Marc Cathey, President Emeritus

Compiled by:
Meteorological Evaluation Services Co., Inc.

Underwriting by:
American Horticultural Society
Goldsmith Seed Company
Horticultural Research Institute of the
American Nursery and Landscape Association
Monrovia
Time Life Inc.

Kauai

Oahu

Molokai

Lanai   Maui

Hawaii

Scale for Hawaii

0   100 Miles
0   100 Kilometers

Scale for Alaska

0   500 Miles
0   500 Kilometers

Copyright © 1997 by the American Horticultural Society

Plate 1. The new AHS Heat Zone Map will assist in the selection of plants for heat tolerance. Courtesy of the American Horticultural Society

Plate 2. *Rhododendron* 'Groovy', Delp Hybrid. Although Delp Hybrids are not yet widely available, I present some here to introduce readers to these excellent plants. Photograph by Paul James

Plate 3. *Rhododendron* 'Reckless', Delp Hybrid. Photograph by Paul James

Plate 4. *Rhododendron* 'Ghost', Delp Hybrid. Photograph by Paul James

Plate 5. *Rhododendron* 'Rhody Romance', Delp Hybrid. Photograph by Paul James

Plate 6. *Rhododendron* 'Delp's Quest', Delp Hybrid. Photograph by Paul James

Plate 7. *Rhododendron* 'Red Hot Mama', Delp Hybrid. Photograph by Paul James

Plate 8. *Rhododendron* 'Beauty Master', Delp Hybrid. Photograph by Paul James

Plate 9. *Rhododendron* 'Masterblend', Delp Hybrid. Photograph by Paul James

Plate 10. *Rhododendron strigillosum*. Photograph courtesy of Rhododendron Species Foundation

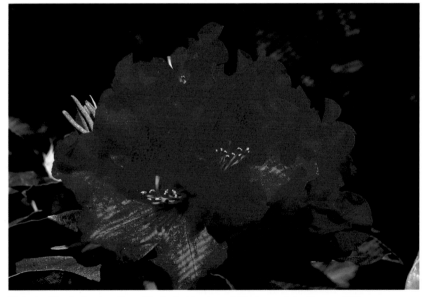

Plate 11. *Rhododendron* 'Jean Marie de Montague'. Photograph by Eleanor Philp

Plate 12. *Rhododendron* 'Queen Nefertite'. Photograph by Eleanor Philp

Plate 13. *Rhododendron* 'Unique'. Photograph by Eleanor Philp

Plate 14. *Rhododendron* 'Gomer Waterer'. Photograph by Eleanor Philp

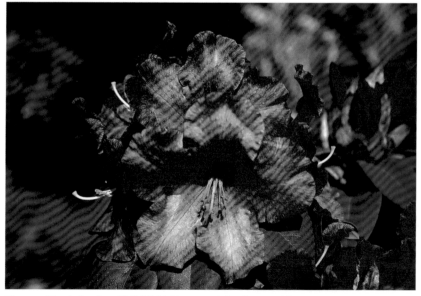

Plate 15. *Rhododendron* 'Hallelujah'. Photograph by Eleanor Philp

Plate 16. *Rhododendron* 'Fastuosum Flore Pleno'. Photograph by Eleanor Philp

Plate 17. *Rhododendron* 'Percy Wiseman'. Photograph by Eleanor Philp

Plate 18. *Rhododendron* 'Trude Webster'. Photograph by Eleanor Philp

Plate 19. *Rhododendron* 'Taurus'. Photograph by Eleanor Philp

Plate 20. *Rhododendron* 'Chocheco Bright Star'. Photograph by Joe Parks

Plate 21. *Rhododendron kaempferi* 'Semper Florans'. Photograph courtesy of the Rhododendron Species Foundation

Plate 22. *Rhododendron* 'Carrie Amanda', a new Schroeder Hybrid. Photograph by H. Edward Reiley

Plate 23. *Rhododendron* 'Elsie Lee'. Photograph by H. Edward Reiley

Plate 24. *Rhododendron* 'Capistrano', a new very cold hardy yellow. Photograph by Stephen Krebs

Plate 25. *Rhododendron* 'Midnight Ruby'. Photograph by Wayne Mezitt

Plate 26. *Rhododendron* 'Flasher', Delp Hybrid. Photograph by Paul James

Plate 27. *Rhododendron* 'Red Quest' and *R.* 'Checkmate' growing at Weston Nurseries. Photograph by Wayne Mezitt

Plate 28. *Rhododendron keiskei.*
Photograph courtesy of
Rhododendron Species Foundation

Plate 29. *Rhododendron* 'Little Olga'. Photograph by Wayne Mezitt

Plate 30. *Rhododendron* 'A. Bedford'. Photograph by Eleanor Philp

Plate 31. *Rhododendron* 'Hilda Niblett'. Photograph by H. Edward Reiley

Plate 32. *Rhododendron* 'Hershey's Red'. Photograph by H. Edward Reiley

Plate 33. *Rhododendron* 'Bellringer'. Photograph by H. Edward Reiley

Plate 34. *Rhododendron* 'Mist Maiden'. Photograph by H. Edward Reiley

Plate 35. *Rhododendron schlippenbachii*. Photograph by H. Edward Reiley

Plate 36. *Rhododendron* 'Gilbert Myers'. Photograph by H. Edward Reiley

Plate 37. *Rhododendron* 'Gibraltar'. Photograph by H. Edward Reiley

Plate 38. *Rhododendron* 'Sham's Yellow'. Photograph by H. Edward Reiley

Plate 39. *Rhododendron* 'Sherwood Red'. Photograph by H. Edward Reiley

Plate 40. *Rhododendron* 'Spring Parade'. Photograph by H. Edward Reiley

Plate 41. *Rhododendron fortunei*. Photograph by H. Edward Reiley

Plate 42. *Rhododendron* 'Autumn Bravo'. Photograph courtesy of Flowerwood Nursery, photographer unknown

Plate 43. *Rhododendron* 'Girard's Border Gem'. Photograph by H. Edward Reiley

Plate 44. *Rhododendron* 'Girard's Double Purple'. Photograph by H. Edward Reiley

Plate 45. *Rhododendron* 'Tiana'. Photograph by H. Edward Reiley

Plate 46. *Rhododendron* 'Fantastica'. Photograph by H. Edward Reiley

Plate 47. *Rhododendron* 'Parker's Pink'. Photograph by H. Edward Reiley

Plate 48. *Rhododendron* 'Scarlet Romance'. Photograph by H. Edward Reiley

Plate 49. *Rhododendron* 'Delaware Valley White'. Photograph by H. Edward Reiley

Plate 50. *Rhododendron* 'Mary Fleming'. Photograph by H. Edward Reiley

Plate 51. *Rhododendron ripense* var. *mucronatum*. Photograph by H. Edward Reiley

Plate 52. *Rhododendron* 'Dora Amateis'. Photograph by H. Edward Reiley

Plate 53. *Rhododendron* 'Hino Crimson'. Photograph by H. Edward Reiley

Plate 54. *Rhododendron* 'Lem's Stormcloud'. Photograph by H. Edward Reiley

Plate 55. *Rhododendron* 'Ken Janeck'. Photograph by H. Edward Reiley

Plate 56. *Rhododendron arborescens*. Photograph by Don Hyatt

Plate 57. *Rhododendron vaseyi*. Photograph by Don Hyatt

Plate 58. *Rhododendron austrinum*. Photograph by Don Hyatt

Plate 59. *Rhododendron calendulaceum*. Photograph by Don Hyatt

Plate 60. *Rhododendron prunifolium*. Photograph by Don Hyatt

Plate 61. Rhododendrons used to border an open area in Ted and Betty Anderson's garden in Washington State. Photograph by H. Edward Reiley

Plate 62. A group planting of rhododendrons in the author's garden. Notice how the use of white provides balance. Photograph by H. Edward Reiley

Plate 63. The light-colored flowers of *Rhododendron* 'Caroline' contrast well with the dark background of pines in the author's garden. Photograph by H. Edward Reiley

Plate 64. Beautiful specimen plants spaced apart as individuals contrast with the green lawn and dark background. Photographer unknown

Plate 65. *Rhododendron* 'Mist Maiden' forms a beautiful specimen plant in the author's garden. Photograph by H. Edward Reiley

Plate 66. Azaleas provide an accent point in the author's garden. Photograph by H. Edward Reiley

Plate 67. A large group planting of rhododendrons in the author's garden. Photograph by H. Edward Reiley

Plate 68. *Rhododendron* 'Pinnacle' used to provide needed height behind the azaleas *R.* 'Helen Curtis' and *R.* 'Elsie Lee' in the author's garden. Photograph by H. Edward Reiley

Plate 69. Rhododendrons used as a transition between the woods and a lawn area in the author's garden. Photograph by H. Edward Reiley

Plate 70. *Rhododendron* 'Windbeam' and *R.* 'Spring Parade' separate the lawn area from the driveway in the author's garden. Photograph by H. Edward Reiley

Plate 71. Rhododendrons and azaleas planted under ideal light conditions in the author's garden. Notice the dappled shade pattern and windbreaks provided by trees. Photograph by H. Edward Reiley

Plate 72. Azaleas used to hide a tree stump in the author's garden. Photograph by H. Edward Reiley

Plate 73. Beltsville dwarf azaleas used as a hedge. Photograph by H. Edward Reiley

Plate 74. *Rhododendron thomsonii* in Dot and Ken Gibson's garden in British Columbia, Canada. The red exfoliating bark of this species is an added feature. Photograph by H. Edward Reiley

Plate 75. Azaleas line the pathway through the woods at the National Arboretum, Washington, D.C. Photograph by H. Edward Reiley

Plate 76. An extended foundation planting of rhododendron and azaleas at the Anderson home in Washington State. Photograph by H. Edward Reiley

Plate 77. A more formal planting using red azaleas and hosta as companion plants. Photograph by H. Edward Reiley

Plate 78. New Weston Hybrids *Rhododendron* 'Blue Baron' and *R.* 'Landmark' make an eye-catching combination. Photograph by Wayne Mezitt

Plate 79. A mass of color brightens the woodland in the author's garden. Photograph by H. Edward Reiley

Plate 80. The beautiful white of *Cornus florida* provides contrast to the early spring landscape and is a good companion in the rhododendron garden. Photograph by H. Edward Reiley

Plate 81. Azaleas provide a transition between a lawn area to a background of trees in the author's garden. Photograph by H. Edward Reiley

Plate 82. *Rhododendron* 'Windbeam' and *R.* 'Girard's Roberta' intertwine to form a good blend of colors in the author's garden. Photograph by H. Edward Reiley

Plate 83. Gable's *Rhododendron* 'Madfort' against the dark green of Norway spruce trees. *Rhododendron* 'Madfort' is also very fragrant placed beside a path in the author's garden. Photograph by H. Edward Reiley

Plate 84. Fall color can be added to the rhododendron garden using Japanese maples. Photograph by H. Edward Reiley

Plate 85. Snow-covered rhododendrons and pines present an attractive winter view of the author's rhododendron garden. Photograph by H. Edward Reiley

Plate 86. Symptoms of *Phytophthora* root rot. Leaves roll downward toward the midrib and eventually wilt, and the entire plant then wilts. Leaves and stems may not become necrotic for weeks. Courtesy of The American Phytopathological Society

Plate 87. Typical V-shaped zone necrosis associated with *Phytophthora* dieback is different from root rot. Leaves abscise within one to two weeks. This dieback is usually associated with young nursery plants. Courtesy of The American Phytopathological Society

Plate 88. Slimy, limp, water-soaked flowers infected with petal blight. Courtesy of The American Phytopathological Society

Plate 89. Leaf gall is most commonly found on azalea leaves and branches. Shown here are gall-coated leaves with white fungus growth and affected leaves turning brown. Galls should be removed before they turn white. Courtesy of The American Phytopathological Society

Plate 90. *Phomopsis* dieback of azalea. Individual branches die. Courtesy of The American Phytopathological Society

Plate 91. Lace bug adult on a leaf. Courtesy of The American Phytopathological Society

Plate 92. Lace bug damage to azalea leaves. Courtesy of The American Phytopathological Society

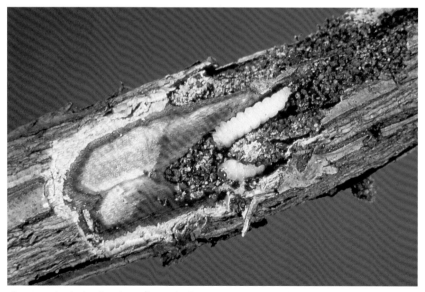

Plate 93. Rhododendron borer larvae in the stem. Courtesy of The American Phytopathological Society

Plate 94. Rhododendron borer adult. Notice the three yellow bands on the abdomen that distinguish this clearwing moth from other borers. Courtesy of The American Phytopathological Society

Plate 95. Marginal leaf notching caused by black vine weevil. Courtesy of The American Phytopathological Society

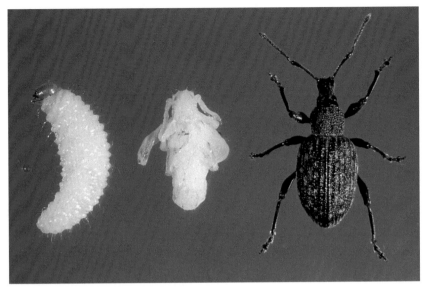

Plate 96. Black vine weevil larva, pupa, and adult. Courtesy of The American Phytopathological Society

Plate 97. Leaf injury from pesticide. Courtesy of The American Phytopathological Society

Plate 98. Bark split on an azalea. Notice the bark has completely separated from the stem near the ground. Photograph by H. Edward Reiley

Plate 99. Chlorotic leaves showing iron deficiency. Some other deficiencies show similar symptoms. Courtesy of The American Phytopathological Society

Plate 100. Foliage burn showing desiccation in the plant top where heat from the sun dried leaves out during winter as roots were damaged by voles and could not replenish the moisture loss. Photograph by H. Edward Reiley

Plate 101. The optimal distance apart to seed. The small white specs on the medium surface are the seeds. Do not cover seeds with medium. Photograph by H. Edward Reiley

Plate 102. Small seedlings, just sending out the seed cotyledons. No true leaves exist at this point. Photograph by H. Edward Reiley

Plate 103. Seedlings now have true leaves and are ready for transplanting. Photograph by H. Edward Reiley

Plate 104. A seedling held by a leaf, ready for transplanting. Photograph by H. Edward Reiley

Plate 105. Seedlings transplanted for further growth. Photograph by H. Edward Reiley

Plate 106. Trusses being assembled for a competitive show. Photograph by Helen Myers

Plate 107. Did you ever see a more beautiful welcome to the flower show than this fiftieth anniversary show in Tacoma, Washington? Photograph by H. Edward Reiley

Plate 108. Display of plants for sale, Mason-Dixon ARS Chapter Show. Photograph by Helen Myers

Plate 109. A beautiful display garden at an ARS flower show. Plants are labeled, which adds to the educational value of the display. Photograph by H. Edward Reiley

Plate 110. A top-quality rhododendron truss. Note how perfect foliage frames a perfect truss. Photograph by H. Edward Reiley

Plate 111. Prospective winning azalea spray of *Rhododendron ripense* var. *mucronatum*. Photograph by H. Edward Reiley

4

Native Azaleas

Donald W. Hyatt

In the United States, the term *native azalea* usually applies to the North American deciduous azalea species and their natural hybrids. Surely, these plants are among the most charming and versatile of our native flowering shrubs. Their delicate blossoms come in a wide range of colors, from pure white through shades of pink to deep rose and lavender tones as well as warmer hues of yellow, apricot, orange, coral, and scarlet, often with contrasting flares of yellow or gold. Many native azalea species are extremely fragrant. Individual plants usually bloom over many weeks as fresh buds open up to replace spent blooms. Because different species flower at different times of the year, it is possible to have native azaleas in bloom from early spring throughout the growing season into late summer or fall.

From an evolutionary standpoint, the native azaleas are quite old and have remained relatively unchanged for millions of years, managing to grow and survive as the continents drifted apart and ice ages gripped the hemispheres. There are species growing wild in Turkey, China, and Japan that are very similar to many of the forms native to the United States. Early plant explorers were enamored by the beauty of the azalea species they discovered when first exploring North America. By the middle of the 1800s, hybridizers in Europe had already started using these species to develop many outstanding deciduous azalea strains, including the popular Ghent, Knap Hill, and Exbury Hybrids.

Today's gardeners are beginning to rediscover the charm and beauty of the native azaleas, and there is increased interest in using them in naturalized plantings and landscape designs. Horticulturists continue to investigate their potential in developing new strains of hardy plants for our gardens because many of the natives are extremely winter hardy and others are adapted to high summer heat and humidity. Although many people assume that new botanical discoveries are only made in remote locations of the world such as the tropical rain forests, modern plant explorers have surprised us by finding exciting new forms of native azaleas right here in the United States. The native azalea species may be very old, but there is much to learn about these amazing plants even today.

Native Azalea Species

There are sixteen azalea species native to the United States, fifteen of which are found along the east coast and one on the west. To help distinguish among the various species, they are grouped below following Dr. Kathleen Kron's recommendation into three color classifications: white, pink, and orange (Kron 1996). By using these general groupings, along with other criteria cited within the descriptions, it is easier to tell the different species apart. However, be aware that species in the wild show much diversity. Even within an isolated population there can be significant variations in flower color, size, and shape. There can also be striking differences in foliage quality, plant habit, and season of bloom. In the wild, natural hybrids between species may grow in close proximity to one another, so the purity of a species form is often in question. Whether a pure species or hybrid, a native azalea will make a wonderful landscape plant that will bring enjoyment for many years.

The White Group

Six species that fall into the white group. Although some forms of these species are actually pink, when large populations are observed, the majority of the plants will have flowers that are white to blush and pink forms are relatively rare.

Rhododendron alabamense—The delicate white flowers of this medium-sized species have a yellow blotch and a distinctive lemon-spice fragrance. A midseason bloomer, the species has 1-in. (0.4-cm) wide flowers that open as the new foliage is expanding. Although individual blossoms are small in comparison to some of the other species, this native azalea can make a wonderful focal point in a landscape because of its heavy bloom and compact habit. *Rhododendron alabamense* is heat tolerant but may not be as hardy for northern gardens, where temperatures regularly fall much below 0°F (−18°C).

Rhododendron arborescens—Among the most fragrant of our native azaleas, this species is a delightful addition to any garden (Plate 56). In the wild, people will usually smell its wonderful heliotrope-like fragrance long before they spot the actual plant in bloom. In the landscape, a single specimen can perfume an entire garden. The 1.5- to 2-in. (0.6- to 0.8-cm) wide flowers are typically pure white to blush pink and have very distinctive stamens of a contrasting deep red. This species usually blooms in June, long after the foliage has fully expanded. Another unique feature is its smooth stems that are devoid of hairs typical in other azalea species, which is why it is known as the smooth azalea. The plant does well in a moist location and is often found growing along streams or in damp areas in the wild. In the landscape, *R. arborescens* forms a medium-sized shrub, although it can get tall in shady locations. The varietal form *richardsonii* is more spreading and compact.

Rhododendron atlanticum—A relatively low grower that can tolerate heavy pruning, this species can be a great landscape plant for a rock garden or foreground accent. The plant is stoloniferous and will spread by underground stems to form large populations in sandy soils in the wild, but the habit is more restrained in heavier soils. The sweetly fragrant flowers open in midseason before or with the expanding foliage. The tubular funnel shaped blossoms are about 1.5–2 in. (3.8–5 cm) long and 1–1.5 in. (2.5–3.8 cm) wide, white brushed with pink on the outside of the corolla, and covered with sticky glandular hairs on the back. The attractive foliage has a very distinctive blue-green cast. Previously listed as hybrids, the Choptank azaleas and the clone 'Marydel' are now considered by many to be pure selections of the species.

Rhododendron eastmanii—This species was recently discovered and is very rare, found only in two counties of South Carolina. Its existence was first documented in the literature in November 1999, and at that time there were only about 500 plants known in the wild (Kron and Creel 1999). The delightfully fragrant flowers are about 1.5 in. (3.8 cm) across and white with a yellow blotch. They appear after the foliage has expanded. *Rhododendron eastmanii* has not been widely tested to determine its hardiness or adaptability in the garden, but considering the merit of the other native species, it certainly deserves testing. As is true for all wild plants, never dig plants in their native habitats but purchase from reliable nurseries that are propagating and distributing rare species with conservation in mind.

Rhododendron occidentale—This is the only azalea native to the west coast of the United States. It has long been admired not only for its beautiful flowers but also for its wonderful fragrance. An excellent landscape plant in the cooler gardens of the Pacific Northwest and United Kingdom, *Rhododendron occidentale* is unfortunately difficult to grow in the warm and humid gardens of the southeastern United States. It flowers in late midseason after the foliage has expanded. The flower buds are often red but open to large white to pink blossoms measuring from 1.5 in. (3.8 cm) to more than 3.0 in. (7.5 cm) across, often with a prominent yellow to orange blotch. Some selections have frilled flowers and others are even double. There are many excellent forms in the trade, including the natural selection called 'Leonard Frisbee' that has 3.5-in. (1.4-cm) flowers in trusses of twenty or more blossoms.

Rhododendron viscosum—Taxonomists have recently lumped several previously identified species into a single designation so that now both *R. serrulatum* and *R. oblongifolium* are considered to be variations of *viscosum*. The white to pale pink flowers are delightfully fragrant and open extremely late in the season after the foliage has fully expanded. The flower tube of this species is about 1.5–2.0 in. (3.8–5 cm) long, quite narrow, and opening to about 1 in. (2.5 cm) wide at the end. They are covered with sticky glandular hairs. Although the flowers may not be as dramatic as some species, *R. viscosum* has many interesting forms with unique qualities. The plant is also very adaptable and grows well in moist locations. The form of the species known as *serrulatum* is a midsummer bloomer, typically flowering in July.

The Pink Group

There are five species in the pink group. Although flowers are supposed to be various shades of pink, there are also pure white, or alba, forms for most of these species, many of which are highly prized as landscape plants. As before, when one observes large populations of species classified under this heading, the majority of the plants will be medium to deeper shades of pink to rosy lavender rather than white.

Rhododendron canadense—Originally considered a completely separate genus, *Rhodora*, this rhododendron species has small flowers, about 1 in. (2.5 cm) across, that are purplish pink. The species blooms in early spring before the leaves have expanded, and the flower shape is most unusual because the top three petals are fused into a single lobe while the bottom two petals flare widely. Also, the flowers have ten stamens rather than the typical five found in most of the native azaleas. Growing along stream banks and in swamps from Pennsylvania to Labrador, *R. canadense* is very winter hardy but can be difficult in southern gardens.

***Rhododendron canescens*—**Also known as the piedmont or Florida Pinxter azalea, the natural range of this species is generally more southern. In the wild, *R. canescens* ranges from northern Florida, Georgia, and the southeast coast of North and South Carolina westward in a broad swath to eastern Texas. The fragrant flowers are 1.0–1.5 in. (2.5–3.8 cm) across and come in shades of white to pink, often with deeper pink to red floral tubes covered with sticky glandular hairs. Appearing in many-flowered trusses, the blossoms open before or with the expanding foliage and have very long stamens. A reliable and heat-tolerant native azalea for gardens where winter temperatures do not often go too far below 0°F (−18°C), this native makes a striking landscape plant. Several excellent named selections have been introduced into the nursery trade, including 'Vernadoe's Pink' and 'Camilla's Blush'.

***Rhododendron periclymenoides*—**Previously know as *R. nudiflorum*, this species is very common in the lower Appalachian Mountains eastward to the piedmont and coastal plains of the eastern United States, extending all the way from Massachusetts down to northern Georgia. Known by many common names such as Pinxterbloom, or wild honeysuckles in colonial times, this species has delicate flowers of white to pale pink, often with pink to red floral tubes. The fragrant blossoms measure 1.0–1.5 in. (2.5–3.8 cm) across and have very long stamens that are usually twice the length of the corolla. Appearing before or with the newly expanding foliage, the flowers are easily confused with those of *R. canescens*. One distinguishing characteristic of *R. periclymenoides* is that the floral tubes usually have fuzzy hairs on the back rather than sticky glandules. The plant is hardy and adaptable, making an excellent landscape shrub for the woodland garden.

***Rhododendron prinophyllum*—**This species, formerly known as *R. roseum*, is very winter hardy. Its natural range is from southern Quebec, New England, and northern Ohio, southward through the upper elevations of the Appalachian Mountains. Although similar to *R. periclymenoides* and *R. canescens* in many ways, the flowers of *R. prinophyllum* are usually a deeper shade of rose pink, about 1.5 in. (3.8 cm) across, but with a shorter floral tube. One of the most distinctive features of this species is its wonderful cinnamon to clovelike fragrance, which can perfume an entire garden in midspring. This native azalea is a wonderful landscape plant for cooler gardens, but it does not do well in the hot, humid summers of the southeastern United States. Exceptionally winter hardy, this species has figured prominently in the background of many azaleas in the Northern Lights Series developed at the University of Minnesota.

Rhododendron vaseyi—This charming species has widely funnel-shaped flowers, about 1.5–2.0 in. (3.8–5 cm) across, that range from pale to deep rose with some brown to green spotting on the upper lobes (Plate 57). There are significant variations in flower color among plants in the wild, including very deep pink to almost red forms as well as pale blush and even pure white selections. 'White Find' is a popular form in the trade with pure white flowers. With typically seven stamens rather than the usual five found in most of the other native azaleas, this species is genetically quite different from the other species and does not hybridize with them. *Rhododendron vaseyi* has a very limited natural range, found in the wild in only four mountainous counties of western North Carolina at elevations above 3000 ft. (900 m). Surprisingly, plants have proven to be quite adaptable at lower elevations including many warmer gardens in the southeastern United States.

The Orange Group

Although this group is classified as orange, it really includes a broad range of colors from yellow through gold to orange, orange-red, and scarlet. There are no white forms found among the species in this group.

Rhododendron austrinum—With a natural range from southern Alabama and Georgia to northern Florida, this species is often referred to as the Florida azalea (Plate 58). Because of its southern habitat, the plant has proven remarkably heat tolerant. The wonderfully fragrant flowers are 1.0–1.5 in. (2.5–3.8 cm) across, usually yellow to gold, with a long floral tube that is often flushed with red and covered with sticky glandular hairs. It also has exceptionally long stamens. The species blooms in early midseason, just as the new growth begins to expand. *Rhododendron austrinum* can make a stunning landscape specimen in southeastern gardens, and some forms have proven remarkably hardy farther north, especially in gardens where the winters do not often fall much below 0°F (−18°C). The species has been known to hybridize readily with other native azaleas in the wild, especially *R. canescens*, which blooms at about the same time. Natural hybrids come in many lovely shades of yellow, gold, peach, orange, and coral. Plant breeders are now using *R. austrinum* to impart heat resistance to many newer deciduous azalea hybrids. Some excellent selections of the species are currently being introduced into the trade, including the deep gold 'Escatawpa' and the bicolor 'Millie Mac'.

Rhododendron calendulaceum—Commonly known as the flame azalea, this species is considered by many horticulturists to be the one of the most spectacular flowering shrubs in the Appalachian Mountains (Plate 59). When the species is in bloom in the wild, entire hillsides can be awash in color. Blossoms are larger than most of the other native azaleas, usually measuring 1.5–2.5 in. (3.8–6.3 cm) across, and some forms observed in the wild have exceeded 3 in. (7.5 cm) in diameter. The flower color can range from clear yellow to deep gold through apricot and salmon to brilliant orange and orange-red to scarlet. Many forms have a prominent yellow to gold blotch on the upper lobe. The flowers open in late midseason while the new growth is still expanding, but unfortunately they are not fragrant. As a landscape plant, *R. calendulaceum* is very winter hardy and an excellent choice in a wide range of garden climates. However, it is not as tolerant of strong heat and has proven difficult in the Deep South. Because this species is a tetraploid having twice the normal number of chromosomes, it does not cross as readily with the other native species, and such hybrids can be sterile.

Rhododendron cumberlandense—This species, formerly known as *R. bakeri*, is frequently confused with *R. calendulaceum*, the flame azalea. Certainly the two species are very similar, but there are some distinguishing characteristics that can help tell them apart. In the wild, the usual color range for *R. cumberlandense* tends more toward the orange-red and red shades rather than orange. Also, the flowers are usually smaller, about 1.5 in. (3.8 cm) across, and appear later in the season after the new growth has fully expanded. It has a relatively isolated natural range on the Cumberland Plateau in Kentucky southward to Tennessee and the mountains of Georgia, Alabama, and North Carolina. *Rhododendron cumberlandense* makes an excellent landscape plant, providing a burst of color in the garden in early summer when few other plants are in bloom. Because *R. cumberlandense* has the normal diploid number of chromosomes, it crosses readily with many of the other species found in its range in the wild. The magnificent hybrid swarm of native azaleas on Gregory Bald in the Great Smokey Mountains probably owes much of its wide color variation to this lovely species. An orange-red selection of the species known as 'Camp's Red' has been in the trade for many years.

Rhododendron flammeum—The natural range for this species is rather small, primarily limited to the mountainous regions of Georgia and South Carolina. Formerly know as *R. speciosum*, this native azalea is another one of the more heat-tolerant species and an excellent choice for southern gardeners. The flowers are not fragrant and only modest in size, approximately 1.5 in. (3.8 cm) across, but they are often held in spectacular ball-shaped trusses. The color range is similar to R. *calendulaceum* in shades of orange-yellow to orange and deep red, often with a prominent gold or yellow blotch. The species blooms in mid to late spring while the new growth is still expanding. It hybridizes readily with other natives, especially R. *canescens*, and the resulting hybrids come in many wonderful blends of yellow, pink, and coral to orange-red. There are also a few named varieties in the trade such as the clear yellow 'Hazel Hamilton', but R. *flammeum* is notoriously difficult to propagate by cuttings so named forms are scarce.

Rhododendron prunifolium—This wonderful native azalea is one of the last species in the garden to flower (Plate 60). Usually blooming in the summer months from July into August, some selections have been known to flower as late September or even early October. The flowers measure 1.5–2.0 in. (3.8–5 cm) across and are usually from orange-red to coral and deep red, often with a noticeable orange blotch. The flowers are not fragrant. Originally, the species was considered very rare because it was only found in a small, isolated area of southwestern Georgia and eastern Alabama. However, through conservation efforts and because it propagates easily from both cuttings and seed, R. *prunifolium* is now widely available in the nursery trade.

Cultural Requirements

Most native azaleas prefer a rich, well-drained soil with ample moisture and at least several hours of direct sun each day to bloom well. Plants in the wild do flower best in full sun, but blossoms will last longer in warmer weather if given some afternoon shade. Plants are relatively disease and insect resistant when grown under conditions matching their natural environments and usually require little special care.

Landscape Uses

Native azaleas make excellent landscape plants. By selecting a number of different species, a gardener can have something in bloom for much of the growing season. Being deciduous, native azaleas do lose their leaves during the winter, so it is often recommended to associate them with other evergreen shrubs or trees. Most native azaleas have colorful fall foliage in shades of yellow, orange, or red, which adds to their interest in the landscape.

Propagation

Like many other deciduous azaleas, native azaleas are often difficult to propagate by cuttings. For best success, take cutting from the new growth in late spring or early summer, treat with a standard rooting hormone, and then place them under artificial lights with long-day conditions. Cuttings will often form roots, but if they do not send out new growth before the autumn, they will usually fail. Even though roots have formed, the plant refuses to grow and eventually dies.

Native azaleas propagate easily by seed. Because of genetic variability, seedlings will not be identical to the parent plants, but most of them will be excellent representatives of the species with attractive flowers. Plants can reach blooming age in just two to three years from seed if given good growing conditions.

Approximate Sequence of Bloom

Early to early midseason: *canadense, periclymenoides, vaseyi*

Midseason: *alabamense, atlanticum, austrinum, canescens, prinophyllum*

Late midseason: *calendulaceum, eastmanii, flammeum, occidentale*

Late: *arborescens, cumberlandense, viscosum*

Very late: *prunifolium*

Hardiness and Adaptability

Hardy in zones 4 to 5 (−25°F, −32°C): *calendulaceum, canadense, prinophyllum*

Hardy in zones 5 to 6 (−15°F, −26°C): *arborescens, atlanticum, calendulaceum, canadense, cumberlandense, periclymenoides, prinophyllum, vaseyi, viscosum*

Heat tolerant: *austrinum, alabamense, canescens, flammeum, prunifolium, viscosum*

Moisture loving: *arborescens, austrinum, canadense, canescens, viscosum*

Fragrance

Light: *alabamense, periclymenoides*

Medium: *atlanticum, canescens, eastmanii, viscosum*

Strong: *arborescens, austrinum, occidentale, prinophyllum*

Size

Low (up to 3 ft., 0.9 m): *arborescens* var. *richardsonii, atlanticum, canadense*

Medium (4–5 ft., 1.2–1.5 m): *alabamense, arborescens, cumberlandense, eastmanii, flammeum, occidentale, prinophyllum, periclymenoides, vaseyi, viscosum*

Tall (6 ft., 1.8 m or more): *austrinum, calendulaceum, canescens, prunifolium*

5

Use in the Landscape

Rhododendrons and azaleas are available in such diversity of flower color, foliage texture, form, season of bloom, and plant size as to fit almost any landscape. A landscape plan is necessary to coordinate the planting with the architecture of buildings, roadways, paths, existing trees, and any other existing features of the landscape and to determine how many and type of plants needed. As soon as the desired effect is defined and the various elements coordinated, plants can be selected to fit the plan. A landscape plan should be designed for easy maintenance in terms of mowing, pruning, mulching, and so on, providing easy access with as little hand care, such as weeding, pruning, and movement of material, as possible. The plant collector (a category into which most gardeners fall from time to time) may need to set aside a separate area for collected items that do not fit into the landscape plan yet are so desirable as to deserve space for evaluation or just enjoyment for their own beauty.

Only some basics of landscaping are presented here, together with suggested uses for rhododendrons and azaleas. These are accompanied by illustrations of their application in the landscape. This material is included to assist those new to planning and developing landscape plans and will potentially reduce costly errors of judgment. I would recommend seeking professional help if the development involves a total landscape plan in a new planting area.

When developing the landscape plan, a primary decision is whether the garden is to have a formal or informal effect. The trend today is toward informal plantings, edging property in gradual curves and grouping plants. Rhododendrons and azaleas are at their best in such informal settings. Plants grow naturally in rather informal groups with graceful curves. There are no square corners in nature's creations, and perhaps the landscape planner is well advised to reflect this design trait. Plantings may be made using gradual, graceful curves around the foundations of buildings, along boundaries, walks, roads, or circling large trees. A very effective method for laying out the boundary of curves and circles is to use a garden hose laid out on the ground to define the shape of the desired bed. The hose can be moved until the desired shape is created. This method permits the gardener to visualize each bed as the landscape plan is being drawn up. Large open areas can be left for lawn and recreational use (Plate 61). The landscape design needs to please the user, and no one plan best serves all.

I do not believe the entire garden should be planted solidly to any one type or texture of plant, even though large groups are sometimes very effective. The differing textures and colors of needled evergreens, deciduous trees and shrubs, and perennial and annual flowering plants are needed to provide visual relief in the landscape and will also broaden the highlights when the garden has something in flower.

While walking through the garden, the realization came to me that the landscape is much like a home. There are numerous rooms, open spaces where we pause to rest and enjoy the area around us, and halls or walkways taking us from one room to the other. There may be furniture in the rooms for sitting and resting or talking. Open or closed doorways exist in the form of trellises, which separate open areas from pathways or other open spaces. Rooms are restful places where we stop or slow down in the garden tour, and paths move us along more quickly in anticipation of the next open space. Curves or corners in paths hide what is ahead and add mystique to the journey. Shrubbery of dense trees also block the view and have the same effect. Plants catch our attention and move us on to enjoy their beauty, as well as serving to block the view of other areas.

When considering design one must think of masses of plants or of open spaces for walking or congregating. Plants and buildings surround open spaces. Low enclosures, which cannot be seen over or through, cause a space to seem smaller, whereas large trees with high limbs open spaces up, making them appear larger. Some gardeners prefer small, private nooks, others more open areas. The landscape should include plants of differing textures and color or tone of foliage, especially among evergreens, which will display foliage year-round.

Color Guidelines

The integration of flower color is important to the harmony of any landscape design. Observing a few general guidelines can reward the gardener many times over.

Bright colors, such as orange and red, are much more difficult to blend into group plantings.

It is usually more effective to use a group of at least three plants of a particular kind rather than to have single plants as little spots of many colors.

White flowers very effectively separate colors that might otherwise clash, such as the bright orange of some deciduous azaleas and some of the brilliant reds. Orange seems particularly difficult to blend into plantings, so it must either be massed or separated from other plants by plants with white flowers. Plate 62 is a good example of using white to balance stronger colors.

Colors that are lost or clash with buildings need to be carefully sited. Brick walls are poor backdrops for oranges and light pinks.

Light pinks and whites are striking in the woodland or in front of evergreen trees where light intensity is low. Rhododendron and azaleas with light pink or white flowers can be grown in mass planting in such locations (Plate 63).

Bright reds can be mixed with pinks and whites in groups of three or five but should not make up more than a third of the total planting.

To minimize surprise color clashes, the final planting needs to be fully visualized before any actual groundwork is done. Planting while plants are in bloom will make it easier to harmonize or blend colors and will make it easier to consider which plants bloom at the same time. Planting when shrubs are in flower requires that plants receive extra shading and watering in the first growing season. Fortunately, rhododendrons and azaleas transplant fairly easily, and if a mistake in placement is noticed, plants can easily be moved later.

The flowering times of the plants used in the landscape need careful consideration as well. Plants flowering very early in the season are best placed in view of a window so they can be enjoyed from inside the house. As the weather warms and becomes more suited to outside activity, plants that flower later can be placed in view of the principal areas of outdoor activity.

Specific Uses in the Landscape

Azaleas, especially the low-growing members of the evergreen group, make excellent foundation plants as do many of the dwarf rhododendrons. Some selections of both rhododendrons and azaleas do well as border plants, acting to separate areas in the landscape, while the larger forms are supreme in the open landscape and especially in open wooded areas. The very low-growing cultivars of both rhododendrons and azaleas are quite useful in rock gardens and as ground covers. Many of the large rhododendrons form stunning specimen and accent plants.

Specimen and Accent Plants

Some of the large rhododendrons and azaleas make excellent specimen plants, as they can be attractive year-round. When appropriately placed in the landscape such plants are breathtakingly beautiful, especially when viewed against backgrounds of large evergreens or a dark green lawn (Plate 64). White, light pink, yellow, or bright red flowers contrast well with a dark green background and will add an eye-catching accent, attracting attention to that point in the landscape. Even the small-leaved rhododendron 'P.J.M.', which matures into a large plant, may be used as a specimen plant. When 'P.J.M.' is in full flower in early spring with drifts of daffodils in front or beside, it offers a sight not soon forgotten.

Plants considered dwarf or slow growing in nature, such as *R. degronianum* ssp. *yakushimanum*, also form excellent specimen plants for close viewing (Plate 65). Specimen plants draw attention to themselves and to the area and should be placed near areas of activity, near paths in the landscape, or in view from the house or road. Specimen plants should be spaced by themselves and far enough from other plants to allow full development of the natural shape of the individual plant.

Accent plants are also used to heighten interest in a portion of the landscape. They differ from specimen plantings in that accent plants are used with other plants, either in a border planting or a grouping, whereas specimen plants stand alone in the landscape. When in flower, both rhododendrons and azaleas provide a blast of color quite capable of accenting any point. Care must be taken not to overwork this quality to the point of monotony or to let plantings overpower the rest of the landscape. Plate 66 shows an effective accent planting.

Group Plantings of Rhododendron

It is in groups that rhododendrons and azaleas perform at their best, both in relation to the landscape and the effect on the well-being of plants and their performance. The group provides shade, interrupts wind, and receives mulch as leaves fall, all of which benefit all the plants in the group.

Shrubs appear more interesting when planted in odd numbers partly because odd numbers lend themselves to circles and curves, resulting in more natural-looking beds. Group plantings may be made around building foundations, along walks or roads, around trees, or around the edge of the landscape, as dividers or privacy screens or as a large accent area. Beds or groups may be planted with all the same cultivar or with several, taking care to blend or match flower color, plant texture, flowering date, and plant height. A sufficient number of plants of the same flowering date, color, size, and texture will provide a smooth transition rather than giving a shotgun effect. Even small groups require at least three of the same cultivar. If bold colors, such as bright reds and oranges, are used, additional plants to provide the light colors of pink and white may be required to blend all colors together. It is often wiser to make solid plantings of bold colors in separate beds.

Spacing of plants within a group depends on the rate of growth, mature size of each plant, and the landscape effect desired. If the group is to be solidly planted with rhododendrons and azaleas, with no interplanting of annuals or other plants, a spacing of 3 ft. (0.9 m) results in a completed, more mature effect quickly. When using plants maturing at 6 ft. (1.8 m) in ten years, an initial 6-ft. spacing will not produce a solid planting for ten years. Decisions on plant spacing depend in part on how quickly a solid mass of plants is desired. Closer spacing will require more funds to purchase the larger number of plants needed.

Plant height must also be considered in selecting plants for group plantings to keep the group in proper scale within itself and with the rest of the landscape. Rhododendrons are sometimes described as tall, which usually means over 6 ft. (1.8 m); medium, 4–6 ft. (1.2–1.8 m); and low, 3 ft. (0.9 m) or less. Azaleas have similar descriptions of upright, spreading, low growing, and so forth. Plate 67 illustrates a large group planting in scale with the landscape.

Where large groups are planted, tall forms need to be placed to the center or back, with lower growing plants on the outside or in front. This allows for maximum viewing of all plants and provides the planting with a multilevel effect, especially when in flower (Plate 68).

Border Plantings, Screens, and Hedges

Borders are used to delineate areas in the landscape. They are used to separate property lines, a service area from the rest of the landscape, the parking area from a lawn, the lawn from the garden, or to create secluded areas. Because most are evergreen plants, rhododendrons and azaleas make excellent border plants in those locations where the wind is not too severe and some afternoon shade is available (Plates 69–71).

Natural screens—The dense evergreen foliage of rhododendrons and some azaleas makes them especially useful in screening undesirable landscape features.

For example, a mass planting of evergreen azaleas is used very effectively to obscure a large tree stump in my garden (Plate 72). Other situations may require screening activity areas from garbage cans or a compost pile or creating a privacy screen around a swimming pool.

If plants are to be developed as a low hedge or border, well-branched and naturally compact plants are required. Evergreen azaleas and some of the small-leaved rhododendrons are very suitable as small hedges. Elepidote rhododendrons are not generally suitable for large formal hedges because their growth habit will not present an attractive appearance if the plants are heavily and regularly pruned, as formal hedges require. If there is plenty of room to accommodate natural growth, however, the larger broad-leaved rhododendrons can make a most attractive border. Rhododendrons and azaleas cannot be used as windbreaks because they do not tolerate wind well; other plants such as yews, pines, spruce, and hollies are better suited to this role in the landscape (Plate 73).

Woodland Plantings

It is in the open woodland where rhododendrons and azaleas can truly reign supreme. The informal setting and the backdrop and overstory of trees provide a pleasing landscape effect, yet also produce the benign climate native to many of these species. The high shade and humidity of the forest, its gift of mulch each year, its windbreak qualities, and the vertical emphasis of the tree trunks all serve to enhance the visual effects while proving an environmental benefit to the landscape planting.

In nature one or two plants of a species are seldom seen growing in one spot, and plants tend to develop large circular or irregular groupings. Thus, it is best to mass plant in the woodland. The larger forms of rhododendrons and azaleas are in better scale for a woodland setting. Smaller species and cultivars are easily lost, and when viewed from a distance they may appear merely as small dots in the extensive scale of the woodland. Small, low-growing plants may be used to best advantage if massed along woodland paths, where observers can come in close contact with them. Plants with fragrant flowers are also more effective when placed near paths, where their fragrance can be enjoyed. I think the fragrance of such plants as R. *fortunei* requires that it not be restricted to woodlands, but rather be planted close to foot traffic, upwind of the residence or along activity areas such as patios.

I recently received an unusual compliment from a carload of sightseers. They had stopped to get their shovel out of the trunk to lift a rhododendron from my woodland planting along the road. When I confronted them, they responded with "We thought they were growing wild!" This is certainly not a valid reason to dig plants, yet I had to feel gratified. The point was that I'd made a naturalistic planting that appeared to have evolved by itself. And this is what I consider a successful woodland planting.

As noted earlier, the large woodland tends to overwhelm not only small plants but plantings small in scope as well. To create a satisfactory display, a rather large area containing at least twenty plants needs to be included in the original plan. And, if at all feasible, the area should be expanded as soon as possible. Plants may be spaced more widely apart in woodland settings to provide growing room for years of undisturbed growth. Irregular spacing, rather than a precise distance between plants, also adds to the natural appearance. The large hybrids can be spaced 6–9 ft. (1.8–2.7 m) apart with smaller growing azaleas and dwarf rhododendrons spaced closer. Check the size in ten years, as given in appendix A, to determine distances for individual cultivars, and see Plate 75 for a successful woodland planting of azaleas.

Container Growing and Bonsai

The smaller rhododendrons and azaleas may be grown easily in containers and, for example, be placed around the patio or in permanent raised planters next to buildings or walkways. Take care to provide a well-drained container and planting mix. A mixture of 50 percent perlite, pine bark, or coarse sand and 50 percent sphagnum peat moss or other coarse mix works well. Because these materials contain little in the way of plant nutrients or even the minor elements, a complete plant food needs to be used regularly.

Rhododendron roots are much more cold sensitive than is the top growth and can be damaged by temperatures below 20°F (–7°C). Provide winter protection for the roots of containerized plants wherever temperatures regularly drop below this level. This is best done by insulating the container with bark or other material or by moving the container to a protected winter storage area. While 20°F (–7°C) is a general rule of thumb, there are a few species and cultivars that can withstand lower root temperatures (Table 5.1). Clearly, container size will vary by the size of plant. Also, expect that as the plant grows older and larger, it will require transplanting to a larger container.

Plants with small leaves, slow growth, and a crooked or spreading growth habit provide the most suitable forms for bonsai. The small-leaved azaleas and dwarf rhododendrons make ideal plants for miniaturizing. Older plants that have already developed twisted or gnarled stems are superior to immature whips. If only young whips are available, it is still possible to obtain the desired

Table 5.1. *Rhododendron* species and cultivars that can withstand root temperatures lower than 20°F (−7°C)

Species or cultivar	Root-killing temperature	
	°F	°C
R. prunifolium	20	−7
R. 'Hino Crimson'	19	−7
Exbury Hybrids	17	−8
R. schlippenbachii	15	−9
R. 'Purple Gem'	15	−9
R. 'Gibraltar'	10	−12
R. 'Hinode giri'	10	−12
R. minus (Carolinianum Group)	0	−18
R. catawbiense	0	−18
R. 'P.J.M.'	−9	−23

From Harvis (1976) and Steponkus et al. (1976)

shape by pruning and wiring over a period of years. (I will not attempt to detail the means and objectives of creating a bonsai *Rhododendron*.) Not all bonsai plants need to be in containers. Many of the smaller, low-growing plant species at home in the rock garden are quite suitable for bonsai development.

Foundation Plantings and Companion Plants

Foundation plantings also seem to require groups of plants. The commonly seen single row of plants lined along a foundation wall is not as interesting as groups that curve out from and in toward the building and add depth to the area. For maintenance and structural purposes, plants should be placed no closer to a building than 3 ft. (0.9 m). Also, if plants are sited under a roof overhang, they will be more susceptible to drought damage as precipitation will not reach the root area.

The size of the plants to be used in foundation plantings must be coordinated with the size of the building, especially its height. A single-story home requires low-growing plants (especially under windows), while the same plants would be out of scale for a multistory building. The tall forms, including the large, broad-leaved rhododendrons, complement taller buildings especially when large landscape trees can unite the planting to the building. The importance of plant selection means it is not a hit-or-miss activity, and a well-conceived landscape plan specifies such things as textures and sizes of plants to be used in all situations. Plate 76 illustrates an extended foundation planting.

Other plants are often used together with rhododendrons and azaleas in foundation plantings, and they can provide an occasion to blend foliage textures and colors. Extreme opposites can blend together well. For example, the needlelike foliage of a pine or yew, perhaps used on a windy corner as a windbreak, serves well as a background for the broad-leaved foliage and flowers of rhododendrons and azaleas. Plate 77 shows azaleas used in a more formal setting, bordered by *Hosta* in front. Companion plants are used to tie rhododendrons and azaleas into the total landscape, creating a natural looking, smoothly flowing vision. They can add contrast in height, texture, color, and season of flowering, and fill the spaces between plants to give a look of completion and maturity to the planting.

Carefully selected trees can add a sense of height to the landscape and provide the light-filtered shade so well suited to many understory plants including rhododendrons. Selection criteria for trees include deep root systems that will not seriously compete for water with the more shallow-rooted *Rhododendron*. Tree foliage needs to allow adequate light to reach understory plants. Trees and shrubs producing flowers or fruit, such as dogwoods (*Cornus*), crab apples (*Malus*), *Viburnum*, and hollies (*Ilex*) possess yet another useful quality by extending the season of color and providing food and shelter for birds and other wildlife. Needled evergreens such as fir (*Abies*), pine (*Pinus*), and hemlock (*Tsuga*), with their fine-textured foliage and light green color, provide a pleasing contrast to rhododendrons and azaleas.

Like the flowering trees, flowering shrubs that bloom earlier or later than the rhododendrons make good companions by extending the period of color in the landscape not only with flowers but with seeds as well. Shrubs can also provide transitions in size and texture between trees and lower azaleas and rhododendrons.

Many native flowers are adapted to the same environmental conditions as are rhododendrons and azaleas. Any wildflowers native to the woodland make excellent companion plants. Specifically, this would be plants such as *Hosta*, *Liriope*, lily-of-the-valley (*Convallaria majalis*), bloodroot (*Sanguinaria canadensis*), wood hyacinth (*Endymion nonscriptus*), ferns (various species), lady's slipper (*Cypripedium*), and Solomon's seal (*Polygonatum*). They could be planted between and in front of rhododendrons and azaleas. Purchase such native plants only from businesses selling plants propagated in the nursery. Collected plants should not be purchased, as this practice adds to the pressures leading to the destruction of wild plants.

Bulbs may be used to delicately extend the flowering season before, during, or after the flowering period of rhododendrons. Early-flowering plants such as snowdrops (*Galanthus*), wood hyacinth or grape hyacinth (*Muscari*), lily-of-the-valley, daffodils (*Narcissus*), and tulips (*Tulipa*) add color early in the flowering season and are not highly competitive for nutrients, water, or space. Daffodils planted in front of or beside early-flowering rhododendrons such as 'P.J.M.' or azaleas such as 'Springtime' add another dimension to the color scheme. Lilies (*Lilium*) can extend the flowering season into summer. The lighter shades of white, pink, and yellow contrast well with the dark green foliage of rhododendrons.

Well-chosen ground covers between plantings of rhododendrons and azaleas can smoothly unite the planting with a lawn or pathway area. While some root competition may develop, it would not be sufficiently severe to restrict the use of closely grown ground covers when they can add so much to the landscape picture.

The genus *Rhododendron* is particularly well suited to a wide range of uses in the landscape thanks to the range of shape, size, flower color, and foliage texture. A gardener may consider using rhododendrons and azaleas wherever the site ensures their well-being and wherever they fit into the landscape plan. Where the situation is right, no other plant can give as much beauty for so little effort.

As landscape needs are determined through one's plan, plant selection can be guided by use of the Good Doer information in chapter 3 and appendix A to identify rhododendrons of proper size, flower color, flowering date, and adaptability. Plates 78–85 show additional examples of landscape uses of rhododendrons, azaleas, and companion plants.

6

Transplanting to the Landscape

Properly planting rhododendrons and azaleas is more critical than for some other garden additions because they are somewhat more exacting in their requirements. But if these requirements are met, the results will be at least as successful as with other types of plants. In this chapter I discuss those requirements necessary to succeed.

Only plants adequately mature to survive the rigors of the new landscape environment need be purchased. Dwarf species and cultivars can transplant well at a rather small size because age or maturity is best used as the criterion for selection. Such plants may be only 2 in. (5 cm) tall, yet will be sufficiently mature with hardened wood to survive the landscape environment. When purchasing larger forms, look for azaleas at least 12–15 in. (30–38 cm) and rhododendrons 18–36 in. (45–90 cm) because they will transplant easier, survive better, and are less costly than larger plants.

Care must be given to the time of planting, particularly in regions or sites less favorable to the growth of rhododendrons and azaleas. In all but the most benign sites, where they can be transplanted in virtually any season, two seasons are best suited for transplanting rhododendrons and azaleas: spring and fall, when plant foliage is not in active growth. *Rhododendron* are sometimes planted as late as the flowering time, but I believe this is usually too late, except for the early-flowering plants. Spring planting can be done as soon as hard freezes have passed and the soil is sufficiently dry to work without damaging soil structure.

Fall planting is gaining in favor both among nursery people and gardeners because roots have the opportunity to work their way into the prepared soil before the onslaught of winter. Fall planting is most successfully undertaken in those regions in which the soil does not freeze to such a depth that the entire root ball of the transplanted plant is likely to get frozen. In less harsh regions, roots can develop quickly in early fall because all the plant's resources can be directed to root growth, as top growth is no longer active. Lack of tender top growth also reduces moisture demand on the newly transplanted root system. As days shorten and the soil cools, roots continue to grow even well into the fall and until the soil freezes. This will result in plants better able to support new top growth the following spring and to survive the hot dry conditions the following summer. Fall planting must be completed at least one month, and preferably three to four months, before the soil freezes.

Preparing to Plant

Chapter 2 outlines how to select the planting site and modify the soil. Questions as to the size of the hole that must be dug and whether raised beds should be used are dependent to a large extent on soil type. In a heavy, poorly drained soil, plants should *not* be fit into small holes in the soil. This is akin to setting them in a container having little or no drainage. On the other hand, smaller holes may be used in well-drained soils. In no case should a planting hole be used that is smaller than twice the diameter of the existing root ball. Plantings in heavy soils need to be raised somewhat above the existing soil level or, if internal soil drainage is determined to be very poor, need to be made entirely on top of the existing soil in an amended soil mix.

When too small of a planting hole is dug in heavy clay soil and is then amended only in this area, water enters the amended medium (that is, the small planting hole) faster than the surrounding native clay soil; it is blocked by the unamended, impervious sides and bottom of the hole. Standing water can then damage the plant roots. The solution would be to dig a larger, wider hole at least 4 ft. (1.2 m) wide and amend all this soil with 50 percent organic matter. The entire planting bed should be raised above the existing soil level by adding topsoil to raise the bed 12–18 in. (30–45 cm). The result is an amended rooting medium that drains well and will encourage rhododendron and azalea root extension. This extended area will encompass enough space for several years of normal growth before the unamended soil is encountered. The continued extension of the roots, beyond the amended medium, can be further encouraged by the use of a good mulch extending beyond the interface point.

Organic amendments not only improve soil drainage, except in sandy soils, but also offer other improvements to the soil environment. One result is to encourage mycorrhizae, the fungi that form a symbiotic association with the roots of ericaceous plants, an association that in turn increases the moisture and nutrients available to the plant. Organic matter with fine particles improves structure of clay soils better than coarse material. The fine particles of pine fines and sphagnum peat moss help separate the clay platelets and the humic acid contributes to improved soil aggregation. To improve moisture-holding capacity of sandy soils, use a larger percentage of coarse organic matter. This is because oxidation of organic materials is faster in well-aerated sandy soils, and coarse material will remain in the soil longer. I recommend a combination of sphagnum peat and fine pine bark in both types of soils.

These planting instructions apply to planting an individual *Rhododendron* in the landscape. However, rhododendrons and azaleas are generally more attractive in the landscape and seem to perform better when planted in groups of three or five or more. In this case an entire bed can be prepared and amended with organic material as discussed in chapter 2. Again, raise the bed above the soil level in very poorly drained soils or construct a bed on top of the native soil.

Rhododendrons and azaleas are shallow-rooted plants, so it is not necessary to dig a very deep hole or bed; 8 in. (20 cm), the usual depth a rototiller works, is deep enough. It is much more effective to prepare the soil area extending around the plant than to prepare the soil area extending much below the plant. This is true even in well-drained loam soils. If the subsoil is well drained and nutrients are available, the roots will grow downward below the cultivated soil in most cases (Figure 6.1). If the subsoil is poorly drained, the roots will in no case grow downward. Rhododendron and azalea roots will extend only as deeply as oxygen is available. The only justification for deep soil preparation might be in areas where soils freeze deeply. This would increase aeration at greater depths and allow deeper root penetration. Use of mulch to prevent deep freezing of the soil is an alternative to deep digging in this circumstance.

It may be difficult to understand why rhododendron roots do not extend deeply in sandy soils. There is adequate aeration and oxygen deep down into the soil, unless a high water table exists, and yet rhododendrons and mountain laurel (*Kalmia latifolia*) root systems are often very shallow on such soils. This is a result of the very low nutrient levels in sand. There are usually very few, if any, earthworms in sand to move organic matter down, so the most favorable area for root development is in the shallow layer of organic material on top of the soil.

Figure 6.1. A rhododendron with a deep root system grown in a well-drained soil. The bed was amended only 8 in. (20 cm) deep, and the root system is now well developed to an 11-in. (27.5-cm) depth. Photograph by H. Edward Reiley

Caution must be exercised in planting rhododendrons near buildings with concrete foundations as they tolerate lime poorly. Contractors often bury additional concrete, plaster, and other lime-based materials around the building site. These materials greatly affect soil pH, raising it dramatically to alkaline levels. In such cases a poor-to-intolerable environment for azaleas and rhododendrons results. Furthermore, simple aging of concrete or cement block foundations causes lime to leach into the nearby soil. New concrete foundations can be sealed with asphalt or other waterproofing material to reduce or eliminate the lime problem. Whatever the situation, always plant at least 3 ft. (0.9 m) from any foundation wall or other concrete structure.

If areas are prepared at least a week prior to planting, the loosened soil will have time to settle. This reduces the likelihood that either the plant or the soil level will change and alter the desired planting hole depth.

Fertilizer use is mentioned here only to make the point that it is safe to dig organics (including urea formaldehyde as a source of nitrogen) or natural minerals, but not chemical fertilizers, into the soil at planting time. If chemical fertilizers are used they must be dug in at least one week before planting and dissolved through the soil with at least 1 in. (2.5 cm) of water. If the planting area has been prepared as suggested in chapter 2, no additional fertilizer is needed at planting time. Research has shown that adding nitrogen fertilizer at planting time actually decreases root growth on dogwood trees. I am not aware of a similar study using rhododendron.

Planting

When digging the planting hole in the bed, attention must be paid to depth, which means the distance from the surface of the planting bed, whether raised above the soil level or not, to the bottom of the planting hole. Rhododendron and azaleas need to be planted about level with the top of the root ball; leaving the top 1 in. (2.5 cm) of the ball above soil level is even better. Under no circumstances should the soil surface be higher than the top of the root ball. The hole therefore needs to be dug to a depth 1 in. (2.5 cm) less than the vertical dimension of the root ball. If the root ball is longer than 8 in. (20 cm), which was recommended earlier as rototiller depth and adequate to prepare a planting area, dig a deeper hole in well-drained soil just large enough to place the root mass. If planting in poorly drained soil, cut off the bottom of the root ball to reduce the dimension. Some readers may be horrified by the latter suggestion, yet it is known that container-grown plants benefit from removing the pot-bound roots circling the bottom. Conversely, if the bottom of the planting remains in the loose, prepared soil, tamp the bottom surface to forestall settling after planting.

In poorly drained soil the root ball must develop on top of the native soil (see chapter 2). In these situations the planting medium is placed around the ball for a distance of about 4 ft. (1.2 m), resulting in a raised bed as high as the root ball. The native soil beneath the plant requires no digging or amendments and will remain stable, not allowing the root ball to settle below the correct planting depth. Similarly, planting depth is more readily secure if the hole in prepared beds is not dug any deeper than the root ball. The diameter of the planting hole in prepared beds needs to be about twice the width of the root ball. This will allow easy access to pack the amended soil in and around the root ball and to spread the plant roots out into the soil.

Planting considerations are also determined by whether the transplant has been field grown or container grown. Container plants are grown in coarse-textured, soilless media and are often seriously pot-bound. The resulting roots are tightly packed and may circle the inside walls of the container. These two factors present a couple of transplanting hazards. First, rhododendrons and azalea roots prefer the ease of penetrating the coarse, soilless mix to the far less hospitable planting soil and will resist growing into the latter. The gardener must do something to encourage root extension out into the surrounding soil. If the container plant is not pot-bound, the roots may simply be pulled out of the mix and spread in the hole at planting time. A sharp garden weeding tool is helpful in digging away the outer edge of the rooting medium to expose the roots. Extend the roots so they are out of the potting mix by at least 2 in. (5cm).

When filling the hole after the roots have been prepared, hold the plant in position and gradually fill the hole to each succeeding root level. Place extended roots on top of the soil and firm the soil below the extended roots so it does not settle and roots remain in a horizontal position after filling above them. Continue this root-covering procedure as the hole is filled. If this procedure is not followed, the exposed roots may be forced back into the original root mass as the hole is filled with growing medium. If container-grown plants are planted on top of the soil and a totally organic mix is used around them, or they are simply transplanted into larger containers filled with a soilless medium, roots will quickly extend into such media, but it is still necessary to spread the roots when transplanting. The transplanting method described here requires a little more time but has been the most successful in my garden.

Another problem often encountered with container-grown plants is the drying out of the root ball. The coarse potting mix dries out more rapidly than the surrounding soil and water cannot move from the finer textured soil back into the root ball. The result is a dry root zone surrounded by a moist soil. Frequent watering of the root ball is necessary to prevent damage to the plant, yet only the root ball should be watered. The surrounding soil is moist, and watering it further can result in a soil too wet to encourage root extension. Additionally, as the root ball dries it will shrink, losing contact with the surrounding soil and making it even more difficult for roots to cross the interface into the surrounding soil. It is in part for this reason that roots are spread when planting. The failure of container-grown plants to survive in the landscape can most often be traced to the drying out of the root ball. This results in root death before roots are able to extend into the surrounding soil.

In 1998 I started a trial planting to evaluate five methods of root-ball treatment of container-grown plants and subsequent growth. At planting time plants were all moderately root bound, with circling roots around the root ball, but not so badly that roots could not be straightened out. Plants of the same size and cultivar were planted in a nursery bed in which the silt loam soil was amended with 2.5 in. (6.3 cm) of pine bark fines (0.25 in., 0.63 cm, or less in size) and 1 in (2.5 cm) of light-colored sphagnum peat moss. (Dark-colored sphagnum peat moss is too decomposed to support biocontrol microorganisms in the soil, although it will improve soil texture.) The composted organic matter was dug into an 8-in. (20-cm) depth with a rototiller. Plants were properly watered, that is, the root ball was not allowed to dry out nor did plants receive too much water. The bed was shaded with 30 percent shade and surrounded by a snow fence windbreak; probably better care than most gardeners would provide. After three years the plants were dug and enough soil removed from the roots to evaluate root extension and growth. Top growth was also evaluated. The five treatments and results are as follows:

> For those planted with no root-ball disturbance, roots did extend out 4–5 in. (10–12.5 cm) into the amended soil. Top growth was satisfactory. The center root ball remained intact, and the circling roots may cause girdling problems in the future.

> For some plants, the root ball was sliced down the sides with a knife, 1 in. (2.5 cm) deep at 3-in. (7.5-cm) intervals around the ball. This is the treatment most often recommended for transplanting container-grown plants, but it resulted in the poorest performance in the trial. The plant lost branches to die back and was discarded after the three-year trial, barely alive and certainly not worthy of anyone's landscape. These results did not surprise me because this method actually severs most roots from the plant.

> For other plants, potting medium was dug off around the edge of the root ball and roots were exposed about 2–3 in. (5–7.5 cm). Planting was done by holding roots up and placing them horizontally on top of firmed fill as the hole was filled. (If roots are not lifted up and placed horizontally they will be pushed back against the root ball as the hole is filled.) This method resulted in a plant that was superior in all ways. Top growth was 30 percent larger and roots had extended out into the soil farther. This procedure requires a little more time and getting down on your knees to properly plant but is worth the extra effort. Rhododendrons are long-lived plants and should be planted properly.

> The last two were nearly identical methods, only differing in the percent of roots washed clean. In one case potting medium was washed from the roots so plants were essentially bare root, and in the other the center 50 percent of the potting medium was left around the roots. These plants survived but did not grow well, lost branches, and were discarded.

Plants that experienced no root-ball disturbance and those whose roots were placed horizontally while planting were transplanted to the landscape and are growing well. Evaluation of these will continue with special interest in subsequent growth. I must say I was surprised that planting an undisturbed container root ball was successful, but there may be a future problem with root girdling. This plant, however, was not tightly root bound. The importance of placing roots out into the amended soil, as was done in the third treatment, is that root ends are placed into the soil that will not dry out as rapidly as the coarse, organic mix container plants are grown in. Root extension also straightens out circling roots, thus preventing future girdling.

Some containers are now treated with a copper hydroxide compound. This chemical prevents root circling by killing root ends as they touch the pot. The process does work, but research has shown that growth of 'Hershey's Red' azaleas was delayed the first year after transplanting to the landscape. This does not solve the problem of container plant root balls drying out quickly.

Field-grown plants already growing in a soil similar to the soil at the new planting site can be placed directly into the planting hole after the burlap or other root covering is removed. The soil can simply be packed firmly around the roots to remove any air pockets. If soil texture of the root ball is widely different from that of the planting site (for example, sand versus clay), the roots need to be exposed and spread as explained previously. This is especially true when the soil in the root ball is of a coarser texture than the new soil environment. Field-grown plants are always handled by the root ball and not by the plant stem to avoid damaging roots. The soil in the root ball is heavy and roots may be torn loose from the stem area if plants are moved or carried by the stem. A field-grown plant will require less frequent watering than a container transplant as the soil in the root ball will not dry out as quickly, but do not allow root balls to dry out.

After the plants, whether container or field grown, are planted, the soil needs to be packed firmly around the root ball with the hands, not tamped in with the feet. The planting depth should be rechecked and adjusted. A circle of soil, called a berm, about 3 in. (7.5 cm) high and with a radius about 6 in. (15 cm) outside the root ball will facilitate watering (Figure 6.2).

The entire planting area can then be mulched with about a 3 in. (7.5 cm) covering and watered to settle the soil around the root ball. Do not water when the planting hole is partially filled, only after planting and mulching is completed. Do not place any mulch within 2 in. (5 cm) of the plant stem. An overly deep mulch will restrict oxygen supply to the roots and is a major cause of death to rhododendrons, azaleas, boxwoods, and other plants requiring high oxygen levels around their roots. Do not tamp, pack, or walk on the planting area after watering, as this will cause a loss of soil structure and thus a loss of soil aeration due to compaction.

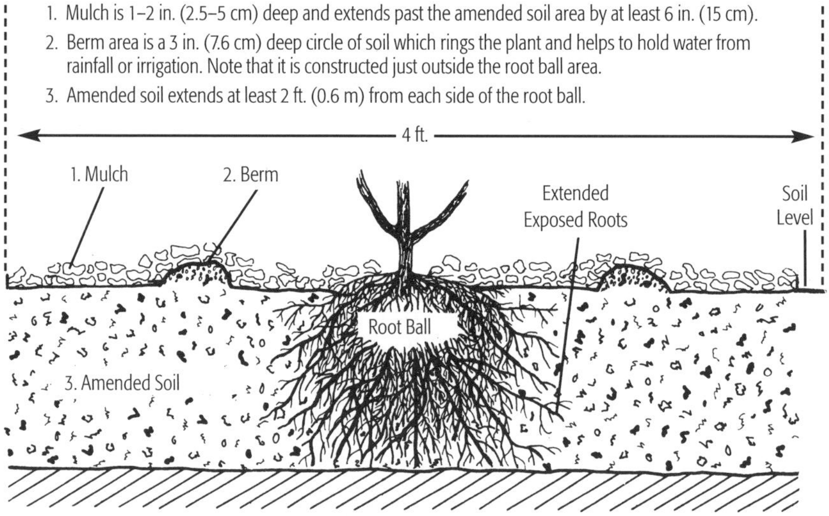

1. Mulch is 1–2 in. (2.5–5 cm) deep and extends past the amended soil area by at least 6 in. (15 cm).
2. Berm area is a 3 in. (7.6 cm) deep circle of soil which rings the plant and helps to hold water from rainfall or irrigation. Note that it is constructed just outside the root ball area.
3. Amended soil extends at least 2 ft. (0.6 m) from each side of the root ball.

Figure 6.2. Cross section of a properly planted *Rhododendron* in well-drained soil. Mulch is 1–2 in. (2.5–5 cm) deep and extends past the amended soil area by at least 6 in. (15 cm). The berm area is a 3-in. (7.5-cm) deep circle of soil that rings the plant and helps to hold water from rainfall or irrigation. Note that it is constructed just outside the root ball area. Amended soil extends at least 2 ft. (0.6 m) from each side of the root ball.

Aftercare

Rhododendrons and azaleas require more attention for the first year after planting—and perhaps for the first three to five years—than is required by established plants. *Rhododendron* seem to need this much time to establish a root system adequate to provide the moisture and nutrient requirements of the plant. Older and well-established rhododendrons suffer little from periods of drought, whereas newly planted plants are severely affected. New, tender growth on plants of all ages may exhibit some wilting in the heat of the day in full sun. If the foliage does not recover a few hours after sundown, this would be an indication of damaging water stress. Misting or fogging with an irrigation system is beneficial even for established plants to control wilting under conditions of extreme or prolonged heat. Provide mist or fog during the hottest part of the day, usually from noon until 4:00 or 5:00 P.M. Misting with a garden hose is equally helpful if an irrigation system is not available.

Field-grown transplants need about 1 in. (2.5 cm) of water, rainfall plus irrigation, per week. Container-grown plants, because their root balls dry out faster, need more water more often, usually every two or three days to keep the root ball moist. Obviously, more water is needed more often under sunny, hot, low-humidity conditions than during periods of cool, cloudy weather.

The watering regime in a woodland area varies much more than for plantings in an open bed. Rhododendrons planted very close to the stump of a tree cut out to thin the area enjoy a generous supply of soil moisture because the area is no longer having moisture pulled for tree growth. Conversely, plants placed within the root zone of a large, actively growing tree have serious competition for water. Given the differing water needs by plant placement in a woodland area, the need for irrigation varies. If all plants receive the same irrigation, some will be watered too much and suffer root damage, whereas others will not receive enough and suffer from drought stress.

Temporary windbreaks and sunshades are most helpful in the first year and especially through the first winter for newly planted rhododendrons. Such protection reduces the need for moisture and thus improves the likelihood of a successful new planting. Figure 6.3 shows burlap used both as a very effective windbreak and as a sunshade for a newly planted rhododendron.

Some protection is advisable for newly transplanted plants even in regions not experiencing extremely cold winters. Protection is most commonly provided to reduce moisture loss and the consequent drying out of the plant, which is the most frequent cause of death in newly transplanted plants. The

Figure 6.3. Burlap sunshade and windbreak around a newly planted rhododendron. This is particularly helpful for the first year after transplanting, especially during the plant's first winter. Photograph by H. Edward Reiley

lack of an extensive root system prevents new transplants from absorbing sufficient moisture to replenish transpiration losses through the leaves. Protection needs to be continued until the root system has extended out into the surrounding soil and the plant is making good top growth annually, perhaps three years or more. There are several measures a gardener can take to bring moisture loss (transpiration) and intake (root function) into balance.

Sunlight raises foliage temperature and results in a more rapid loss of moisture from the leaves. Shading the plant, therefore, reduces moisture loss. Burlap, snow fencing, or any similar material breaks the sun's rays and reduces heat stress. Do not allow the shade material to touch the foliage, as foliage damage will develop. Air movement across the plant also increases moisture loss through the leaves, except when the relative humidity is 100 percent. Reducing wind velocity will help sustain moisture levels.

During the winter months plant protection is directed toward the fact that roots cannot absorb moisture as the soil freezes, changing soil moisture to ice. Because the plant is unable to absorb water, it dries out just as surely as it does in constantly high temperatures. Mulching modifies deep soil freezing; when coupled with a windbreak and shading, it will go far in improving plant survival. Once plants have established a good root system, extensive protection is no longer necessary.

To summarize, when transplanting to the landscape:

- ▶ use plants of adequate maturity or size;
- ▶ plant during the best season for the local area;
- ▶ prepare the planting hole properly (keeping good drainage in mind);
- ▶ use only organic fertilizers initially;
- ▶ prepare the root ball to encourage root extension;
- ▶ plant at the proper depth;
- ▶ mulch and water well;
- ▶ provide shade and wind protection;
- ▶ and never allow the root ball to dry out.

Transplanting Large *Rhododendron*

Large rhododendrons or azaleas are usually transplanted for one of several reasons. The most common is to achieve an immediate landscape effect, which would otherwise require years of waiting. Another might be to better site a plant that has outgrown its place in the landscape, usually as a result of improper plant selection. Or plants being grown for the landscape may have been left in the garden nursery area too long. Whatever the reason, large plants with a fully developed root ball are very difficult to move manually. A power-driven tree spade simplifies the task and is the most efficient. But gardeners seldom have access to such a large, specialized piece of equipment and must do the job by hand. I use the following method.

As a general reference, a plant 5 ft. (1.5 m) tall requires a root ball about 3 ft. (90 cm) in diameter. *American Standards for Nursery Stock*, a publication sponsored by the American Association of Nurserymen, suggests that a grown, broad-leaved, evergreen plant 5–6 ft. (1.5–1.8 m) tall with a well-branched root system requires a root ball with a minimum diameter of 20 in. (50 cm). The 3 ft. (90 cm) ball I recommend is preferable if it can be physically handled, as more roots are retained to support the plant in its difficult two to three years following transplanting.

Dig the trench 12–18 in. (30–45 cm) deep around the root ball. At this point undercut the root ball, that is, sever the roots from the underlying soil. In sandy soils that tend to fall apart easily, burlap can be pulled around the ball and wrapped tightly with rope to hold the ball together before the plant is undercut. This is seldom necessary in silt or clay loam soils. Undercutting can be done either by pulling a piece of ¼-in. (0.6-cm) steel cable under the root ball with a tractor or by using a shovel and a digging iron around the ball repeatedly until all the roots are severed. With either method the resulting root ball will probably be only 8–12 in. (20–30 cm) deep, which is sufficient.

Drill two holes near the edge of a ½-in. (1.3-cm) piece of plywood. Tilt the plant to one side, slide the piece of plywood under the root ball, and set the plant back down on the plywood. Rope or cable run through two holes previously drilled in the uphill edge of the plywood can be used to pull the plant to its new site. Pull the plywood directly over and slightly past the prepared new planting site, tilt the plant back, and slide the plywood from underneath it. Finally, place soil around the root ball. Care must be given as previously described for all transplants.

7

Care in the Landscape

If gardeners select the proper planting site, prepare the soil well, and choose suitable cultivars, rhododendrons and azaleas will be well equipped to survive. As soon as the root system has extended well into the surrounding soil, usually about three years after transplanting, very little aftercare will be needed.

Watering

By virtue of their broad leaves, rhododendrons and azaleas are constantly losing water through transpiration. The first priority in their maintenance is supplying an adequate supply of water, that is, maintaining a uniformly moist soil. In hot, dry areas where moisture loss is high, a steady, dependable source of water is required.

Old, established plants can survive long periods of drought in late summer, when they are no longer in active growth. Though leaves may wilt, no damage is indicated as long as the foliage is turgid again by morning. If foliage is still wilted in the morning, a deep, soaking is called for. Misting can lower foliage temperature and moisture loss considerably. Misting the foliage of established plants during the heat of the day can extend the period between watering. Mist nozzles controlled by a timer set to the appropriate cycle to prevent serious wilting require relatively small volumes of water.

Sustained daytime wilting over lengthy periods, even though turgor returns overnight, will stress established plants. Consequences of such stress may be the appearance of disease, twig blight, or dieback, as well as symptoms of mineral deficiency in the leaves. A water-stressed plant is more susceptible to insect and disease attack because it is not absorbing the soluble nutrients necessary for good health. Selecting more appropriate plants sometimes reduces problems induced by water stress. Gables' 'Caroline' and many of the *Rhododendron yakushimanum* species or first generation *R. yakushimanum* hybrids seem to seldom suffer dieback or twig blight under severe stress.

Newly transplanted plants require close attention to watering. They cannot be allowed to wilt for any extended period of time. When in active growth, soft, new foliage may wilt on hot afternoons, especially in full sun, but if the foliage recovers an hour or two after sundown, no serious damage will result. Misting new growth during the heat of the afternoon is very beneficial and poses no threat of creating overly wet soil. The root ball and soil around and below newly transplanted plants need to always be kept moist. The amount of water needed to achieve this condition varies with ambient and soil temperatures, evaporation, and other factors, so check the soil beneath the mulch weekly to be sure the soil is moist but not wet.

Watering newly transplanted container-grown plants differs somewhat from that suitable for field-grown plants. The soil around the roots of field-grown plants dries out more slowly, and thus plants require less frequent watering. Conversely, the coarse medium surrounding the roots of container-grown plants holds little water and will dry out quickly. Container-grown plants must therefore be watered every two to three days with just enough water to thoroughly wet the root ball. The soil around the root ball needs to be watered only when it starts to dry out—not nearly as frequently as the root ball.

The death of newly transplanted plants, and especially container-grown plants, can most often be traced to improper watering and hence drying out or over watering of the root ball. Extra attention to the water needs of newly transplanted plants is necessary for up to three years, depending on how quickly the roots extend out into the soil. The intensity of care declines each year, and the frequency and quantity of water can be lessened as the root system develops.

Reduced watering of both old and new plants in late summer and early fall is necessary so that a new growth cycle is not encouraged late in the season. Tender, new growth induced by watering late in the growing season cannot harden off before freezing weather. Vigilance is still in order in the case of new transplants, and in the event that continued heat and sunlight lead to extremely dry soil conditions, water will be needed to maintain plant health and continued root development.

Water quality needs monitoring if extensive irrigation is required. Water with a high pH will cause soil pH to move above the level suitable for best plant growth (pH 5.0–6.0). Water from sources containing root rot organisms or herbicides should not be used. The water quality of flowing streams is usually sufficiently high that no serious problems arise; yet it is best to consult local growers or other knowledgeable persons to be certain.

Mulching

Mulches, which maintain a more consistent soil temperature and moisture level, are typically associated with the native habitat of rhododendrons and azaleas. The same benefits can be derived from mulch when used in the landscape. A loose, coarse mulch extending beyond the root system is of great value in the landscape and helps prevent many problems.

By shading the soil, and thus lowering soil temperature, the mulch greatly reduces moisture loss. The soil moisture level is maintained at a more consistent level, which leads to uninterrupted root development. Because water loss is reduced, the need for irrigation is also reduced. Soil organisms producing root rot in rhododendrons and azaleas require both high soil temperatures and wet soils to become infectious. The cooling benefits provided by mulch can act as a disease-prevention measure. (Specific disease control is discussed in chapter 8.) As they decompose, organic mulches also provide plant nutrients and help maintain levels of soil organic matter. Another benefit is leaching of humic acid into the soil, resulting in soil aggregation and improved soil tilth. Proper mulching is a must throughout the life of the plant and is second only in importance to proper watering, the number one maintenance practice.

Apply new mulch each year late in the fall or early winter, after the plants have hardened off and rodents have found other winter homes. Only coarse materials such as wood chips, bark, leaves of most deciduous tree species, or pine needles should be used because they allow better oxygen exchange between the roots and the air. Maple leaves, grass clippings, or peat moss are not good mulching materials as they can pack down too tightly. Peat moss also encourages root growth into the mulch; when dry, it is very difficult to wet and sheds water away from the plant roots. Very coarse materials such as oak leaves and pine needles can be applied 3 in. (7.5 cm) deep. Finer materials, such as ground pine bark ¼ in. (0.6 cm) in diameter, are applied only 1 in. (2.5 cm) deep because oxygen does not pass through them as readily. Keep mulch a few inches away from the main stem of the plant to avoid an environment conducive to crown rot and vole damage. Because there are no feeder roots this close to the plant stem, any drying out of the soil in this area is of little consequence.

Mulches are often applied too deeply in the landscape, which leads to severe root damage and death for any number of plants including rhododendrons and azaleas. According to Dr. Francis R. Gouin, University of Maryland, not only is overmulching a waste of mulch, but it is rapidly becoming the number one cause of death to azaleas, rhododendrons, dogwood, andromeda, boxwood, mountain laurel, hollies, cherry trees, ash, linden, and spruce. Repeated applications of mulch cause suffocation of the roots of shallow-rooted species. The symptoms of overmulching are the same as others indicative of root damage: chlorosis, mineral deficiencies, poor growth, dieback, and plant death in extreme cases. Deep mulch may keep the soil frozen longer in spring, thus preventing roots from absorbing water on warm days when leaves are transpiring moisture.

Nutritional Needs

Rhododendrons growing well in the landscape, exhibiting dark green foliage, normal growth rate, and flowering well, require little if any fertilizer. The nutrients released by decaying mulch usually provide sufficient nourishment to maintain healthy, active growth. Soil properly prepared with adequate amounts of organic material encourages the growth and establishment of the symbiotic mycorrhizae in the roots of rhododendrons and azaleas. This mutually beneficial association results in a more efficient transfer of soil nutrients into plant roots so that plant growth is normalized even in soils of low fertility. The need for intensive fertilization is therefore reduced. The fertilizer needs of landscape plantings differ from the needs of plants in a nursery, where rapid growth is stimulated to produce a marketable plant as soon as possible.

If landscape plants do require fertilizer, applications should be made after a killing frost in the fall or in spring after early azaleas flower. To prevent leaching from the soil, nitrogen fertilizer should be applied in organic forms such as soybean meal or synthetic organic urea. If chemical forms are used, ammonium sulfate is the best choice. New slow-release nitrogen forms such as urea formaldehyde or sulfur-coated urea slowly release nitrogen. When a complete fertilizer, containing all of the major plant food elements, is required Osmocote® or other slow-release fertilizers are recommended.

Roots will absorb nutrients in the fall, stimulating root growth. If plants are dormant, they will not be stimulated to produce new shoot growth and lose cold hardiness or dormancy. In warm climates where there is no extended cold period, fall fertilizing should be used cautiously, if at all.

Plant nutrients are the essential elements needed for plant growth. Plant food elements are divided into three groups: (1) major nutrients (or macronutrients) are consumed in large amounts by plants; (2) secondary elements are used in moderate quantities; and (3) minor nutrients (or micronutrients) are required in very small quantities. The macronutrients nitrogen, phosphorus, and potassium are usually the elements in short supply in the soil and the ones that must be added by fertilizing. Secondary elements such as calcium, magnesium, and sulfur are used in moderate quantities by plants and may also be in short supply in some soils. The micronutrients boron, copper, chlorine, iron, manganese, molybdenum, zinc, and nickel are seldom in short supply in loam or clay soils, though shortages do appear in sandy soils. The deficiencies most often seen involve the following nutrients.

Major Elements

Nitrogen—This is one of the major plant food elements. Nitrogen promotes rapid growth and dark green leaf color because it is basic to the production of chlorophyll. Nitrogen also produces the most visible growth response in plants. A deficiency of nitrogen results in plant foliage turning uniformly light green or light yellow, and there is a general reduction in growth rate. Leaves may eventually become red, and in severe cases older leaves drop after turning yellow.

Because nitrogen is the plant food element most rapidly leached from the soil, it is the element most commonly needed. The amount of leaching varies considerably among different forms of nitrogen fertilizers, and this must be considered when determining which form to use. The nitrate form carries a negative charge, as do soil particles, and is leached most rapidly because like charges repel. Furthermore, because ericaceous plants do not prefer nitrogen in the form of nitrate, this form should not be used. Urea or ammonia forms, having a positive charge, do not leach rapidly and are the forms ericaceous plants prefer.

One form of chemical nitrogen recommended for use in the landscape is ammonium sulfate (21 percent actual nitrogen). It releases nitrogen as ammonium ions that do not leach rapidly and are preferred by ericaceous plants. Ammonium sulfate has a further advantage in that it leaves an acidic residue of sulfate ions and continued use will lower soil pH (by removing calcium as calcium sulfate). Because ammonium sulfate is a highly soluble salt, it must be used in small amounts, 0.5–0.75 lb. per 100 sq. ft. (0.2–0.3 kg per 9.3 m²) sprinkled lightly in an area around the outer edge of the plant foliage. Remove any fertilizer accidentally spilled on the leaves, as it will burn foliage. Ammonium sulfate is made available slowly over a period of approximately six weeks. Apply it in early spring and if a deficiency appears, as yellow or light green foliage, again in two months. Do not apply nitrogen after June 1 unless a shortage is evident.

Organic sources of nitrogen are the safest to use because they release nitrogen slowly, which minimizes any likelihood of plant damage. Cottonseed meal (7 percent nitrogen), soybean meal, or alfalfa meal are good but usually expensive organic fertilizers. Apply at a rate of 4 lb. per 100 sq. ft. (1.5 kg per 9.3 m²). There are also commercially prepared organic fertilizers that are specially formulated for rhododendrons and azaleas. If these are used, apply according to the manufacturer's directions.

Urea formaldehyde (38 percent nitrogen) is a synthetic organic fertilizer that releases nitrogen slowly over a period of six months in the form of urea, which in turn breaks down in the soil to ammonium ions. When applied in the fall after the first killing frost or when plants are hardened off for winter, it is a very effective fertilizer. Apply 0.75 lb. per 100 sq. ft. (0.3 kg per 9.3 m²). Urea does not change soil pH.

Mulches release nitrogen slowly as soil organisms break the material down at the soil surface, and they vary considerably in the amount of nitrogen made available in their decomposition. Materials previously recommended for mulching release very small amounts over a long period of time. The two extremes in the nitrogen content of organic mulches are green, uncomposted sawdust and composted animal manures. Fresh sawdust actively withdraws nitrogen from the soil, and nitrogen fertilizer must be applied to prevent nitrogen deficiency. For this reason, sawdust should not be used until it has been well composted. Composted animal manure will add nitrogen to the soil. Cow manure provides the least nitrogen, with horse, hog, sheep, and poultry manure providing progressively more. Composted animal manure used as a summer mulch may result in unwanted succulent growth late in the growing season. All manures must be composted first and are best dug into the soil prior to planting.

To summarize, nitrogen is the plant food element resulting in the greatest growth response. It is leached from the soil as the ammonium ions are slowly converted to nitrates by soil microorganisms. Nitrogen may be added annually as fertilizer or can be added through the natural breakdown of organic mulch.

Phosphorus—This element hastens plant maturity and the hardening-off process, the reverse of the effect of nitrogen. Phosphorus does not readily leach from the soil, and annual applications are not required. Mycorrhizae associated with the roots of ericaceous plants usually absorb sufficient phosphorus to maintain plant health even in phosphorus-deficient soils. Excess phosphorous in the soil can interfere with the health of mycorrhizal fungi.

A deficiency of phosphorus serious enough to affect plant growth in the landscape seldom occurs in loam soils or in soil tested and amended according to the soil laboratory recommendations. However, deficiency symptoms can include stunting or lack of new growth, delayed maturity, abnormally dark green leaves, reddish purple spots on the underside of leaves, older leaves turning brown and dropping, and lighter than normal flower color. If phosphorus is deficient, it can best be applied as superphosphate sprinkled lightly on the surface of the mulch at any time of year.

Potassium—This is most commonly known as its compound potash. Potassium is critical to the formation of strong cell walls and thus strong stems. Potassium is not incorporated directly into plant tissue but plays a key role in the synthesis of plant proteins, starch, cellulose, and lignin. It also participates in the opening and closing of leaf stomata and thus gas exchange between the plant and the atmosphere. Adequate potash also improves a plant's ability to fight disease. Potassium deficiency leads to deficiencies of iron, so symptoms are similar to those for iron deficiency: chlorosis of the leaves between the veins beginning at the leaf edge and tip, rolling up of leaf edges, leaf drop in severe cases, and the appearance of dieback diseases.

Potassium is not as strongly fixed in the soil as phosphorus but does not readily leach except in sandy soils. Most soils contain an adequate supply that is readily available to plants. Potassium in the form of potash can be applied at any time of year because, like phosphorus, it does not stimulate vegetative growth. Sulfate of potash (49 percent potash) is a good form to use with ericaceous plants especially if the acidity of the soil must be lowered. Murate of potash (60 percent potash) is recommended if soil pH is adequately acidic.

Fertilizers specially formulated for rhododendrons and azaleas and containing all three of the major plant food elements are available and highly recommended for use in the landscape.

Secondary Elements

Calcium and magnesium—Deficiencies of these elements mimic the symptoms of iron deficiency and appear as yellowing of the leaf between veins. Calcium deficiency also is displayed by tip burning and brown lesions over the leaf surface and reduced root growth. These symptoms are rarely encountered in loam soils of proper soil pH but may occur in sandy soils. Magnesium is an essential part of chlorophyll and necessary in its production.

Sulfur—Plant proteins contain sulfur, and it is used in the manufacture of chlorophyll. Organic matter contains 70 to 90 percent of soil sulfur. Soluble sulfur is readily leached from the soil. The breakdown of gypsum and organic matter in the soil continually releases soluble sulfur. Plant deficiencies are exhibited as plant stunting and pale color of older leaves.

Minor Elements

Minor elements required for adequate plant growth include boron, copper, chlorine, iron, manganese, molybdenum, zinc, and nickel. Although required in very small quantities, they are considered essential to plant health. Availability of minor elements is affected to a large extent by soil pH, which if not properly controlled can result in minor-element deficiencies in plants. Soil pH must be maintained between 4.5 and 6.0 to make the minor elements specifically required by rhododendrons and azaleas available in the best proportions. A low pH results in manganese toxicity in some soils, whereas a high pH leads to iron deficiency. Minor elements are generally available in adequate supply in properly adjusted soil. The minor elements are used by plants in such small quantities and are generally so toxic in excessive amounts that the average gardener cannot accurately apply them to the soil without running the risk of plant damage. Slow-release fritted trace element compounds especially formulated for rhododendrons and azaleas have been developed and, when carefully used, result in improved plant growth where deficiencies exist. Adequate organic matter in and on the soil surface as mulch is good insurance against minor element deficiencies.

Iron—The symptoms of iron deficiency first appear as a yellowing of leaves between leaf veins while the veins remain dark green. These symptoms usually appear in plants grown in soils with a pH above 6.0. Occasionally iron deficiency results from poorly drained soils. If soils contain high levels of calcium, phosphorus, and potash, this can lead to iron deficiency at pH levels below 5.5. Maintaining proper soil pH is the best remedy for iron deficiency. Iron chelates can be used in either foliar and/or soil applications to correct the deficiency quickly. Chelates should be viewed as only a temporary solution until soil pH can be corrected. If other minor element deficiencies are suspected, soil tests need to be run to specify the problem. The application of soil acidifiers is explained in chapter 2.

Root damage—Plant root damage often imitates symptoms associated with minor-element deficiencies. Too much mulch or a poorly drained soil, both of which reduce oxygen supply to the roots, most often causes root damage. Excessive fertilizer use, insect or vole attack, or mechanical injury resulting from hoeing, cultivating, or compacting the soil by walking on it also damage roots. If symptoms appear, it is advisable to first check soil aeration before applying fertilizer or other soil amendments.

In summary, to provide good nutrition for rhododendrons and azaleas, plant in a well-drained, properly prepared, high-organic soil of pH 4.5–6.0 amended with nutrient elements as recommended by a soil-testing laboratory, and apply a loose organic mulch. These steps, coupled with proper watering to keep the nutrients in solution and available to the plants, can only result in healthy, vigorous growth.

Weeds

Weeds are present in every landscape. The best weed control is to start with clean soil and never allow any weeds to mature and go to seed. A good mulch can be a very important aspect in controlling weeds. Azaleas and rhododendrons should never be tilled due to their shallow root systems, so weeds must be pulled by hand. Weed killers can be used if the weeds are far enough away from garden plants and their roots to allow safe application. Check with your local extension service or horticulture department for the best herbicide to use. The chemical glyphosate has proved very effective in my garden. It kills only what it is applied to, and the active chemical is inactivated in the soil so root absorption is not a problem. When this herbicide is used with a wick type contact applicator, weeds very close to desirable plants can be controlled.

Pruning

Rhododendrons and azaleas present their best appearance as informal plants and generally require very little pruning or shaping in the landscape. This is assuming that the plant has the genetic potential to fit the landscape and that the plant has been properly shaped in the nursery. If plants do need pruning, as a regular part of sanitation maintenance, by all means prune and do so with confidence. Any necessary pruning can be done with three simple tools: a small hand-pruner, a pair of long-handled lopping shears, and a pruning saw.

Plant parts are removed for a number of reasons including deadheading (removal of faded flower trusses), removal of diseased and dead wood, removal of wood to shape or thin the plant or to regenerate an old plant, and root and foliage pruning prior to transplanting a large plant. Pruning needs to be done only for sound reasons, so the objective to be served must be clearly established before any plant parts are removed. While nursery pruning is dealt with later, I note for the benefit of gardeners that growers try to produce a compact plant with many branches. To obtain such a plant, growers disbud and summer prune new growth to produce multiple branches resulting in compact plants.

Pruning Rhododendrons in the Landscape

If a newly purchased plant was properly pruned and shaped in the nursery and flower buds are present on most of the terminals, additional pruning is not required at the time of planting. Terminal vegetative or leaf buds can be pinched out to promote branching if 50 percent or more of the branches have leaf buds rather than flower buds.

The terminal leaf buds of plants, which seldom naturally branch well, require disbudding. If the lateral buds are nearly as large as terminal leaf buds, multiple breaks (branches) will probably develop without pinching. Figure 7.2 illustrates a branch with multiple leaf or vegetative buds of similar size.

Figure 7.1. A nicely branched and compact field-grown plant ready for transplanting with no pruning required. Photograph by H. Edward Reiley

Figure 7.2. A terminal with buds of similar size. All these buds will probably break, and the plant will develop multiple branches without the need for pinching or pruning. Photograph by H. Edward Reiley

This plant will probably branch well without pruning the terminal buds. If terminal buds are not pinched out and only single shoots emerge, these must then be pruned or pinched off to produce multiple branching. If the plant receives adequate light, most terminals will set flower buds on the final flush of growth. It is important to know where to cut on the stem if pruning elepidote (nonscaly, large leaf) rhododendrons is necessary. Unlike azaleas and lepidote rhododendrons (scaly leaf), the elepidotes do not have adventitious buds spread along the stem. Buds are present only where leaves are or were attached to the stem. Pruning cuts should be made just above a whorl of leaves or above the bud scar on the stem where leaves had been in previous years.

Deadheading—Removal of faded flower trusses on large-leaved elepidote rhododendrons is a form of pruning, which pays big dividends because it will encourage greater flower bud set. Lepidote rhododendrons and azaleas do not require deadheading because they flower well every year without it. Elepidote *Rhododendron* should be deadheaded as soon as the flowers in the truss start to fade. Simply grasp the stem of the flower truss at the base of the truss just above the terminal leaves with the thumb and forefinger and twist sideways. If dead-heading is done properly, no leaves or buds will be removed along with the truss.

Removing diseased or dead wood—The immediate removal of diseased or dead branches, whatever the cause, is a necessary task. This form of pruning is simply a good sanitary practice because it also helps control disease and insects in the landscape. Dead, infected branches must always be pruned below the infected area or area damaged by insects and promptly disposed of by burning or hauling away in the garbage. Pruning tools should be disinfected between each cut with alcohol or a 1:9 mix of bleach and water.

Shaping Azaleas

Azaleas can be pruned in early spring by simply cutting back long shoots to the point where branching is desired. Azaleas should not be pruned after July 31 to allow enough time for the plant to set flower buds for the following year. If cultivars have been selected for a particular site and the plants overgrow the space allotted to them, severe pruning is called for and must be repeated periodically. The best time for severe pruning is early spring, after the coldest winter weather has passed, or immediately after flowering.

At times azaleas send up long, straight stems that dramatically affect plant shape. Depending on how formal the planting is, where the plant is located, or the gardener's desire, this growth habit may or may not be viewed as a problem. If necessary, these shoots may simply be cut back to match the height of the rest of the plant; they will branch at this point within a few weeks. Rhododendrons and azaleas sometimes develop too many branches, which result in smaller flowers and the shading out and death of interior branches. If such a situation begins to develop, remove any weak branches with poor foliage until the desired density is restored.

Because azaleas and lepidote rhododendrons have adventitious buds, which break easily, liberally scattered along the stems, they may be cut back to any point. If the azaleas are vigorous, they will branch nicely. Elepidote rhododendrons, however, do not develop adventitious buds nor develop new shoots as readily as azaleas. It is very important that rhododendrons be vigorous and in good health before severe pruning. It may be necessary to carefully fertilize and water weaker plants for a year or more before a heavy pruning to improve vigor.

Various cultivars react more or less favorably to severe pruning. I have pruned a 6 ft. (1.8 m) plant to about 1 ft. (0.3 m) and produced good multiple branching from the crown. Some severely pruned plants, however, may require years to regenerate and on occasion die. The gardener uncertain about a plant's response can use the alternate method of pruning in stages. Remove only a few branches at a time, perhaps one-third of the branches each year, over a three-year period. In pruning to reduce height, remove the branches back far enough to allow the plant to grow for at least five years before the next pruning. Plants cannot tolerate severe pruning at close intervals.

Alternatively, plants may outgrow the width allotted to them, in which case a different type of pruning is required. In this case only the side branches should be removed. Side branches are cut back to the main trunk or to a junction with another branch on the plant. Cuts should be made about ⅛ in. (0.3 cm) from the other branch or trunk leaving a very short stub. This stub will not only heal over more quickly than a larger cut flush with the trunk, but will also minimize tissue death in the trunk.

Rejuvenating an Old or Damaged Plant

As plants age, they lose vigor and often become open and ungainly due to loss of branches over the years. Consequently, they lose much of their value in the landscape. Only major surgery, either a single massive cutback or spread over two to three years, can solve the problem. Although it is surely the more drastic approach—one that terrifies many gardeners—I urge cutting the plant back to the desired height, anywhere from 1 ft. (0.3 m) to 3–4 ft. (0.9–1.2 m) above the soil level in a single session. Such a massive reshaping can be done with more confidence if some small shoots have already appeared below the point of pruning. This is often the case if the plant foliage is thin and has allowed light to penetrate to the center. In virtually every case in which I have pruned a plant in this way, I have been rewarded with a vigorous, compact plant in a few years.

The alternate method of cutting back one-third of the branches each year over a three-year period is preferable if no new shoots are visible at the base of the plant. The successive thinning often encourages new shoots to form as light intensity within the plant increases. In any case, heavy pruning of old plants usually yields much more compact plants within three to four years. If a plant should succumb following such severe pruning, all is not lost because a planting site is opened for one of the newer hybrids, which most gardeners are eager to try.

Large rhododendrons and azaleas can sometimes be badly damaged by strong winds or ice storms felling trees or branches. Damaged *Rhododendron* must be

Figure 7.3. Regrowth after severe pruning of a large rhododendron. Photograph by H. Edward Reiley

cut back to the nearest undamaged branch or trunk, even to soil level. Healthy plants will recover quickly from such damage and the resulting surgery.

Root Pruning

Root pruning is warranted if larger plants need to be moved. It can best be done a year before the move and will induce vigorous root branching. It is done by cutting down into the soil to the length of a spade blade in an entire circle around the plant. The circle needs to be about 6 in. (15 cm) smaller than the diameter of a root ball that can easily be handled in transplanting. If the circle is small enough it will be saturated with old and new roots that will hold the root ball together when moving the plant the following year.

Care of plants in the landscape consists of maintaining proper soil moisture, annual mulching, maintaining proper soil pH and nutritional levels, insect and disease control (see chapter 8), and annual deadheading and other forms of pruning as necessary or desired. Proper plant selection and placement greatly reduces the need for most landscape maintenance, allowing time for gardeners to enjoy the fruits of their labor.

8

Plant Disorders

Plants suffer from three types of disorders. The two most often discussed are infestations and diseases caused by living (or biotic) organisms. The third, physiological (or abiotic) disorders, result from environmental stress factors such as heat, sun damage, drought, poor soil drainage, inappropriate soil pH, root damage, mechanical injury from machines or animals, and allelopathic effects of other plants.

Before appropriate treatment can be administered, the problem must be diagnosed. Symptoms may be similar for biotic or abiotic causes; for example, abiotic conditions such as sun scald or leaf desiccation may exhibit symptoms very similar to damage from biotic fungus diseases. A search for the actual presence of the causal agent is necessary. In the case of biotic problems, a living organism will be present, for instance, an insect or fungal spores. In many cases, more than one agent may be responsible. The primary agent may be abiotic, such as a drought placing plants under stress, resulting in more susceptibility to secondary biotic agents.

No amount of cultural savvy will overcome problems associated with poor plant selection. Check the Good Doer information in chapter 3 and appendix A or check with your local chapter of the ARS for best performers in your area. However, most plant disorders can be markedly reduced by proper site selection, use of adapted plants, and use of cultural practices conducive to growth of the plant (for instance, maintaining soil that is moist but not wet). The best disease control is prevention. A well-nourished, vigorously growing plant is much more resistant to both insects and diseases.

Fortunately, rhododendrons and azaleas have few serious insect and disease problems, not enough to limit their use in the landscape. A few, however, are serious enough to require attention. The first and most effective control is selection of insect- and disease-resistant plants. Another approach is through the use of biocontrol agents, consisting largely of microorganisms in the soil and on leaf and stem surfaces as well as beneficial insects. The last resort is use of chemical controls. Chemicals generally work faster but may result in other problems in the environment.

Considerable variability exists within rhododendrons and azalea cultivars; some resistant plants are listed in this chapter and appendix A. Some deciduous azalea cultivars, for example, have damaged leaves or lose most of their leaves by late summer from powdery mildew, whereas others are not damaged. This difference is a result of genetic resistance in the latter plants. Disease resistance can be increased in most plants through cultural practices as well. Plants that are overfertilized and grow rapidly are more prone to disease and insect attack. Soft, tender tissue is easier for fungus spores to penetrate. When properly managed, plant resistance to insects and diseases can be increased and complete control of some diseases is possible.

Much has been learned about biological control, and many biocontrol agents, such as bacterial and fungi that live in the soil, are as effective as chemical controls without the dangers. Soils high in organic matter are colonized by biocontrol agents, which assist plants in warding off insects and diseases and in absorbing moisture and food elements. Bacteria such as *Bacillus*, *Pseudomonas*, and *Panloea* species are effective against phytophora; fungi such as *Penicillium* act as parasites against disease organisms; and actinomycetes produce chemicals that stop the growth of other organisms, a phenomenon called *antagonism*. These biocontrol agents also produce antibiotics that protect roots from attack by disease organisms. Overuse of chemical fertilizers can destroy some soil microorganisms and thus eliminate their many benefits.

Diseases caused by bacterial and viral agents occasionally attack rhododendrons, yet they are usually of little consequence in the landscape. Fungi cause most of the serious rhododendron diseases. The first line of defense against fungi is maintaining a high level of garden sanitation. A disease organism can produce an infection or become pathogenic only if it is present in the immediate environment, can make contact with a susceptible host, and environmental conditions favor its growth. Control requires altering only one of these three conditions.

Garden sanitation is part of the first line of defense and needs to be an ongoing practice. Diseased plants, including roots and dying branches, must be removed and destroyed immediately to destroy pathogenic organisms before they cause further infections. Weeds may act as alternate hosts and must also be controlled, as must other hiding places for insects such a weevils, slugs, and other pests. Clearing brush to provide air movement will encourage drying of foliage surfaces, which discourage the growth of fungi.

Biocontrol by Soil Microbial Communities

Organic amendments such as green manure, stable manure, and composts can provide the food base for biocontrol agents in the soil and thus facilitate control of diseases and harmful insects. Soil biocontrol agents stimulated by this food source contribute to the suppressive activity on pathogens in four ways: (1) competition for food and space, (2) antagonistic action, (3) parasitism and/or predation, and (4) systemic induced resistance. Availability of nutrients within the soil organic matter plays an important role in regulation of these activities. Composts high in soluble salts, such as manures, must be incorporated into the soil at least three months before planting to allow for leaching of salts. High nitrogen concentrations encourage *Phytophthora*, the agents that cause root rot. Conversely, compost high in carbon and low in nitrogen result in reduced plant growth.

The decomposition level of organic matter also critically affects the composition of bacterial taxa as well as the populations and activities of biocontrol agents. Competition, antibiosis, parasitism, and systemic induced resistance are all affected. Composts can serve as an ideal food base for biocontrol agents and offer an opportunity to introduce and establish specific biocontrol agents into soils, which in turn leads to sustained biological control based on the activities of microbial communities. At various stages of decomposition, organic amendments have different effects on biocontrol agents and therefore biological control:

> Immature composts serve as a food base for both biocontrol agents and plant pathogens, and this often results in increased incidence of disease.

> Following the heat phase of composting, organic matter is fully colonized by soil microorganisms, plant pathogens can no longer compete, and disease is suppressed. An organic mulch maintained by adding some new material each year results in some organic matter being in the proper stage of decomposition to support biocontrol agents in numbers large enough to offer continually effective disease control.

> When organic matter becomes highly decomposed or humidified, availability of soil organic matter to biocontrol agents becomes limited and biocontrol begins to fail.

Most of the beneficial effects from composts are due to the activity of microorganisms found in the soil surrounding roots (the rhizosphere). Composts have a major effect on the type of microorganisms found in the rhizosphere. Some microorganisms produce plant growth hormones, whereas others produce natural chelators that keep elements such as iron in solution even at a pH above 7.0. Still others produce antibiotics that are effective against pathogens. Some parasitize disease-causing agents, and others actively search out and consume pathogens. Some biocontrol agents colonize roots in compost mixes and activate biochemical pathways in plants that lead to resistance to root and foliar diseases.

Plants produced in some compost-amended mixes have higher concentrations of an enzyme related to host defense mechanisms. These plants have higher levels of biochemical activity related to disease control and are better prepared to defend themselves against diseases. Controlled inoculation of composts with biocontrol organisms that induce systemic resistance increases systemic disease control and suppresses foliar diseases as well. These commercial compost inoculants should be applied just after the heat phase of composting. A commercial preparation to inoculate the soil with biocontrol agents after fumigation has been used in Belgium since the late 1980s. It consists of several isolates of *Trichoderma harzianum*, a well-know biocontrol agent, and has been very successful in improving yields and plant health.

Composts containing more lignins, such as in pine bark, are lower in microbial biomass and must be incorporated at higher (50 percent) concentrations. Composted manures, on the other hand, are effective when incorporated at 5–10 percent (v/v). Adding nitrogen in the form of urea to bark or woody materials at the rate of 1 lb. per cubic yard (0.5 kg per m^3) of organic matter speeds up the composting process. Compost so treated must be turned more often. The pile must be kept moist (50–60 percent moisture by weight). Dry composts become colonized exclusively by molds, which repel water and can inhibit plant growth; some molds can be minor fungal pathogens. After about six weeks, it is safe to use the woody material as mulch. If the wood or bark compost no longer gives off an ammonia-like odor and smells like soil, it is ready for use.

Because of their resistance to decomposition, composted pine bark and peat do not release significant quantities of essential plant nutrients. Therefore, essential micronutrients must be incorporated into container mixes. Composted manures supply trace elements. For most effective disease control in the field, compost should be applied at least three months before planting. This allows for salts to leach out and also for beneficial microorganisms to more fully colonize the substrate.

Pythium and *Phytophthora* root rots are among the most easily controlled diseases. Natural composts control these root rots, whether applied as mulches or incorporated into the soil. These root rots can be controlled most effectively in composted, bark-amended container media. While very low in nutrients, sphagnum peat harvested from just under the surface of bogs contains a considerable amount of cellulose and is light in color. When included in potting mixes to raise the pH above 5.3, light sphagnum peat becomes consistently suppressive to *Pythium* and *Phytophthora* root rots while it is colonized by mesophilic microorganisms. Dark-colored sphagnum peat is low in cellulose and not as effective in controlling *Pythium* because concentrations of carbohydrates are lower. The suppressive effect of light peat may last three to six months after potting. Woodland plants requiring mycorrhizae for growth, such as yews and rhododendrons, perform better in soil beds treated with composted bark than in beds treated with methyl bromide, which kills these beneficial fungi.

Biocontrol agents require soil sources of organic matter for sustained activity against *Pythium* and *Phytophthora* root rots. Research by Dr. H. A. J. Hoitink of Ohio State University shows that both the quality and quantity of organic matter are critical to survival and efficacy of biocontrol agents. Rhizosphere deposition products and root exudates do not provide an adequate supply of slow-release biologically available energy to introduced biocontrol agents. A commercially available product containing several isolates of *Trichoderma harzianum* is used to help control pathogenic microorganisms. Results have been promising.

Note of caution—Throughout the rest of this chapter, I mention various chemical controls for diseases and pests. All chemicals mentioned are listed by the appropriate authorities as materials providing control. I recommend none of them specifically to the reader because I have no way of knowing how well equipped the gardener may be to handle pesticides. If proper safety precautions are taken, however, there should be no problem. None of the chemicals mentioned are highly toxic. The reader is strongly advised to always read the label and follow directions exactly.

Fungus Diseases

Fungus diseases are best controlled by sanitation or preventive sprays. The best controls are cultural practices and sanitation directed toward altering any one of the three requirements necessary for fungi to become pathogenic. It is quite difficult, if not impossible, to eliminate or cure a fungus disease once a plant is infected. It is therefore important to carefully monitor and maintain a sanitation program. Remove any known disease organism to prevent or eliminate further contact with plants. In the event sanitation methods fail, chemical control must be initiated as soon as possible after the first sign of infection.

Only the most serious fungal diseases capable of doing extensive damage to rhododendrons and azaleas warrant discussion here. Diseases that produce a few leaf spots but result in little or no lasting damage to the plant are not described.

Root rot (*Phytophthora cinnamomi*)—Commonly called rhododendron wilt because the entire plant wilts, phytophthora root rot can be one of the most serious diseases of rhododendrons and azaleas. It is not a serious problem in cooler climates where the soil temperature is below 50°F (10°C). Most often it is a disease of small plants recently transplanted, or it can be common to nursery situations. The same disease organism also infects *Cornus*, *Pieris*, *Taxus*, *Camellia*, various laurels, *Juniperus*, *Vaccinium*, and *Pinus*, to list only a few. It can infect large landscape-size plants in poorly drained soils, although roots can often regenerate in the well-drained upper soil levels. *Phytophthora cinnamomi* is the most common form of phytophthora affecting rhododendrons. It is most active at soil temperatures of 68–72°F (20–22°C). A low-temperature species exists in California, and it is inhibited at soil temperature above 72°F (22°C).

Phytophthora cinnamomi causes wilting by plugging the conductive tissue in the roots, thus preventing the movement of moisture into the upper parts of the plant. Root rot symptoms can be noticed in the early morning when affected plant foliage remains wilted (Plate 86). In contrast, plants that have wilted from heat or low soil moisture recover by morning in all but the most extreme drought conditions. The foliage of diseased plant will also take on a dull green appearance.

There is no known cure for root rot. Infected plants should be carefully removed, with great care taken to remove all infected roots and leaves. The plant and all its parts need to be burned or disposed of in the garbage. Do not replant any susceptible species and/or hybrid plant in the same area for several years unless composted bark is added and drainage is increased by raising planting beds. Low temperatures do not kill *Phytophthora* oospores.

Systemic fungicides have been developed for prevention of root rot. Metalaxyl used as a soil drench reduces the spread of *Phytophthora* into or among plants, but it does not generally kill the fungus in infected plants. Metalaxyl should be used only according to the manufacturer's instructions for rhododendrons. Continued use may result in chemical-resistant forms of the disease. For use with small landscape plants, approximately 10 sq. ft. (0.9 m²) of soil around each plant needs to be drenched. For large rhododendrons and other large shrubs, 20–30 sq. ft. (1.8–2.7 m²) of soil needs to be drenched. Metalaxyl can be applied with a hose applicator or directly through an irrigation system. Metalaxyl, like all chemical pesticides, must be used with extreme care, especially because it is a systemic and can be absorbed through the skin. A bacterium that kills the *Phytophthora* fungus is also under study.

The best preventive measure, however, is to plant only in well-drained soils because *Phytophthora* fungus requires freestanding water in the soil to become infectious. Poor soil drainage, too much mulch, or any other practice that maintains or encourages high soil moisture and low soil oxygen levels provides favorable conditions for root rot. *Phytophthora* is not necessarily a fatal problem in northerly regions where soils remain cool. The best means of prevention are the following:

Purchase disease-free plants from a reputable nursery. Avoid selecting plants lacking normal dark green foliage or those that remain wilted when the soil around the roots is moist.

Plant only in a well-drained site. In heavy soils dig in a porous material such as pine bark to improve drainage and plant in raised beds.

Plant at the same depth or 1 in. (2.5 cm) above the soil level in which the plant was grown in the nursery, in well-drained soils.

Place container plants on a bed of gravel with good drainage, not on plastic.

Select plants bred for disease resistance.

In summary, control of root rot depends upon using the following control measures, in this order of importance. First, plant in well-drained sites or in raised beds. Second, select disease resistant plants. Third, use compost for biocontrol (*Phytophthora* is one of the easiest diseases to control with compost). Finally, use chemical control as a last resort. Chemicals are more preventive and not always effective as a control.

The plants most resistant are 'Caroline', 'Professor Hugo de Vries', 'Red Head', and *R. minus* Carolinianum Group. 'English Roseum' is moderately resistant. Resistant species include *R. davidsonianum*, *R. hyperythrum* (very resistant), and *R. pseudochrysanthum*. *Rhododendron yedoense* var. *poukhanense* is a resistant azalea.

***Armillaria* root rot (*Armillaria mellea*)**—Plants suffering from this disease exhibit no specific symptoms, making diagnosis difficult. Rather, the plants just appear weak and less thrifty and the leaves wilt, turn yellow, and drop. Plant death may be sudden or may take years. It is most common to areas in England and the Pacific Northwest. According to University of California researcher Robert D. Raable, the fungus can be identified by the presence of a layer of white fungus tissue between the bark and the wood of the main stem at or below the soil line or beneath the bark of large roots. Control is best achieved by removal and disposal of all infected plant parts. Other less important root rot diseases such as crown rot (*Phytophthora cryptogeal*) are best controlled by providing good soil aeration and maintaining cool soil temperatures with mulches.

Twig blight (*Botryosphaeria dothidea*)—*Botryosphaeria* dieback is the most important disease of rhododendrons in the landscape. It is seldom seen in container plants in nurseries but may occur on field-grown plants. Infection can take place through wounds or cuts, bark cracks, fresh leaf scars, and other areas not well protected by bark. Heat and drought stress can increase incidence of the disease. Plants in full sun are more often infected. Plants are also more susceptible for the first two years after transplanting.

Twig blight infects larger branches of landscape plants. The first symptoms of the disease are leaf wilting on only one or several branches. The entire plant does not wilt, as is the case with root rots. Leaves also take on a dull green appearance. Stems turn brown and, if the bark is scraped off, a reddish brown discoloration is found underneath.

Pruning out all infected branches best controls twig blight. Branches must be removed below any diseased tissue and the pruning tool sterilized between each cut with rubbing alcohol or a 1:9 solution of bleach and water. Burn all infected branches after pruning. Deadheading seems to help control this disease.

Dieback—This is primarily a disease of nurseries, especially among container-grown plants, where it can be devastating. *Phytophthora nicotina* var. *parasitica*, *P. hevacea*, *P. cactorum*, *P. cirticola*, and *P. cinnamomi* (see root rot) have all been isolated from plants exhibiting symptoms (Plate 87). The disease first appears on young foliage as water-soaked areas on the leaves. This is followed by foliage drying up and dropping off. The disease then moves down the stem and can kill a young liner-size plant in a few days. A film of water and warm weather are needed for infection to occur, which makes prolonged periods of rain in the summer ideal for its spread. Table 8.1 contrasts symptoms for diagnosing *Rhododendron* dieback caused by *Botryosphaeria* and *Phytophthora*.

Table 8.1. Diagnosing *Rhododendron* branch damage caused by *Botryosphaeria* and *Phytophthora*

Botryosphaeria	*Phytophthora*
Mostly in landscape	Mostly in container nurseries
Entire branch or section of plant wilts quickly (one to two days) and dies	Attacks individual shoots
Attacks older wood	Attacks succulent leaves and stems
Entire leaf rolls downward parallel to midrib	Leaf does not roll
Entire leaf turns grayish green then brown	Dark brown to black discoloration progressing in V-shaped pattern from midrib to leaf margins
Leaves remain attached to dead stem	Mature leaves drop from stem quickly
Brown discoloration in wood on one side of stem	Brown discoloration in wood
Moves fast in old stems	Moves fast in succulent stems
Branches die at any time	Shoots usually die during growth flush

From *Plant Pathology Information* by R. K. Jones and D. M. Benson, Note 232, Department of Pathology, North Carolina State University. Revised April 1984.

The incidence of dieback may be reduced or controlled by spraying the foliage with a broad-spectrum fungicide after flowering and again in two weeks. Additional sprays may be necessary if a second flush of new growth occurs, and again in late summer if dry soil conditions cause plant stress. Some of the new systemic fungicides such as Fosethyl® and Metalaxyl® look very promising in control of both twig blight and dieback. Check the label for more information.

Phomopsis **dieback**—This disease is most often associated with azaleas. Symptoms start just after flowering and are seen as a slight chlorosis of all leaves on a twig or branch, finally turning brown and wilting (Plate 90). Usually only a single branch is affected. Leaves remain attached to the stem until late summer or fall, generally falling off before the first frost. *Phomopsis* dieback occurs more frequently on older plants in the landscape. Wounds, including natural wounds such as flower bud and leaf scars as well as pruning wounds, are necessary for infection.

Control is possible through use of systemic fungicides. Pruning out and destroying dead branches can reduce spread of the disease. Cuts should be made below dead portions of branches, and pruners should be disinfected between cuts. According to J. T. Walker, researcher at the University of Georgia, the least susceptible azalea cultivars are 'Delaware Valley White', 'Hershey's Red', 'Pink Gumpo', and 'Snow'.

Bud and twig blights (*Briosia azaleae*)—This disease of young tissue has been reported on many rhododendrons. *Briosia azaleae* is common in the northeastern Unites States but has been observed as far south as North Carolina. Symptoms are dead twigs and small dried-up buds with silvery gray scales. Control is usually possible by eliminating diseased twigs in late autumn or at latest early spring.

Web blight (*Rhizoctonia* spp.)—Web blight is an important disease of evergreen azaleas in nurseries during warm summer months and in liners in heated greenhouses with relatively high humidity. Symptoms are leaf lesions or spots, which may kill entire leaves. Webs form and cause abscised leaves to remain attached to the plant shoots. In severe cases liners may be killed. Control is generally possible through wider plant spacing for better air movement to reduce humidity in the plant canopy and through sanitation.

Blight (*Phythopthora syringae*)—This dieback disease is a cold- or cool-weather fungus disease observed in the Pacific Northwest. It causes a leaf spot similar in appearance to leaf scorch. For long-term control, prune out and destroy infected branches. Metalaxyl used as a drench or foliar spray in mid to late summer gives good chemical control.

Powdery mildew (*Microsphaera penicillata, M. azalea,* and *M. vaccinii*)—Powdery mildew is a serious disease of deciduous azaleas and has more recently been found on rhododendrons. In addition to those *Microsphaera* species listed, *Sphaerotheca pannosa, Erysiphe cruciferarum,* and *Microsphaera izvensis* also have been reported to cause powdery mildew on rhododendrons. The fungus *Microsphaera azalea* is found throughout the Pacific Northwest on garden azalea and rhododendron species and hybrids. *Microsphaera vaccinii* has been found on native *R. occidentale* in the wild.

Symptoms on deciduous azaleas are described well by the disease's name: leaves become covered with a white powdery coating, losing some of their photosynthetic effectiveness and presenting a poor appearance in the landscape. Many deciduous azalea cultivars, especially if grown in climates to which they are not adapted, suffer damage starting in late July or August. This may finally result in early defoliation and a gradual weakening of the plant. Poor air circulation contributes to the problem. Chemical sprays based on wettable sulfur regularly applied from July through August are very effective but should not be used when air temperatures exceed 85°F (29°C).

Where rhododendrons are involved, symptoms are often quite different and variable. Infection occurs in spring and summer, and the disease develops late in the summer. Colonies have been found throughout the winter on leaf undersides. Small black, spherical sexual spores are produced in fall in great numbers on azaleas and less frequently on rhododendrons. The disease is worse under conditions of high humidity and wet mild winters. The most commonly found symptoms are diffuse pale yellow spots on the upper leaf surface 0.25 to 1 in. (0.6–2.5 cm) in diameter. The leaf undersurface will display purple to brown circular, diffuse feathery areas. Other symptoms may appear as large purple-brown spots on the upper leaf surface, purple ring spots, or green spots. The remainder of the leaf turns yellow. Brown sunken spots are not symptoms of this disease.

Symptoms are influenced more by cultivar than by environment. Some cultivars such as 'Unique' show no symptoms on the leaf top but may have spots or powdery growth on the leaf underside. 'Virginia Richards' and the species *R. campylocarpum* and *R. cinnabarinum* suffer defoliation. Most azaleas and some rhododendrons such as 'Purple Splendor' and 'Vulcan's Flame' display the descriptive white powdery growth on both sides of the leaf.

The most effective control is to select resistant cultivars. Resistant deciduous azaleas include 'Delight', 'Girard's Crimson Tide', 'Girard's Red Pom Pom', 'Girard's Salmon', 'Girard's Yellow Pom Pom', 'Lollipop', 'Northern Hi-Lights', 'Washington State Centennial', and many native hybrids. Resistant rhododendron species include *R. strigillosum* and *R. yakushimanum*.

Spacing plants wider and encouraging better air circulation and planting in more open areas with sunshine also helps control this disease. Spray to protect new growth in the spring at bud break and apply again in two weeks later. Systemic fungicides such as Bayleton® and Strike® (triodimefon), which is labeled for this use, are most effective.

For gardeners not desiring to use these chemicals, some potassium bicarbonate–based products are available, such as Armicarb 100®, First Step®, and Remedy®, which is registered for home use. Safer Garden Fungicide® (14 percent sulfur) is also available but must not be used when temperatures exceed 85°F (29°C). A biological control, A 10®, is not as effective and requires more exact use. According to Hank Becker (*Agricultural Research Magazine*, June 1994), neem oil blocks out spores of powdery mildew, thus preventing infection. Neem oil works as a curative as well as preventive spray. The botanical insecticides Margosan-0® and Bio-Neem® contain azadirachtin but unlike neem oil have no fungicidal activity on powdery mildew. There are also naturally occurring fungal parasites and competitors that compete for growing area, and the fungus *Ampelomyces quisquahs* actually reduces the ability of powdery mildew fungus to reproduce, resulting in its death.

Petal blight (*Ovulinia azaleae*)—*Ovulinia* petal blight is a common disease of azaleas, rhododendrons, and mountain laurel. This disease only attacks flower petal tissue, and the damage does not affect plant vigor or the growth of vegetative parts. When environmental conditions are favorable, *Ovulinia* petal blight can destroy the flowers in a few days (Plate 88). Petal blight ascospores can germinate within a temperature range of 40–80°F (4–27°C); however, primary infection normally occurs at 50–71°F (10–22°C). Petal blight is worse in warm, wet, or humid weather. Early- and late-flowering plants are not affected as much because weather conditions are less favorable for the disease. There are no known resistant plants. (*Botrytis cinerea* will also cause blight of flowers, but the disease progresses more slowly and the flowers are not slimy.)

Petal blight first appears as small, circular, water-soaked spots on the petals. Spots appear white on colored flowers and tan or brown on white flowers. Spots enlarge rapidly and cause the entire flower to collapse. Flowers feel slimy to the touch. Blighted flowers dry and remain attached into summer. At this time, small ⅛ to ¼ in. (30 to 60 mm), dark, hard, lens-shaped sclerotia form in the blighted petals. These spores overwinter in debris under and near the plants. The following spring, small mushroom-like funnel structures sprout from the sclerotia. Microscopic spores shoot from the mushroom-like structures and are blown by wind to infect new flowers.

Control is possible through use of systemic fungicides. (Adding new mulch in an effort to disturb or remove fruiting bodies of the fungus has not been very effective in controlling this disease.) If neighbors have rhododendron and do not spray, you will need to spray every year. Fungicides must be applied as soon as color shows in the flower buds, and during a wet spring spraying may need to be repeated. As later-flowering cultivars show bud color, additional applications must be made. Effective systemic fungicides include Bayleton or Strike (triadimefon) and a new substitute for Benlate® and Tersan®, Cleary's 3336® (dimethyl 4,4'-0-phenylenebis[3-throallophanate]). Also available at most garden centers are Spectricide® and Immunox®. For gardeners concerned about using chemicals, neem oil would probably work. Because it may not be labeled for this disease, however, I cannot legally recommend it. Other biofungicides such as the bicarbonates may also be worth a try if labeled for such use. Check with your local extension horticulturist regarding the best sprays to use in your area.

Leaf gall (*Exobasidium vaccinii*)—Leaf gall affects some rhododendrons and some cultivars of evergreen azaleas, but not all. As the galls reach the reproductive stage, a white coating appears (Plate 89). This disease is not limited to leaves, however, and may appear as thickened swellings on branches, flower parts, or seedpods. Because the fungus can overwinter within the infected plant, control is best achieved by removing and destroying all galls when they first appear and before the galls are coated white. This is not a serious disease, and handpicking is an effective control.

Leaf rust (*Pycnostipanus azalea*)—The common name describes this disease, which appears as a reddish dust on leaves. Leaf rust is seldom a serious problem for plant health, yet it does make for an unattractive landscape. Good air circulation and exposure to sun to quickly dry the foliage following rains or irrigation help control rusts. Some cultivars are resistant, and selection of resistant plants is a good preventive measure. The fungicide triadimefon applied on a weekly basis gives control if the problem becomes acute. Hemlock (*Tsuga canadense*) is an alternate host necessary for rust to complete its life cycle. Therefore, if possible, do not plant rhododendrons or azaleas near hemlocks.

Bud blast (*Pycnostipanus azalea*)—Bud blast is usually first noticed when plants reach their bloom season and flower buds turn brown and fail to open. The actual infection is made through the axils of bud scales during the previous July and August. In the following winter, such infected buds are covered with spores that resemble black bristles. These bristles become the source of infection for next year's buds. Control is by removing dead buds or spraying with a broad-spectrum fungicide applied immediately after flowering.

Insects

Insect pests or rhododendrons and azaleas represent a diverse range of the insect world, including beetles, weevils, true bugs, moths and caterpillars, nematodes, aphids, mites, borers, and scale insects. Only a few of these are of significant importance.

Lace bug (*Stephanotis* spp.)—Two different species of lace bug cause damage to azaleas and rhododendrons. *Stephanitis pyrioides* attacks azaleas, whereas *Stephanitis rhododendri* is a pest of rhododendrons and mountain laurel (*Kalmia latifolia*). For both species, damage is worse in sunny locations and where plant diversity is low. Damage is first noticed as speckled whitening of leaf tops as the insect sucks nutrients and chlorophyll from the leaf (Plate 92). An examination of the leaf underside will reveal sticky, dark, varnish-like excrement and the insects themselves.

Lace bugs overwinter as eggs, usually attached along the midvein of leaves. Nymphs hatch in spring, around mid-May in the mid-Atlantic region. There are from two to four generations a year depending on length of growing season. Adults are about $\frac{1}{8}$ in. (3 mm) long with a dark body and lacy wings (Plate 91). If adults are found in fall, it is safe to assume eggs are present for the following spring's first generation. Adults are long lived and persist until severe freezing occurs. In a study by Neal and Douglas (1988), females were found to live from 48 to 253 days, longer during cooler weather.

Recent research points to the importance of site selection in the control of lace bugs on azaleas. The results can probably also be applied to the rhododendron lace bug. Paula M. Shrewsbury and Michael J. Raupp (2000) observed that the best habitat predictors for lace bug abundance was structural complexity (plant diversity) and light exposure. The best predictor was an overstory of trees; the more overstory trees the fewer lace bugs. A diverse mixture of plant species also had a positive effect in decreasing lace bug populations, probably because more predators exist under these conditions. Robert B. Trumble et al. (1995) found that lace bugs are more abundant and cause more damage in open, sunny locations than in shade. Again, this is not because they prefer these conditions, rather because there are fewer predators under sunny, open conditions. A higher level of arthropod predators, such as spiders, in shaded habitat reduce lace bug survival. Another natural predator of lace bug, the Japanese plant bug (*Stethoconus japonicus*), has been found in the eastern United States by USDA researchers, who hope it will become an effective control agent in the future. We can thus conclude that a more complex landscape has fewer pest outbreaks than simple ones and that the most important single factor limiting lace bug abundance is the presence of an overstory tree layer.

The most effective chemical controls I have used are acephate (Orthene®) and imidacloprid sold as Merit® or Marathon®. Imidacloprid applied as a foliar spray, a soil drench, or granules watered into the soil gives good control the entire season. Both chemicals are systemic insecticides, so direct contact with the insect is not necessary as long as the leaves are wet with spray or granules watered into the soil. Nontoxic materials include insecticidal soap, the new highly refined spray oils for year-round use, and neem oil.

Research by Deborah Smith Fale of Rutgers Cooperative Extension Service revealed that azaleas differ widely in their susceptibility or resistance to attack by the lace bug. The Rutgers publication *Resistant Cultivars* lists the following: 'Cavalier', 'Dawn', 'Dream', 'Elsie Lee', 'Eureka', 'Macrantha', 'Marilee', 'Pink Fancy', 'Pink Star', 'Red Wing', and 'Salmon Pink'. Moderately resistant cultivars include 'Coral Bells', 'Jan Cochran', 'Karen's', 'Kathy', 'Mary Lyrin', 'Nancy', and 'Rachel'. Some very susceptible cultivars are 'Blaauw's Pink', 'Gigi', 'Girard's Rose', 'Gloria', 'Hershey's Pink', 'Hershey's Red', 'H. H. Hume', 'Mother's Day', 'Mrs. L. C. Fisher', and 'Sweetheart Surprise'. The most resistant deciduous azaleas include *Rhododendron canescens* and *R. prunifolium*, whereas *R. alabamense* and *R. calendulaceum* are the most susceptible.

Whiteflies—Two whiteflies are pests on a few azaleas (*Pealius azaleae*) and rhododendrons (*Dialeurodes chittendeni*). The small, white insects are easily seen by shaking a branch to make them fly. Damage is indicated by a gradual yellowing of leaves, the result of plant juices being sucked from the underside of the leaf. Whiteflies also exude honeydew, which results in the growth of a black mold on the leaf surface. The mold is harmful only in that it decreases the amount of light to the leaves, thus reducing photosynthesis. Whitefly damage is greatest in dry weather and may be especially intense in greenhouses.

The new pyrethrin pesticides are relatively safe to use and result in good control if applied in the evening, as sunlight will destroy pyrethrin's effectiveness. Whiteflies are attracted to the color yellow and also can be trapped on yellow sticky strips. Spraying the underside of leaves with horticultural oil or soap is effective.

Midge (*Clinodiptosis rhododendri*)—The midge is a minor pest on rhododendron. The signs that midges are present are stunted and distorted new growth and downward-turned leaf tips; leaf edges may be spotted red or brown. The small larvae feed beneath the leaf edges and are hidden under the edges as the leaves curl. Damage to tender growth from cold temperatures appears much like midge damage.

Removing and destroying infected growth by hand can control midges. Two years of surveillance and removal are required for complete control. Acephate applied just as the new growth is expanding is also very effective. A fall soil application of the systemic insecticide imidacloprid (Merit or Marathon) washed into the soil provides a full year of protection. Sun breaks down this chemical, so it must be incorporated into the soil, covered by mulch, or washed into the soil with at least 1 in. (2.5 cm) of water. Another tactic that has proven successful is handpicking midges and burning new growth that shows signs of midge damage. This techniques may need to be continued for several years to completely eliminate the problem.

Thrips (*Heliothrips haemorrhoidalis*)—Greenhouse thrip damage appears very similar to damage from the lace bug, with white blotches forming on leaf tops. The underside of the leaf becomes silvery with small black spots of excrement (frass). Damage is usually worse in hot weather. Thrips lay eggs in early spring, with a life cycle of about a month when egg laying is repeated. This brief life cycle results in a rapid population buildup of thrips in a short time. During the height of thrip activity, acephate gives control in two applications, one week apart.

Mites (*Oligonychus ilicis*)—Southern red mites are dry-weather pests and almost invisible to the naked eye. They are not insects and belong to the same family as spiders, which also have eight legs. Damage is first noticed as plant foliage becomes bronze, brown, or pale green. A magnifier will be needed to locate mites, which is most easily done by shaking the leaves over a white piece of paper. Any mites present will fall onto the paper, which can then be examined with the magnifier.

Simply blasting mites from a plant with the full force of a garden hose is usually effective. The new, highly refined spray oils are also very effective; because they are nontoxic, I recommend their use over toxic chemicals. Apply oil sprays at temperatures below 80°F (27°C).

Leaf miners (*Caloptilia azaleella*)—Leaf miners may occasionally be a problem, especially on azaleas. Miners tunnel through the leaves and contribute to premature leaf drop. The chemical used to control lace bugs (acephate and imidacloprid) will also control leaf miners. Repeat the application of acephate in ten days.

Azalea bark scale (*Eriococus azaleae*)—Several scale insects attack azaleas and rhododendrons, but only occasionally do they become a serious problem. Scale insects first appear as white egg sacs in twig forks in May and June (in Maryland). Adults appear as small, white, cottony masses on stems, twigs, and leaves. If these masses are crushed, moist red liquid appears if the adult is alive. Scale populations appear as small raised bumps on the twig or leaf. They feed on leaves and stems, and the first symptom is yellow or red spotting on the leaf or on the bark of twigs. Azalea bark scale produces one generation per year in the northern part of its range and two in the south.

Scale insects usually produce a waxy protective coating over their body, which makes them difficult to kill with contact sprays. Very effective chemical control can be achieved with the new, highly refined spray oil. The oil penetrates the insects' protective coating and kills them by suffocation. These oils work best if used when the temperature is below 80°F (27°C) to prevent injury to the plant.

Rhododendron borer (*Synanthedon rhododendri*)—The rhododendron borer attacks rhododendron, kalmia, and deciduous azaleas. This borer is indigenous to North America and is found primarily in the eastern United States. There is one generation per year. Adult moths emerge from mid-June until about mid-July and deposit eggs in cracks and crevices of bark, usually near or in bark crotches. The larvae chew holes to the inner bark and sapwood, where they overwinter (Plate 93). Larvae feed from March until May, when they pupate just under the bark. Rhododendron borer moths are active when the following plants are in flower: American holly (*Ilex opaca*) in full bloom, *Rhododendron catawbiense* in full bloom, white fringe tree (*Chionanthus virginicus*) in full bloom, Kousa dogwood (*Cornus kousa*), and smoke bush (*Cotinus* spp.).

The rhododendron borer larva, a white grub with a brown head, is 0.5 in. (1.3 cm) long at maturity. The adult is a clearwing moth ⅜ in. (0.9 cm) long, which resembles a wasp more than a moth (Plate 94). It is steel blue or coppery black with three narrow gold dorsal bands on abdominal segment 2, 4, and 5. There is a tuft of black scales on the end of the abdomen.

Plant symptoms may appear similar to those for branch blight; leaves first turn dull green then brown. Small branches and young plants may break off or be completely killed. Injured branches have holes, scars, and sawdust on the bark and on the ground below holes. Adults emerge in June, leaving an empty pupal case protruding from the bark. Activity of moths can be monitored with pheromone traps, which trap adult males. Traps should be placed two weeks before the first moths are expected.

Control is targeted at the newly hatched larvae before they bore into the bark. The date to begin control should be based on pheromone trap monitoring and should begin ten to fourteen days after the first male is trapped, sometime between mid-June and late July. Egg laying starts within three to four days of emergence and hatching in ten to fourteen days. Spray should be directed toward leaves, woody stems, branches, and the trunk using chlorpyrifos to coincide with larvae hatch. According to Neal and Douglas (1984), two applications of chlorpyrifos gives complete control. Lindane provides limited control, and acephate gives poor control. One application of chlorpyrifos gives better control than two applications of lindane. Thorough coverage of woody plant parts is important. Control is not effective once larvae enter the plant stem. Spraying should be applied to runoff on all bark and leaf surfaces. Spraying the entire plant contacts adults, eggs, and newly hatched larvae.

Stem borer (*Oberea myops*)—The adult stem borer is a small long-horned beetle that emerges in mid to late spring. The beetle is approximately 0.5 in. (1.3 cm) long with a yellowish head and thorax with three black spots. Wing covers are grayish to yellow. The damage is done by the larvae and is very similar to that of the rhododendron borer. However, stem borers enter the plant only through young twigs of the current season's growth.

To destroy the borer and prevent further damage, cut twigs off as soon as wilting is noticed. If not controlled the first year, the larvae tunnel downward the second year and may travel to the base of the plant, where a pupal chamber is hollowed out. Plants become so weakened at this point that they are easily broken off. Prune out infected twigs and spray when adults are present. Control by spraying is difficult, however, because the adult is active for only about a week.

Weevils—Several weevils attack both azaleas and rhododendrons. These include the black vine weevil (*Otiorhynchus sulcatus*), the strawberry root weevil (*Otiorhynchus ovatus*), the two-banded Japanese weevil (*Callirhopalus bifarciatus*), and the woods weevil (*Nemocestes incomptus*). The black vine weevil is native to Europe and most often encountered in the northern half of the United States and southern Canada, as is the woods weevil. The strawberry root weevil and several other *Otiorhynchus* inhabit the Pacific Northwest and regions with similar climates in Europe and Australia. The damage done and the control measures needed are similar for all weevils.

Weevils that attack rhododendron and azaleas are flightless and are all female. Each female lays about 200 eggs in rough bark or under litter on the soil surface. Adults are up to 0.5 in. (1.3 cm) long and are nocturnal, hiding under cover on the soil surface during daylight. Black vine weevil larvae have no legs, which is very distinctive in identification.

Damage is first noticed as a pattern of overlapping notches on the leaf edges of rhododendrons and is the result of the nocturnal feeding habit of the weevil (Plates 95, 96). Other methods of determining adult emergence are placing a white cloth under plants and shaking the plant vigorously. Weevils will fall off onto the cloth and play dead. This must be done at dusk or after dark, when weevils are active. Another detection method is placing burlap around the plant stem or placing boards on the soil surface under the plant, where adults hide during daylight hours.

Although leaf damage is often the first noticeable symptom, it is not nearly as significant as the root damage the larva activity inflicts during the fall and early spring. Plants may be severely weakened or killed due to the loss of feeding roots and the girdling of larger roots. As a consequence, plants wilt or exhibit symptoms associated with a severe drought or root rot. By the time these symptoms are noticed, it is too late for effective control.

Weevils can be controlled at the adult stage when they emerge in early summer. Chemical spray application needs to start three weeks after the first adults emerge, as egg laying begins about a month after emergence. Delayed spraying allows time for most of the adults to emerge and be killed by one or two spray applications. If a daytime hiding place at the base of plants is provided, such as a piece of bark or a board, adults will collect there. Monitoring the situation daily will indicate the first adult emergence date. First visible leaf damage is another indicator of adults being present. Dan Herms of the Ohio Agricultural Research and Development Center determined that black vine weevil adults tend to emerge a month earlier than previously thought in northern Ohio, closely corresponding with the blooming of black locust (*Robinia pseudoacacia*) trees. Previously, nurserymen in the area were spraying after the weevil had laid eggs and were experiencing poor control. Thus, you may need to watch for earlier than anticipated emergence in your area and look for weevil adults when the black locust flowers.

Acephate applied in the evening to the entire plant is an effective chemical spray, yet it remains lethal for only two or three days. A second application in two weeks and a third in four weeks is required. Imidacloprid (Merit and Marathon) is effective both sprayed on foliage and as a soil drench. Soil applications of any insecticide, however, kills natural predators such as predatory ground beetles (carabids), which roam through ground litter in search of insects. Thus, chemical sprays sometimes become counterproductive.

Dr. Richard S. Cowles of the Connecticut Experimental Station suggests biological control through the use of pathogenic nematodes (*Steinernema carpocapsae* and *Heterorhabditis bacteriophora*) plus native predators such as beetles as the best approach. Nematodes are most effective when applied in May and late August, when many hosts are available in the soil. The nematodes do overwinter in cold climates throughout the continental United States. Nematodes must be watered into the soil and not be exposed to sun or dry conditions. They survive from year to year as long as some hosts are available; however, they offer more effective control if added each year to increase their population in the soil.

Control of weevils in container plants is best accomplished by mixing the pesticide Talstar® (bifenthrin) into the potting media. Talstar is degraded by sunlight in one day, but when incorporated into potting media and protected from sunlight, its half-life is between three and four years.

Rhododendron 'P.J.M.' shows 100 percent resistance to adult feeding of weevils, and shows no root damage as well. Others showing resistance include 'Jock', 'Sapphire', *R. dauricum*, *R. minus*, and *R. scintillans*.

Rhododendron bud moth—The bud moth occurs naturally on native azaleas in California and native rhododendrons in Oregon. The small moths lay eggs in July on leaves where the emerging larvae will feed. Bud moths overwinter in the larval stage and in spring eat their way into flower buds and small shoots. Infected flower buds only partially open or fail to develop entirely. The bud moth is still a minor pest in landscapes, so handpicking of infested flower trusses and twigs offers the best control.

Other root pests—Other types of grubs may occasionally damage azalea or rhododendron roots if plantings are made in areas that were recently in sod. Japanese beetle, June beetle, and others spend their pupal life in the soil eating roots. These pests are most numerous in sodded areas because they prefer to feed on grass roots. Milky spore disease, a biocontrol agent targeted towards Japanese beetle grubs, is very effective but will not control other types of grubs such as June beetle. See your local extension horticulturist for specific control. If sod areas are prepared a year ahead of planting a landscape, the grub problem will be greatly reduced. Imidacloprid will control most soil grubs. Soils may also contain damaging nematodes or other garden pests with potential for damage. Check with your local extension service to see if there are such problems in your area and, if so, how to resolve them.

Caterpillars—Moth and butterfly larvae can be especially destructive to young tender growth and are serious pests of deciduous azaleas. Several types of loopers and other caterpillars are responsible for this damage. *Bacillus thuringiensis*, a naturally occurring bacteria, is an effective means of control when caterpillars are small. Later instar stages must be treated with neem oil or nearly any insecticide labeled for caterpillars.

Table 8.2. *Rhododendron* pest management calendar

PESTS	IMPORTANCE[1]	APPLICATIONS[2]	FEB[3]	MAR	APR	MAY	JUN	JUL	AUG	SEPT	OCT
Azalea stem borer	N	1		—S—			——————P————				
Black vine weevil	I	3	—G—			————S————					
Japanese weevil	N	1 or 2					—S—				
Lace bugs	N	1 or 2					——————S——				
Rhododendron borer	N	1		—S—			————P				
Rhododendron tip midge	N	2			—S—		—S—				

[1]Degree of importance of pest: I, important pest, high probability of occurrence; N, treat as needed.
[2]Number of applications needed for most effective control. It is usually best to wait ten to fourteen days between applications in cool weather and seven to ten days between applications in warm weather.
[3]G, apply granular pesticide; P, prune out infested twigs or branches; S, spray application of pesticides. See your local cooperative extension agent or garden center for recommended pesticides.
Adapted from Department of Entomology, North Carolina State University Insect Note 58; prepared by James R. Baker, extension entomologist.

Mammalian pests—In urban and suburban neighborhoods, dogs can cause the yellowing and eventual death of branches on small plants by urinating on them. Rabbits are fond of azaleas, preferring some cultivars to others; they cut shoots off at or near ground level. Deer can severely damage azaleas and occasionally rhododendrons. Rodents such as voles cause root and stem damage.

Live trapping and relocation can at least temporarily solve any rabbit problem. Voles can be poisoned with appropriate bait set in their tunnels. Deer might be controlled with repellents, unless the deer population is under such pressure that they are eating anything to survive. Deer detest the smell of eggs, which is the effective ingredient in some repellents. I have achieved adequate control on rhododendrons by spraying with a sticker spreader in December using six beaten eggs added to 1 gallon (3.7 L) of water. My deer population has a large area to feed over, and this method may not work where deer are confined to a smaller area. When deer are present in large numbers, the only effective controls are an 8- to 10-ft. (2.4- to 3-m) fence or a well-trained dog.

Physiological Problems

The sudden onset of cold weather early in the fall before plants are fully hardened off can cause bark splitting, which severely damages any split stems (Plate 98). To remedy this, push the bark back tightly against the stem before it has dried out and wrap the split portions with grafting tape to hold the bark tightly against the stem. The splits may also be coated with grafting wax to prevent drying out or damage from the entry of rainwater. Mulching in early fall contributes to bark split because it holds heat in the soil and stems get colder. Later in the season after stems have hardened off this is not a problem.

Any foliage or buds not fully hardened off in fall may also be seriously damaged by the first hard freeze. Symptoms are similar to the foliage drying in summer from excess heat or drought. In both situations, death of foliage and buds results. Low temperatures in spring, as new growth starts, cause symptoms of leaf twisting and rolling similar to that caused by midge.

Winter sun striking only the south side of stems results in widely fluctuating stem temperatures. Severe stem damage may result from heating by sunlight during the day followed by sudden chilling after sundown. This causes the stem bark to first expand and then contract faster than the underlying stem, resulting in a condition known as stem canker. Damage appears as dead areas on the southwest side of the stems as the bark loosens from the stem and is shed. Shading the plant, wrapping the trunk with tree tape, or painting trunks white with diluted latex paint all give protection from stem canker.

Sunscald is often mistaken as a disease because at times secondary fungus infections occur in damaged tissue. It appears as if the fungus caused the problem when the origin is actually sunscald. Primary damage occurs when the sun overheats plant foliage. Symptoms are off-color leaves turning yellow with browning developing on the edges and tips as damage progresses. Badly damaged leaves drop from the plant. Sunscald is caused by dehydration of the leaves as a result of an increase in temperature. Moisture is lost through transpiration faster than the roots can replenish it. This occurs both in summer and winter as the sun heats plant foliage and is more detrimental to new transplants prior to root establishment (Plate 100). Shading the foliage to reduce temperature usually remedies the situation. Note that some cultivars are more susceptible to sunscald than others.

Allelopathic Effects on Plants

Another little-known problem is allelopathy. Some plants secret chemicals into the soil from their roots or leaves; these chemicals have adverse and often deadly effects on other plants growing within their root zone or leaf-drop area. This is a natural defense mechanism plants use to reduce competition.

Black walnut (*Juglans nigra*) is a major problem in this regard, as are English walnut (*Juglans regia*) and hickories and pecans (*Carya* spp.). These plants all produce hydrojuglone. When exposed to the air and soil, hydrojuglone is oxidized into the highly toxic allelochemical juglone. Symptoms of damage from juglone include leaf wilting and yellowing and possible death of a plant. Rhododendrons, azaleas, and mountain laurel (*Kalmia latifolia*) are all damaged by juglone. Some other trees with allelopathic properties include American elm (*Ulmus americana*), American sycamore (*Platanus occidentalis*), black locust (*Robinia pseudoacacia*), cherry (*Prunus* spp.), cottonwood (*Populus fremontii*), red oak (*Quercus rubra*), sassafras (*Sassafras albidum*), and tree of heaven (*Ailanthus altissima*).

9

Propagation

The propagation and hybridizing of rhododendrons and azaleas are two of the more rewarding activities a gardener can undertake. Most gardeners are familiar with propagation by seed, a sexual process, but many fewer are aware of the almost magical process of asexual propagation. To follow the progress of a stem cutting developing roots, a root cutting developing a new top, parts of two or more individual plants growing together in a graft, or entire plantlets developing in a test tube from a single cell is a wonder to behold. Of all the world's multicellular organisms, only plants possess the unique ability to regenerate the entire viable organism from a single cell or plant part. This unique ability results from the potential of every new plant cell, whether from root tip, stem tip, bud, or cambium, to produce multitudes of undifferentiated cells that in turn develop into leaves, stems, or roots, regardless of origin. Undifferentiated tissue is triggered to develop into the full array of plant parts by hormones and environmental factors.

Propagating does require a commitment of time and energy and a small outlay of capital for the equipment necessary to root cuttings, heal grafts, and so on. In addition, the propagator must have access to plants from which cuttings, scion wood, and other parts can be used. Much of this material can be acquired through the generosity of fellow gardeners, most of whom willingly share propagation material.

Rhododendron and azalea species may be propagated from seed with some variation in offspring. Such sexual propagation cannot be used for cultivars, however, because they do not breed true to form. All cultivars must be propagated by one of the asexual processes.

Prior to the ready availability of rooting hormones, rhododendron species and hybrids were difficult to propagate from cuttings, although both could be grafted. Some deciduous azaleas are as easily rooted, yet they require special handling to promote shoot development. Tissue culture, or micropropagation, the most recently devised asexual method of propagation, is becoming a major technique for the rapid reproduction of all rhododendrons and azaleas. It is especially useful for those that are difficult to root from cuttings, such as some deciduous azaleas. This procedure requires a sterile laboratory, however, and is not recommended for the amateur.

Despite the widespread and growing use of micropropagation, the most common propagation method in North America remains stem cuttings. Grafting remains the propagation mainstay in Europe. Few plants are now propagated by layering because it is a slow process that yields only a limited number of plants. Some deciduous azaleas, which are difficult to propagate by stem cuttings, continue to be propagated by root cuttings or by tissue culture.

Cutting Basics

The availability of clear polyethylene plastic, rooting hormones, rooting media, and fluorescent lights and the knowledge needed to coordinate these elements into a propagation program make it possible for any gardener to successfully root a high percentage of cuttings. By virtue of being an asexual method, propagation by cuttings results in no genetic change in the resulting plants; all are identical to the parent plant as they are clones of the parent. The use of cuttings is one of the most satisfactory methods of propagating many woody plants, including *Rhododendron*.

Some relatively simple criteria must be met to root stem cuttings successfully:

Cutting wood must be of proper maturity—before the new season's growth has turned woody yet after the leaves are fully mature. Wood taken from juvenile plants roots in higher percentages. Wood taken near the roots of older plants also roots better, whereas wood from old branches roots more slowly.

Cuttings must be taken from vigorous, insect- and disease-free plants.

The rooting medium must remain moist yet well aerated.

The container must drain well.

The medium and container must be free of pathogenic organisms.

Cuttings must be treated with a proper rooting hormone.

The atmosphere around the cuttings must contain 100 percent relative humidity.

Ample light, but not direct sunlight, must be provided. Red light stimulates rooting.

Ambient temperatures of 60–75°F (16–24°C) must be maintained for a satisfactory rooting percentage. Providing bottom heat hastens rooting.

Facilities

Stem cuttings can be rooted using one of two facilities: a closed container or a greenhouse with a mist or fog system (Figure 9.1). The closed container is best suited for the gardener wishing to propagate a few plants because it requires neither a significant investment nor skilled management, yet the results can equal those of the more complex systems. The container used can be of any size or shape as long as it is sterile, is at least 4 in. (10 cm) deep to allow space for root development, and has adequate drainage. The container covering must be able to maintain 100 percent relative humidity and allow maximum light. The gardener wishing to root only a few cuttings can make a satisfactory container out of a Styrofoam soup bowl, a milk jug, or a sterilized flowerpot.

Figure 9.1. A homemade rooting facility. Cuttings are placed in a cut-off milk jug, labeled, and ready to be covered with polyethylene plastic for rooting. Photograph by H. Edward Reiley

Figure 9.2. Quonset hut propagation unit. The flats are placed under fluorescent lights. The moisture collecting on the inside surface of the plastic indicates 100 percent relative humidity. Photograph by H. Edward Reiley

Flats may be converted into small Quonset huts (Figure 9.2). Bend three pieces of no. 9 wire (each about 30 in., 75 cm long) into a hemisphere. Insert the ends into predrilled holes in the flats or in the medium and wire them together. After the cuttings are set in and watered, the flats are covered with clear polyethylene plastic supported on the wires. Tie string around the bottom to maintain proper moisture levels.

If a greenhouse is available, a bench can be covered with plastic in the same way as suggested above for flats. A Nearing frame (Figure 9.3) is another highly effective rooting structure, requiring very little management. Figure 9.4 provides construction details for a Nearing frame.

Mist systems are commonly used in greenhouses to root cuttings. A covering is not required as long as 100 percent relative humidity is maintained. Cuttings are set directly in the greenhouse bench with a periodic mist sprayed over the benches. Cycles are regulated with electric timers, electronic leaves, evaporative pans, or photo cells. Fogging systems similar to mist systems have recently been developed to maintain a constant 100 percent relative humidity in the propagation area. The difference between the two systems is that fogging produces smaller water droplets that remain suspended in the air longer. Foggers can easily maintain proper moisture conditions over the entire greenhouse.

Figure 9.3. An inside view of one side of a Nearing frame filled with cuttings. Photograph by H. Edward Reiley

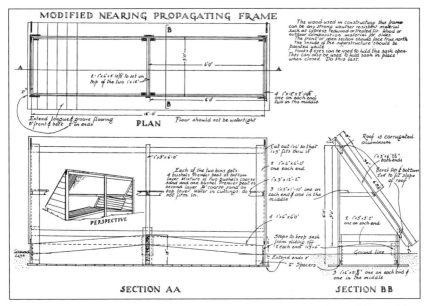

Figure 9.4. Building plans for a Nearing frame. From Leach, *Rhododendrons of the World* (1961, 323). Printed with permission.

It is important that cuttings are not water stressed. Under such conditions stomata close and the exchange of gases slows or stops. Carbon dioxide, which is essential to photosynthesis and the formation of carbohydrates, is excluded when stomata are closed. Carbohydrates, in turn, provide the energy for root development.

Media

There is little consensus as to the absolute best rooting medium. Any formulation that is sterile, holds moisture, and is well aerated will produce satisfactory results. However, rooting medium under mist or fogging systems must drain better than those used in a closed container because the medium is constantly being wetted. As a result, horticultural perlite is often used as the sole rooting medium under mist propagation systems.

A very effective, widely used container medium consists of 50 percent coarse sphagnum peat moss and 50 percent horticultural perlite or Styrofoam beads by volume. (Use light-colored sphagnum peat moss, which is less decomposed then darker moss.) After thoroughly mixing the medium, wet it completely. If dry sphagnum moss is used, it will require considerable water. Test for saturation by breaking a piece of the sphagnum moss; if thoroughly wet, the color will be a uniform brown throughout. After wetting, squeeze the propagating mix by hand to force out excess water.

Fill the container level with the top, then firm but do not pack the medium to about 1 in. (2.5 cm) below the top. If using a Nearing frame, fill the rooting bin to within 6 in. (15 cm) of the top to allow space below the sash for cuttings. The top of the medium must be level to assure uniform watering of the cuttings.

Taking Cuttings

Stem cuttings are usually collected from late June to mid-August before new stem growth has become woody. Select cuttings from new growth found at the terminal branch ends. Wood of medium diameter and vigor typical of the plant will root better than the thin, weak, wood or large, overly vigorous wood. Parent plants need to be clearly identified and in good health. To prevent confusion and mislabeling at a later date, cuttings taken from different plants must be placed in separate bags or containers and labeled.

Traditionally, gardeners have been advised to collect cuttings in the early morning when stems are turgid. During periods of drought, parent plants may need to be thoroughly watered the evening before cuttings are taken to insure turgidity. Some gardeners, however, have experienced excellent rooting results using wilted cuttings from, for example, broken branches. As long as the cutting wood regains turgid status when placed in water, the cuttings root well—and some propagators claim perhaps better than cutting that never wilted. This has not been proven in a scientific experiment, but may be worthy of trial and comparison.

Place each cutting in a moistened bag or container maintained at 100 percent relative humidity. To avoid overheating, do not expose cuttings to direct sunlight. Cuttings are best placed in the rooting medium as soon as possible after collection. However, if cuttings need to be held for a few days, they can be stored in a closed container in the refrigerator for up to a week. There will be little or no loss of viability.

Disease Control

A medium of sphagnum peat and perlite is quite effective in preventing root rot diseases. Spraying the cuttings and the entire surface of the medium with a broad-spectrum fungicide, however, also will prevent mold or algae from growing on the surface. Fungicide sprays are also used to protect the tops of tender softwood cuttings of deciduous azaleas from rot. (Follow all label instructions when using fungicides.) Soaking rhododendron cuttings in a 9:1 solution of water and bleach for five minutes will prevent foliar disease during the rooting process. Rinse after the five-minute soak.

Light

Higher rooting percentages result if cuttings are placed in good light but not direct sunlight. Keeping the covering on all rooting containers clean will maximize light to cuttings and result in faster rooting. One can use fluorescent lights that are 4 ft. (1.2 m) long, each containing two 40-watt tubes, placed about 12 in. (30 cm) above the cuttings. These are set to be on for sixteen hours continuously each day and provide excellent light for indoor rooting of cuttings. Small containers can be placed in north-facing windows or on the north side of a building. A Nearing frame should be placed in full sun with the front, or open side, oriented exactly true north. True north can be established on a clear night by aligning one side of the frame with the North Star.

If cuttings are rooted in the greenhouse in a closed container, shade must be provided if the interior heats to above 80°F (27°C). If they are rooted under mist or fog in a greenhouse, no shade is necessary unless the entire greenhouse heats up to 80°F (27°C), in which case shade compound or cloth should be used.

Rooting temperature is not critical, as this process normally occurs over a wide temperature range. Rooting can, however, be sped up in cool weather by placing heat tapes or cables—and in larger operations hot water tubes—under the rooting medium. Set to maintain a temperature range of 70–75°F (21–24°C).

Watering

Cuttings may be watered when first placed in the container to settle the medium around the roots. Watering may wash the rooting hormone off cuttings, especially if powder formulations are used. When in an atmosphere of 100 percent relative humidity, cuttings may not require additional watering until they have rooted. Small containers usually require no additional water until roots develop, as long as the medium remains moist and the plastic covering continues to display water droplets. (The condensation on the plastic is an indication that 100 percent humidity is being maintained.) Check the medium about every four weeks. Moisture can be lost if condensation is not being totally recycled within the container. When using a Nearing frame, add water once a week to wash oxygen down through the rooting medium, as air exchange through the bottom of the frame is low. Cuttings under mist or fog need no water applied after that initially used to settle the medium.

Hardening Off

This is a necessary step to enable cuttings to adapt to the harsher, yet normal, growing conditions of the landscape. As soon as cuttings have developed a root ball of more than 2 in. (5 cm) in diameter, they are ready to begin the hardening-off process.

In situations using mist propagation, hardening off is accomplished by gradually reducing the mist cycle until an average watering sequence is reached. Hardening off for cuttings in other situations involves opening the cover on closed containers a bit wider each day. After one week the plants can be fully exposed to the outside environment.

During hardening off the cuttings must be watered and fertilized. For strong growth, fertilize every third watering with a half strength solution of neutral rhododendron fertilizer or the equivalent. Cuttings rooted under mist will require more fertilizer because the nutrients constantly leach from the leaves, and plants may even require mineral fertilization prior to rooting. If the foliage of plants under mist progressively loses its dark green color, fertilizer at half normal rates should be applied to maintain the health of the cuttings.

Aftercare

After the cuttings have rooted and been hardened off (Figure 9.5), they can be transplanted to flats, beds, or pots for further development (Figure 9.6). The transplant medium should be a combination of bark, sphagnum peat moss, and perlite or the same medium the cuttings were rooted in (50 percent sphagnum peat and 50 percent perlite).

In a greenhouse, cuttings are transplanted into flats or benches at a spacing of about 3 in. (7.5 cm) on center to develop through the winter months. If interior temperatures exceed 40°F (4°C), the cuttings will start to grow and will require adequate light, increased spacing, fertilizer, and water. Rooted cuttings not being grown in the greenhouse must be overwintered in shade and protected from the wind. In cold climates, place them in a shaded, closed cold frame, under Microfoam®, a plastic-covered cold house, or in a pit to protect roots against cold and to prevent drying out. In areas where the temperature drops below 20°F (–7°C), cuttings in flats and pots should never be overwintered on top of the ground fully exposed to the elements.

Figure 9.5. A well-rooted cutting being removed for transplanting. Photograph by H. Edward Reiley

Figure 9.6. Flats of transplanted cuttings. Photograph by H. Edward Reiley

While these general principles are common to rooting all stem cuttings, there are some important differences in methodology in rooting stem cuttings of evergreen and deciduous azaleas or rhododendrons. Therefore, I discuss the propagation specifics for each group separately.

Evergreen Azaleas

These are the easiest of the *Rhododendrons* to root from cuttings, both in terms of the time required and the success rate. The range in maturity of evergreen azalea cuttings used for rooting is wide. Wood taken when too soft, however, may rot or not root at all, and older, harder wood develops roots very slowly, if at all. Cutting wood is best taken from current season's growth that has partially hardened off. Wood needs to be firm enough at the base to break when bent, yet be less firm in the upper part of its length.

The exact date that cuttings are taken is more significant to management concerns than to rooting percentages. Cuttings taken in June will be well rooted by late summer and can be transplanted. If spaced widely enough in the rooting frame (3 in., 7.5 cm apart) cuttings may be overwintered in the same container. This spacing will be needed for continued development of the root system. Cuttings taken later than June may not be well rooted by the time cold weather arrives and will need additional protection. Such cuttings also may not be developed enough to survive in growing beds the following spring. These later cuttings may require overwintering in a heated greenhouse to promote sufficient development for spring planting.

Taking Cuttings

Take cuttings 3 in. (7.5 cm) long from the terminal end of the current season's growth. Immediately place these in a moist plastic bag with any excess water removed. Close the bag to prevent the cutting from drying out. If several different cuttings are made, keep each type separate and carefully labeled. Larger, better-branched plants develop more quickly from cuttings with several side shoots. The wood at the base of such cuttings should be the current season's growth.

To prepare cuttings for the rooting medium, strip the leaves from the lower half of the cutting and pinch off the tip of each cutting to prevent flowering and to stimulate branching (Figure 9.7).

Dip the cuttings in a rooting hormone containing approximately 0.1 percent active rooting hormone or according to the directions for softwood cuttings.

Figure 9.7. Evergreen azalea cuttings prepared for insertion into the rooting medium. Photograph by H. Edward Reiley

If a liquid rooting material is used, immerse cuttings 1 in. (2.5 cm) deep for five seconds. If a talc dip is used, immerse to 1 in. (2.5 cm) and then tap the cutting to remove excess material. Do not immerse cuttings in the hormone container, but rather transfer the rooting hormone to another container, as dipping the cutting will contaminate the material. Excess rooting material should be disposed of as indicated on the label.

Place the dipped cuttings in the rooting medium about 2 in. (5 cm) apart and 1.5 in. (3.8 cm) deep. Carefully label each group as they are inserted. Mist the cuttings during this process to prevent stress until they are placed under cover. As soon as the flat or other container is completely filled with cuttings, water it well to settle the rooting medium. Do not pack the medium tightly around the cuttings.

At this point, many growers spray the cuttings and surface of the rooting medium with a fungicide as a preventative measure against root rot.

Cover small containers with polyethylene plastic or glass to provide a watertight seal. If using the Quonset hut flat, pull the previously cut plastic over the wire hoops and tuck it under the bottom or secure with string. If placed on a greenhouse bench without a mist system, cover with large sheets of polyethylene plastic, using wire or other material to hold the plastic up off the cuttings. Shade must be provided on top of this plastic cover if the sun heats up the green house bench during the summer months. If a Nearing frame is used, simply close the north-facing sash.

If the propagating containers or facilities are properly sealed and able to maintain 100 percent relative humidity, evergreen azalea cuttings should root in six to eight weeks. If the inside surface of the plastic or glass covering is consistently covered with small droplets of condensed water throughout the rooting period, the proper humidity level can be assumed. If rooted in a greenhouse, the misting cycle must be of sufficient length and frequency to keep the foliage of the cuttings moist at all times.

After six weeks use a narrow tool to lift a cutting from the medium and check for roots. When cuttings have developed a 2-in. (5-cm) root ball, start hardening off in preparation for transplanting or overwintering the small plants.

Deciduous Azaleas

Numerous propagation methods are used for deciduous azaleas. A few species of deciduous azaleas are difficult to propagate and some gardeners propagate only from seed. Although some deciduous azaleas are reluctant to root from stem cuttings, most can be propagated in this way if given proper attention. In this section I describe stem cuttings, division, and root cuttings. Mound layering is another method used for deciduous azaleas, and both seed propagation and mound layering are discussed later in this chapter.

A few significant differences set the procedure for rooting stem cuttings of deciduous azaleas apart from those used with evergreen azaleas. Cuttings from the evergreen azaleas are taken over a wide period of time and hard cutting wood will root and grow easily. By contrast, the deciduous azalea must be propagated from softwood taken early in the growing season. Great care must be taken to keep these cuttings in water from the time of pruning to placement in the rooting container. Deciduous azalea cuttings are taken as softwood cuttings because they will root more easily and because early rooting will allow more time during the same growing season for the cuttings to develop new vegetative growth.

Sometimes rooted cuttings of deciduous azaleas, which do not grow vegetatively during the season in which they are rooted, also seem reluctant to initiate shoot growth at the proper time the following year, even when well rooted. I have found that if left intact in the rooting medium, many reluctant cuttings send out shoots about a month later than cuttings that did grow vegetatively the previous year.

Taking Cuttings

Take cuttings and immediately place the cut ends in 1–2 in. (2.5–5 cm) of water in a collecting container. Use a separate container, such as a plastic bag, for each different cultivar to reduce the chances for improper labeling. Containers and media used to root the cuttings are identical to those used for evergreen azalea cuttings.

Rooting hormone should not be used because it seems to delay vegetative growth later in the summer and is not necessary for rooting to occur. However, the native azalea *R. calendulaceum* roots better when dipped in 0.8 percent rooting hormone.

Dip the cut ends in a broad-spectrum fungicide to control fungal diseases.

Because the cuttings are soft and easily damaged, prepare holes 1.5 in. (3.8 cm) deep into the rooting medium, spaced 3 in. (7.5 cm) apart, and place a cutting in each hole. The spacing is wider than recommended for evergreen azaleas, both to accommodate the larger leaves of deciduous azaleas and to encourage new vegetative growth. If the tips of the cuttings were not pinched prior to collecting, they should be pinched when placing them in the rooting medium. Water the cuttings to settle the medium around them and then spray thoroughly with a fungicide. Close the rooting container in the same way as for evergreen azaleas, and place it in strong light but not direct sunlight.

Deciduous azalea cuttings must be observed carefully for the first few days to check for unusual wilting. Mist the foliage of any wilted cuttings in closed containers for the first few days.

After about six weeks, lift and check one of the cuttings for formation of the root ball. If well rooted, apply a one-quarter strength soluble fertilizer, especially formulated for azaleas, to the foliage and medium. Fertilize again with one-half strength fertilizer if no new growth has appeared by early August. This second application usually produces new vegetative growth by autumn and thus assures that the cuttings will grow. Extending day length from sixteen to eighteen hours of light immediately after the cuttings have rooted will also help promote growth.

Deciduous azaleas are best overwintered in the rooting container. If overwintering outdoors, cuttings need to be stored under Microfoam, in a cold frame, or a Nearing frame to protect from wind, winter sun, and freezing and thawing if the climate so dictates. Growing-on is carried out in the same way as recommended for evergreen azaleas.

Propagation by Division

This method is especially appropriate for the stoloniferous species of deciduous azaleas. The crown of the plant can be divided at any point where shoots with roots attached can be separated. Shoots arising from roots at a distance from the parent plant also can be dug as separate plants. Division is best done in the fall at the time the leaves start to fall. The separated parts are treated as individual plants and planted in nursery beds for closer attention until a more extensive root system develops. Recent research has indicated that the severe pruning of transplanted plants, often recommended on the theory of balancing top growth with the size of the root system, actually reduces growth and survival in many cases. As long as the top remains turgid, it should not be pruned.

Propagation by Root Cuttings

Deciduous azaleas are also often propagated by root cuttings. Use sections of root from pencil to finger size in diameter, about 4 in. (10 cm) long, and containing some fibrous roots. These cuttings are taken by gently digging around the parent plant or by lifting the parent to expose roots from which the cuttings are taken. Root cuttings should be taken in late fall or early spring and immediately placed in the soil or a propagating bed. To prevent the entrance of root rot organisms, treat the cut ends with a wettable sulfur powder before planting. A mixture of 50 percent peat and 50 percent perlite makes a quite satisfactory medium for root cuttings. Place the cuttings horizontally, cover with only 1 in. (2.5 cm) of soil, and mulch to prevent frost heaving. Alternatively, they may be planted in flats and placed in a greenhouse or under lights to grow. In about six to eight weeks, shoots emerge from the large end and roots develop at the smaller end. Root cuttings grow new roots on the shoots that sprout from the cuttings. These shoots can be removed and rooted separately as softwood cuttings.

Rhododendrons

In North America, rhododendrons are generally propagated from stem cuttings, whereas most European growers use grafts, as they believe this method produces more uniform, compact plants. Another advantage claimed by European growers is that a widely adaptable rootstock is better suited to sustain grafted plants in a wider range of soils. Some rhododendron species are propagated from seed, and all can be propagated by layering.

Stem Cuttings

Rhododendron cuttings are taken when the current season's growth is semihard. In the case of the large-leaved forms, this is usually July, although cuttings may be taken again in September. Cutting wood of the small-leaved rhododendrons, especially the early-flowering types, is usually sufficiently mature to be taken in June through July and again in September. Cutting wood needs to be mature enough to break when bent sharply but not completely hardened off. 'P.J.M.' and some other *R. dauricum* hybrids root and grow on better, however, if cuttings are made after the leaves take on their winter color, which indicates the complete hardening off of the wood. Such cuttings must be rooted in a heated building or greenhouse.

Cuttings are made from current season's growth. Medium-size stems are best and are usually found on branches with two or more terminal shoots. Cuttings taken from branches lower on the plant, closer to the root system, appear to root better, and cuttings from juvenile plants root much better. Large, thick, single shoots often take longer to root and take up more space in the propagating frame even when leaves are trimmed. Cuttings with flower buds root readily. If such stems are used, remove the flower buds so that energy won't be used for flower production. It is best not to cut more than 30 percent of the current season's wood from any parent plant. Only one or two cuttings should be taken from branches bearing two to four terminals.

Taking Cuttings

Remove cuttings from the plant at the point where the current season's flush of growth started so no stubs remain on the parent plant. The cuttings need to be long enough to insure that they extend into the medium to stand up and hold the leaves above the medium. Use a sharp knife in preparing cuttings so that the tissue is cut, not torn. Cuttings must be carefully labeled and kept separate in containers with 100 percent relative humidity, as explained for azaleas.

Shorten the cutting to a length of about 2.5 in. (6.3 cm) and remove all lower leaves. The top rosette of four or five leaves on cuttings with average-sized leaves, such as R. *catawbiense*, can be left. Leave more top foliage on cuttings of plants with small leaves and fewer on larger-leaved types. To conserve space in the rooting frame, large leaves are also usually reduced to one-half of their length.

On two sides of the cutting, remove a thin sliver of bark and wood starting 1 in. (2.5 cm) from the bottom. This wounding results in better root development along the full length of the cut (Figure 9.8).

Dip the cutting in liquid or powder rooting hormone to a depth of 1 in. (2.5 cm). Because rhododendrons are more difficult to root than azaleas, rhododendrons require a stronger hormone formulation (0.8 percent active ingredient). The types of rooting containers and media used are identical to those described for azaleas.

Punch holes about 2.5 in. (6.3 cm) apart and 1.5 in. (3.8 cm) deep into the medium and insert the cuttings. Firm the rooting medium around cuttings only enough to maintain their erect position. Spacing may need to be modified to insure that leaves of cuttings do not overlap.

Label the cuttings as they are inserted into the container. Apply a fungicide for use on shrubbery as directed on the label.

Close the rooting container or place the cuttings under a mist system as explained for azaleas.

Aftercare is much the same as described earlier for azaleas. Most important is that the rooting medium remains moist. Most rhododendron cuttings

Figure 9.8. Left: A rhododendron cutting as removed from the parent plant. Right: A cutting properly prepared for rooting. Note how leaves have been stripped and trimmed and the stem bark removed. Photograph by H. Edward Reiley

develop roots in about twelve weeks and need to be checked at this time for root development. Some cuttings may require more time, and as long as the foliage remains turgid and green, they will eventually root. After any watering needs are met, close the container or turn the sprinkler system back on. Wait until at least a 2-in. (5-cm) root ball has developed to start the hardening-off process as explained earlier for azaleas. Figure 9.5 shows a well-rooted rhododendron cutting.

Rhododendron cuttings do require one additional step in their aftercare. All terminal buds should be pinched out in the fall after cuttings are hardened off. This stimulates lateral bud development and encourages multiple branching to develop earlier the following spring. Rooted rhododendron cuttings are overwintered in the same manner as described earlier for azaleas.

Grafting

Most European nurserymen view grafting as the best means for propagating rhododendrons, and there are indeed some advantages. By using a strong-growing, widely adapted rootstock under all plants, the survival of the resulting plants in a wide variety of conditions is better assured. *Rhododendron* 'Cunningham's White' is widely used as an understock for grafting in Europe because it tolerates higher soil pH and adapts readily to a wide range of soil and climatic conditions. A new superior rootstock, Inkarho®, is now used for grafting in Europe. Grafting is also thought to produce more compact plants. The principal disadvantages of grafting are the tendency of the rootstocks to produce suckers, which frequently engulf the scion, and the fact that graft incompatibility may result in poor growth or separation of the graft union.

Amateur gardeners seeking to augment their collection of species or cultivars or produce duplicates of a rare plant should consider grafting. It is a quite effective way to propagate a limited number of plants and provides another propagation challenge, especially for plants difficult to root by cuttings. Grafting requires a greenhouse or other indoor growth chamber similar to that used for rooting cuttings, including lights or bright natural light. The most commonly used grafting methods for rhododendrons are the saddle graft, cleft graft, and side graft (Figure 9.9).

Rootstocks for grafting are rooted cuttings from a cultivar selected for the vigor of its roots and its adaptability, such as the new Inkarho® rootstock developed in Europe. The rooted cuttings need to attain a size of 1/4 to 3/8 in. (0.6 to 0.9 cm) in diameter before grafting is undertaken. The rootstock is more easily handled if potted in 4- to 5-in. (10- to 12.5-cm) pots at least a month

A. The Saddle Graft

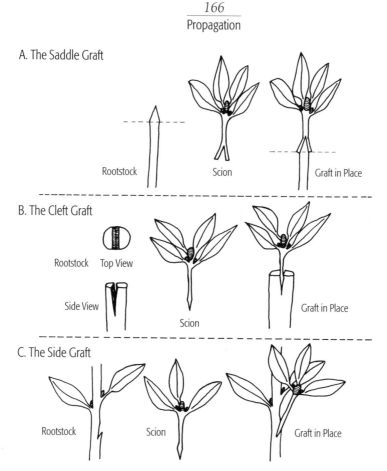

Rootstock   Scion   Graft in Place

B. The Cleft Graft

Rootstock   Top View

Side View   Graft in Place

Scion

C. The Side Graft

Rootstock   Scion   Graft in Place

Figure 9.9. Grafting techniques

before grafting. Place pots in a growing environment of about 65–75°F (18–24°C) to encourage active root growth. It is important that the roots be actively growing before a graft is attempted. Grafting is best done in December and January, when the scion wood is mature and dormant.

Side Graft

Cut scions 3–4 in. (7.5–10 cm) long from the plant to be propagated. Scions are cut from the pervious season's growth. Place immediately in a cool, moist environment to prevent moisture loss. If the scions are not grafted immediately, store in a cool environment of 100 percent relative humidity until grafted.

Remove all leaves from the lower 3 in. (7.5 cm) of the rootstock stem.

With a sharp knife, slit the rootstock stem on one side for a distance of 1 in. (2.5 cm) to just above the soil line. Slant the cut slightly toward but not to the exact center of the stem. Move the knife back and forth slightly while cutting to reduce the downward pressure on the stem. This will avoid tearing the roots off the small plant.

Reduce the number of leaves on the scion piece to three or four. If a large-leaved form is used as the scion, cut away the terminal half of each leaf. Then remove a 1 in. (2.5 cm) long slice on each side of the bottom stem end to make a wedge shape to fit the cut previously made in the rootstock. All cuts must be straight and smooth so contact between the scion and rootstock is continuous along the matching surfaces.

Slide the scion into the slit on the rootstock, being careful to place both cambium layers to match on at least one side. The cambium is a very thin layer of cells separating the wood (xylem) of the stem from the bark (phloem) and is located just under the bark. The difference between the wood, bark, and cambium layer is easily identified. Precise alignment of the cambium is important because it is the tissue where new cells are formed. This will permit the scion and rootstock to grow together to form new xylem and phloem for the transport of water and nutrients from root to shoot and back.

While holding the scion in place, tightly wrap with a rubber bud tie. Begin the wrap by overlapping the bud tie at the bottom of the graft and end by tucking the last wrap under the previous one. The joint needs to be wrapped its entire length with no exposed cut surfaces remaining. Check that the cambium layers of the scion and rootstock have remained aligned during tying.

Mist the graft and place it immediately in a grafting case, similar to the containers suggested for cuttings. When using a grafting frame, place a layer of moist (not wet) sphagnum moss in the bottom so the pots are buried in sphagnum deeply enough to cover the grafted area. Alternatively, cover individual pots with a polyethylene plastic bag. Before pulling bags over individual pots, place a handful of moist moss around the graft. The case and/or bag must be sealed watertight. Grafts should be placed under plastic immediately after being completed. Never allow the scions to dry out.

Maintain a temperature of about 50°F (10°C) and an atmosphere of 100 percent relative humidity around the grafted plants, and provide sixteen hours of bright light each day.

In about five weeks, remove the peat moss from around the graft union. Prune away any sprouts emerging from the roots or stem of the rootstock, mist the grafts, and reseal the container.

About three weeks later, reduce the number of leaves on the rootstock by about 50 percent and again remove any sprouts from the rootstock. The temperature now needs to be raised to 65°F (18°C). When the grafts are well callused, hardening off can be initiated.

Open the grafting case or plastic bag slightly and observe carefully for the first week. Mist and, if the grafted scion wilts, close the container. If wilting is not evident, continue to gradually increase the plant's exposure to the outside conditions as outlined in hardening off of cuttings. Plants must be carefully observed during this hardening-off period. Any grafts that have not healed completely can be quickly identified as the scions that wilt. If only a few are

Figure 9.10. Side graft in a transplant container. Note the graft union. Photograph by H. Edward Reiley.

incompletely healed, move them to a separate container for a few more weeks before attempting to harden them off.

Lower the temperature to about 60°F (15°C) when the completely healed plants have been fully hardened off. Remove the rubber bud ties. If the grafts are tightly callused and healed over (Figure 9.10), prune off the upper portion of the rootstock just above the graft union. If the grafts are not fully healed, give the plants more time. There is no need to rush this pruning, but it should be done before the first flush of growth on the scions is completed. All sprouts from the rootstock are again cut or pinched out. The temperature can now be raised to 70–75°F (21–23°C) to stimulate growth.

Saddle Graft

The saddle graft is a very simple and perhaps the best grafting method for rhododendrons. The rootstock is produced in the same way as described for the side graft, except that the stems of the rootstock selected are smaller in diameter—they must fairly closely match the diameter of the scion wood. The scion wood is gathered at the same time and in the same way as for side grafts.

Cut the rootstock off about 2–3 in. (5.0–7.5 cm) above the soil level and below the first rosette of leaves. Less sprouting from the rootstock occurs if the section is taken from below any stem leaves. A straight section of stem at least 1 in. (2.5 cm) long will be needed.

Use a sharp knife or grafting tool to make straight, smooth cuts on opposite sides of the stub about 0.75 in. (1.9 cm) long to form an inverted V shape.

Select a 3-in. (7.5-cm) scion of the current season's growth. Leaves on the scion should be reduced to three to four. If the scion is a large-leaved form, cut the leaves in half laterally.

Split the scion stem up from the cut end for about 1 in. (2.5 cm), or cut a V shape in it to match the rootstock.

Slide the scion down onto the wedge-shaped rootstock, align the cambium on at least one side, and wrap snugly with a rubber bud tie.

Aftercare is as discussed for the side graft.

Cleft Graft

Cut the rootstock off at a right angle 1 in. (2.5 cm) above soil level with a very sharp knife. Split the rootstock stem down the center about 1 in. (2.5 cm). Prepare the scion as for the saddle graft.

Cut a 1-in. (2.5-cm) slice off opposite sides of the scion to make a smooth wedge shape.

Insert the scion in the split stem and align the cambium on at least one side. Push the scion down until no cut wood is exposed, and wrap snugly with rubber grafting tape or a large bud tie. Seal the end of the stem with grafting wax.

Aftercare is the same as recommended for the side and saddle graft, except when a cleft graft is done on a large plant in the landscape. In this situation, clear plastic bags pulled over the grafted branches must be shaded from the sun.

Green Graft

Green grafting is used for propagating both rhododendrons and azaleas and is one of the most successful and easiest methods. Green grafting is used to increase the number of plants of a particular cultivar, as well as in hybridizing programs. This method is done in the summer months and uses easier-to-work green wood taken when both rootstock and scion are in active growth. Cleft and saddle grafting are the most successful forms for green grafting. Hybridizers green graft new seedlings to older plants so they can evaluate flower buds more quickly and also to improve the appearance of older plants by what is called "top-working." The latter simply refers to grafting young vigorous scions of new, superior cultivars to the upper stems of older plants.

Green grafting is undertaken after a flush of growth has hardened off to almost the same degree of maturity as would be used for rooting cuttings. In all cases, current season's growth is used for both rootstock and the scion. If plants are grown to provide rootstock for green grafting, one straight stem near the soil level needs to be encouraged. This is easily done by cutting a young plant back in the early spring to just above the first leaves. As shoots arise, remove all but one new shoot to be used as the rootstock.

Layering

Trench or mound layering is seldom used today because large numbers of rhododendron plants are so easily propagated by cuttings or grafting. Layering is a slow process, and only a limited number of plants can be propagated from a single parent plant. Layering is, however, an excellent method for the gardener needing to propagate only one or two additional specimens of a plant to share or to assure survival of a rare form.

In late summer or early fall, select a propagating branch that is close enough to the soil surface to be bent down and covered with soil. Using a branch on the north side of the plant is best because the soil will be shaded by the parent plant and will retain moisture better.

Dig a trench 2–3 in. (5.0–7.5 cm) deep and about 3 in. (7.5 cm) wide where the current season's growth of the branch can be brought into contact with the ground.

Remove all the bark and cambium in a ring 1 in. (2.5 cm) wide or cut two-thirds of the way through the stem at the point where the branch touches the ground. Both of these procedures will restrict the flow of synthesized food from the leaves back to the roots and result in an accumulation of carbohydrates at the girdled area. Remove any leaves that would be buried with the stem. Apply rooting hormone to the wounded area at the same strength as for cuttings.

Place the girdled or cut portion in the trench and cover with soil rich in organic matter.

Hold the branch in place by putting a brick or stone on top of the soil above the layered branch. Keep the soil in the vicinity of the branch moist but not wet.

Rooting usually occurs in the year following layering. If no roots are evident upon cautious examination the following fall, leave the layer in place for another season.

When a root system has developed, separate the layer from the parent plant and transplant the new plant to a nursery area where it can be given careful attention until it is well established.

Mound layering is often used with deciduous azaleas that are difficult to root from cuttings. The procedure is as follows:

Prune the parent plant close to soil level in early spring to produce as many new shoots as possible growing near the ground.

In the fall, build a mound of soil high in organic matter to a depth such that only the tips of the new shoots remain above the mound.

Maintain good moisture levels throughout the mound.

The following spring, clear the mound down to soil level and remove rooted shoots by cutting them from the parent plant just above ground level. The parent plant will produce more shoots in the course of the summer.

Transplant the rooted shoots to a nursery bed until well established.

Seed Propagation

Rhododendron and azalea cultivars do not propagate true from seed. Some isolated species propagate rather uniformly from seed, but there is nearly always variation among the seedlings. Any variation produced would then be within the limits of natural variation typical of sexual reproduction. Hybrid seeds resulting from crosses do not breed true and must always be sown and grown to maturity to identify any worthwhile offspring.

Rhododendron and azalea seeds are available from the ARS Seed Exchange and some commercial sources. If the gardener wishes to collect seed, do so in early fall before the seedpods open. The seedpods of some rhododendrons open easily soon after they dry, but others must be pried open or crushed. The seed can be separated from the pod debris by sifting through a fine sieve. Store seeds in a clearly labeled container in a cool, dry place until the seeds can be prepared for sowing in early winter. Rhododendron and azalea seeds are extremely small and must be handled very carefully.

The conditions required to grow seed are virtually identical to those required to grow rooted cuttings. Germination is highest at temperatures of 70–75°F (21–24°C) in an atmosphere of 100 percent relative humidity. The growing medium needs to hold moisture well, be well drained, and be fine enough that a smooth surface can be prepared. If the tiny seeds fall into small holes on the soil surface, they may become too deeply covered. I recommend a medium composed of 70 percent sphagnum peat moss and 30 percent horticultural perlite, but other organic mixes may be equally satisfactory. Many propagators use 100 percent milled sphagnum peat moss.

The germinating container must be moisture-tight when sealed, must drain well, and must be at least 4 in. (10 cm) deep. The other dimensions depend entirely upon the number of seeds to be sown. Containers must be clean and preferably made of plastic, metal, or glass. Plastic food storage boxes with clear tops make excellent seedling growing containers. Bottom holes will allow more careful watering once the seedlings are developed. The procedure for seeding is as follows:

Fill the container with growing medium and firm it to provide a smooth, level surface about 1 in. (2.5 cm) below the top of the container.

Water lightly with one-quarter strength rhododendron fertilizer because the medium has essentially no available nutrient content.

Spray the surface with a broad-spectrum fungicide if disease has been a problem. This is seldom necessary, however.

Sprinkle the seeds on top of the medium, being careful not to sow too thickly (see Plate 101). Do not cover the seed with the medium. Spray the surface with a plant mister so there is moisture available for germination.

Cover the container with clear plastic or glass and seal to maintain 100 percent relative humidity inside.

Place the container in a warm (70–75°F, 21–24°C) area for germination. Light is not necessary at this time yet must be provided as soon as the seeds have sprouted. The safest practice may be to place the container under a 40-watt fluorescent light immediately. Germination occurs in two to eight weeks in most cases (see Plate 102).

Seeds of some species, such as *R. yakushimanum*, will germinate better if placed in a cool situation, 40°F (5°C) or below, for six weeks immediately after seeding and before placing under lights.

As soon as the seedlings have two to four true leaves, transplant them to flats or a nursery bed. Plate 103 shows a group of seedlings ready for transplanting. Transplanting must be accomplished before seedlings begin crowding each other. Crowding can result in disease problems or the death of smaller seedlings.

The first step in transplanting is hardening off. Do this by gradually exposing the tender seedlings to normal conditions of humidity, as is done with cuttings and grafts, by gradually opening the container over a period of one to two weeks. Water needs must be carefully monitored during this time to keep the medium moist but not wet. It is best to water from the bottom, as surface watering can wash out or knock over small seedlings.

Once hardened, seedlings can be transplanted into pots or a larger container with a medium of 50 percent coarse sphagnum peat moss and 50 percent perlite or ground Styrofoam. Alternatively they can be transplanted to nursery beds high in organic matter. Handle each seedling by a leaf, not by the stem. If the stem is bruised, the result is death of the plant. Always lift seedlings by prying from underneath the root ball so roots are not torn loose. Plate 104 shows a seedling lifted from the container ready to transplant.

Spacing in the new container needs to be about 1.5–2 in. (3.8–5.0 cm) on center. The seedlings are set at the same depth as they were growing in the germinating container. A small hole punched in the medium for each seedling using a dibble board or a finger will facilitate planting. Gently cover the roots; water the seedlings to settle the medium around the roots (see Plate 105). Mist the transplanted seedlings several times the first day after transplanting.

Place the seedlings under 40-watt fluorescent lights, 12 in. (30 cm) above the plants.

Fertilize by watering with one-quarter strength neutral rhododendron food every third watering.

Aftercare is similar to that for rooted cuttings, except that it will be longer. Seedlings are more tender and cannot be exposed to sun and wind as quickly.

With the knowledge and material available today, a gardener can expect excellent results propagating rhododendrons and azaleas. Not only is it a sound venture economically and in terms of increasing the extent of a collection, but also much personal satisfaction can be derived from propagating and growing one's own plants.

10

Nursery Growing

Nearly all rhododendron and azalea growers will at some time grow very small, tissue-cultured liners, rooted cuttings, or seedlings to landscape size. Scale of operation makes little difference in the proper method for doing this. The systems discussed here are adequate for both the hobbyist and the nurseryman. Two systems used in the nursery production of plants are field growing and container growing, with container growing currently gaining popularity. There are some advantages and disadvantages to both systems, as discussed below.

Field Growing

Field growing has many advantages. Less water is required and it must be less frequently applied because plant roots are in a larger water reserve and soils hold more moisture than soilless mixes. Plant roots become acclimated to the soil, resulting in better root extension, and so develop a better root ball. Plants with soil root balls transplant and survive better in the landscape than container-grown plants grown in coarse, soilless mixes. Nutrient deficiencies, especially deficiencies of minor elements, do not limit growth if soils are properly prepared. Additionally, overfertilizing is less of a problem because the soil environment acts as a buffer. Roots are not injured from summer heat or winter cold, so they do not require protection from either.

Field growing also has disadvantages, however. More labor is required in planting, digging, and potting or balling for market. Root balls are heavier and thus more difficult to handle and transport. It is harder to precisely control growing medium density, aeration, and soil-borne insects and diseases. Plants cannot be dug for market if soils are wet. The root system is reduced during digging. If growing for market, the grower is selling not just a plant but his precious topsoil as well.

Transplanting Liners

One-year-old liners are usually used to begin growth in the nursery field bed. The nurseryman purchases such plants as rooted cuttings or tissue culture liners. In some cases the nursery, using any of the several propagating methods described in chapter 9, produces one-year-old liners. Liners are then rooted in an organic medium and given considerable protection throughout the growing period. Under such favorable conditions, plants are relatively tender. Even after hardening off, plants must be given some protection initially, particularly if planted to field beds.

Two major obstacles are encountered in transplanting small plants into the soil: encouraging root extension into the soil and protecting their foliage. Getting the roots to venture out into the soil from the soilless medium in which they were rooted can be solved in several ways. One way is to amend the soil with at least 50 percent organic material. In so doing, I have found no comparable substitute for amending with coarse sphagnum peat moss. The moss should comprise no less than 25 percent of the organic amendments used. Pine bark, 1/4 in. (0.6 cm) and less in size, may be used to provide the other 75 percent. (Another method to encourage roots is discussed later as part of planting procedures.) The second obstacle is protecting the foliage, especially that of tissue culture plants, which is generally more succulent than foliage of rooted cuttings. Shading, wind protection, and maintaining adequate soil moisture are the most important measures to be taken. Using a modified cold frame most easily solves this situation.

This cold frame is not the glass-covered structure commonly used, but rather the cover is made with snow fence, lath, or shade cloth. Walls are high enough to accommodate the top growth of the plants, and it is not heated. Figure 10.1 depicts a large cold frame covered with snow fencing and used to grow tissue culture liners and rooted cuttings through the first growing season. The walls are constructed of concrete block, the joints between levels overlapped for stability, although joints are not mortared. The bottom row is set about 4 in. (10 cm) below the soil surface to provide additional stability.

The size of the cold frame depends on the number of plants to be grown. An economical width is 14 ft. (4.3 m) wide as an outside dimension with about a 1 ft. (30 cm) path down the center. This provides space for two beds approximately 6 ft. (1.8 m) wide with enough room for seven rows of liners in each

Figure 10.1. A cold frame made from concrete blocks covered with lath. Photograph by H. Edward Reiley

bed spaced 8 in. (20 cm) apart. The plants need to be allowed enough space that the foliage is just touching at the end of the growing season. The center path provides maintenance access for weeding, pruning, and so on. The 14 ft. (4.3 m) width can be spanned with 2 x 4–in. frames, which will require no center support if boards can be set on edge. The frames are then covered with snow fence or lath to provide 30–50 percent shade. Incidentally, a narrower structure may require the same number of blocks for construction but allow less growing space. Both ends of the frame are initially left open to permit passage of a rototiller or other equipment needed to prepare the soil. Plywood ends can be set in place to close the structure after planting. The sash can easily be lifted and stacked by two people when it is necessary to enter the cold frame after planting.

The soil in the cold frame needs to be tested, amended, and in general prepared as for a planting bed. This includes incorporating 1.5 lb. per 100 sq. ft. (0.6 kg per 9.3 m²) of urea formaldehyde and at least 50 percent organic matter. The center path can be about 12 in. (30 cm) wide and 8 in. (20 cm) lower than the planting beds when the path is dug, the soil removed can be placed on each side. Afterward, the two beds are ready to be leveled.

Figure 10.2. A liner plant with extended roots free and ready for the planting bed.
Photograph by H. Edward Reiley

Liners should be transplanted as early in the spring as possible. Planting can begin when the soil and air are still cool and moist yet the soil is sufficiently dry to work without destroying soil structure.

Start rows on one side of the bed using a string to keep them straight. Plant the first row about 8 in. (20 cm) from any walls, spacing plants 8 in. (20 cm) apart in the row. Use a ¾-in. (1.9 cm) plywood board to walk and kneel on while planting to protect the loosely dug soil from compaction. Alternating plants in succeeding rows, spaced midway, will maximize the growing space.

Each liner needs to be prepared immediately prior to planting so roots do not dry out. Prepared liners should be kept in a flat or other container with the roots covered by moist peat moss or mulch until planted. Before setting the liners in the bed, shake or comb off the medium around the roots to expose root ends. If plants are tightly pot-bound, cut off the bottom of the root ball and straighten the roots so they extend from the medium (Figure 10.2). Although preparing the roots takes a little extra time, the better growth of plants is warranted. Place the liner in a hole large enough to permit filling in around and below the extended roots and maintain their extended horizontal position. Firm but do not pack the soil tightly around the tender roots; use water to settle soil around the roots.

Make every effort to prevent root damage. The fine, tender roots of liners are easily torn, pulled from the plant stem, or bruised. This greatly reduces the effectiveness of the developed root system. When removing liners from pots, squeeze or tap the bottom of the plastic pots or hold the pot upside down and tap to shake the plant out. Lift plants from flats by sliding a putty knife or similar tool under the root ball. Cutting between plants in a flat with a sharp knife four to six weeks prior to transplanting greatly facilitates removal from the flat and will also promote a well-branched root system. Never pull the top of the plant to remove it from a container. After careful removal from the container, immediately plant or cover the roots with rooting medium or moist mulch until planting. After planting, mulch the bed from both edges with 1 in. (2.5 cm) of fine pine bark or other suitable material.

When the bed is fully planted and mulched, irrigate to settle the soil around the plant roots and to raise the humidity in the cold frame. If planting is interrupted or when planting a large area that allows time for plant foliage to dry, mist the plants periodically until the entire frame is planted, watered, and mulched. Immediately after planting and watering, place the lath cover or snow fence over the cold frame (see Figure 10.1). During the first week I also add a 50 percent shade cloth over the lath for additional sun and wind protection.

The single most important requirement after planting is proper watering. This is a practice that cannot be overemphasized. The soil, however, should never be overwatered. About 1 in. (2.5 cm) of water per week, as either rain or irrigation or a combination of the two, is a general rule of thumb. Less may be needed in a cold frame covered with shade and a windbreak, so check soil moisture several times a week to determine whether water is needed. The root ball should always feel moist but not wet. To gauge the amount of water the planting bed receives, place a straight-sided container among the plants. Mark a 1 in. (2.5 cm) line on the inside. Check this water gauge regularly to determine when irrigation may be needed.

Newly rooted cuttings or tissue culture plants should not be pruned at planting time, as the leaves are necessary to manufacture food for the development of new roots. Wait several weeks until new feeder roots have become established. At this time, pinch or cut back the tips of azaleas to promote early branching. To promote low branching, cut the azaleas back to 2–4 in. (5–10 cm) from the soil surface. New shoots will emerge on the stem to about 2 in. (5 cm) below the cut. Figure 10.3 illustrates the pruning needs of an azalea.

Figure 10.3. An azalea liner. Mary Reiley holds one of the taller stems where pruning will encourage low branching. Photograph by H. Edward Reiley

Later pruning depends upon plant growth. Pruning can be done as necessary to encourage additional branching. Do not prune after August 1, however, because it will stimulate tender growth and azaleas may not set flower buds. Figure 10.4 shows azaleas after one year of growth. The plant in the center was not pruned; the one to the right was pruned to stimulate low branching. Spring pinching of azalea flower buds from all tips, as soon as they swell enough to be easily removed, will result in more vigorous, uniform top growth. Obviously this would not be done the year the plants are moved to the landscape or marketed.

Rhododendrons have a growth habit different from that of azaleas and require a different approach to pruning. While azaleas grow by continuous extension of stems, rhododendrons grow in rapid growth flushes. Stem elongation is stopped when a whorl of leaves and a terminal bud with lateral buds in the leaf axils are set. Additional growth does not occur in rhododendrons until soft wood has matured. Young plants usually have two such growth flushes each year.

Figure 10.4. Azalea plants after the first year's growth. The center plant has not been properly pruned and shows gangling growth. Photograph by H. Edward Reiley

If terminal buds were removed from rhododendron cuttings the previous fall after rooting, no pruning is required. If terminal buds were not removed, pinch these buds from all cuttings at planting time. During the first flush of growth, additional pinching is necessary only when single shoots are produced. Single shoots can be cut off when they are 1–2 in. (2.5–5 cm) long to promote additional branching. If plants still do not branch well, delay pruning until the first flush of growth has hardened and the root system is developed. Liners with adequate root systems are able to force and support more branches. Figure 10.5 shows a well-branched liner, the result of pruning back a single shoot after adequate root development had occurred. Tissue culture liners usually develop multiple branches at soil level and readily develop as compact, well-branched plants.

Pruning of liners is the most important pruning ever done on a plant. No amount of pruning later in the plant's life can correct mistakes made at this stage of development. The goal is to have three or four branches starting at or near soil level (see Figure 10.6).

Figure 10.5. Rhododendron liner. The single center shoot was pruned, resulting in five new branches originating near the soil surface. Photograph by H. Edward Reiley

Figure 10.6. Multiple branching on a rhododendron liner after one year's growth. This specimen illustrates successful pruning. Photograph by H. Edward Reiley

Close monitoring is needed to control or prevent damage from insects or diseases in the cold frame. If pests such as mites or fungus diseases appear, spray immediately with the proper chemical. See chapter 8 for control recommendations. However, if the plants were free from insects and diseases when planted in the cold frame and good sanitation is maintained, there probably will be no need to use pesticides.

The number and type of weed seeds in the soil of the cold frame primarily determine the extent of any weed problems. The key to successful weed control is to remove weeds when they are small. Their removal long before maturing and reproducing will go far in controlling any current and future weed populations. Except for the very vigorous and tall growing weeds, 1–2 in. (2.5–5.0 cm) of mulch prevents most weeds from getting a start. Nearly all types of weeds require light for germination. Mulch blocks light from reaching the soil surface and thereby discourages weed seed germination from the native soil. The few that do emerge can easily be pulled by hand as soon as they are visible. The mulch layer will not be radically disturbed by this process and so will continue to block most attempts at germination. Chemical weed control is an alternative for use in the cold frame. Contact your local extension horticulturist for recommendations.

In the fall, after the first killing frost or when plants are sufficiently hardened off, apply 0.75 lb. per 100 sq. ft. (0.3 kg per 9.3 m²) of urea formaldehyde to the soil surface. This late-season organic nitrogen application will promote root development in the fall and will result in evergreen azaleas holding more leaves over the winter. Growth the following spring will also be more vigorous as a result of a fall nitrogen application. In warm climates where cold temperatures do not persist, this fertilizer application should not be used.

The lath cover over the cold frame usually provides adequate winter protection. The plywood ends, if removed during the summer, need to be replaced to protect the plants against rodents and wind. No additional care will be needed until transplanting time the following spring.

Second-Year Field Management

After a year spent in the cold frame, the plants are of sufficient size and maturity for transplanting to open field beds for an additional year or two. These beds may be in full sunlight in USDA hardiness zones 5–6 and possibly zone 7. It will be necessary to shade plants in sites where sunlight is intense enough to cause foliage damage and subsequent yellowing of leaves.

Figure 10.7. Field beds in author's nursery in central Maryland ready for planting. Notice the maintenance path in the center area. Each bed is 7 ft. (2.1 m) by 100 ft. (30 m). Beds are raised about 12 in. (30 cm) above the existing soil level. The native soil type is a silt loam. Photograph by H. Edward Reiley

Raised beds greatly reduce the incidence of root rot and are recommended for field-grown plants for all but extremely well-drained soils. For best results beds need to be 12 in. (30 cm) above the existing soil level and gradually taper down at the edges (Figure 10.7). Raised beds may require additional irrigation, yet the benefits to plant health usually will outweigh this consideration.

In general, prepare the soil in the nursery beds as described in chapter 6. A few details are different for nursery field bed preparation because it involves more intense plantings. The soil needs to be slightly higher in organic matter. Dig in a 3- to 4-in. (7.5- to 10-cm) layer of organic amendment. Also, it is necessary to pay closer attention to soil test results. Precise amounts of fertilizer elements are required to produce optimum conditions for plant growth. Because nitrogen is generally not part of soil testing, a general recommendation is 1.5 lb. per 100 sq. ft. (0.6 kg per 9.3 m²) of urea formaldehyde dug in prior to planting.

The practice of preparing beds in the fall for spring planting can free up valuable time. Most gardeners are fully occupied with numerous other springtime chores, and to have the bed ready for planting seems especially valuable. This practice also allows organic amendments in the soil to promote beneficial microorganisms, which aid in soil-borne disease control.

Field beds no more than 6 ft. (1.8 m) wide are easier to weed, prune, and otherwise tend and can accommodate three rows of plants. If the width is increased by only 1 ft. (to 7 ft., 2.1 m), four rows of azaleas can be planted, but the plants in the center of the beds will be difficult to tend. Do not walk in the beds because that will compact the soil and reduce aeration to the roots. Space azaleas 1.5 ft. (0.5 m) apart in each row and rhododendrons 2 ft. (0.6 m) apart; rows should be 1.5 ft. (0.5 m) apart.

Beds can be planted as early in the spring as possible—immediately after the last date on which the soil freezes and once the soil is dry enough to work. Because plants in the cold frame are acclimated to the climate, they are hardened off and will only be frost susceptible at the roots.

Lift each plant from the cold frame bed by cutting around it and prying the root ball loose with a shovel. Handle plants by the root ball, not the top, to avoid tearing roots from the stem. Keep the roots of the newly dug plants covered with mulch or soil until transplanting. Because the plants were grown in a soil mix similar to the soil being transplanted into, no special preparation of the root ball is necessary.

Dig holes just deep enough so that the top of the root ball is level with the bed. The ball should be resting firmly on the bottom of the hole. Using your hands, fill soil around but not on top of the roots. Firm the soil, yet do not tamp tightly. After the bed is planted, mulch with 2 in. (5 cm) of loose mulch, such as pine bark, and water well to settle the soil around the roots. If the bed is planted early in the spring, no sun protection is necessary.

The most critical cultural practice from this point on is proper watering. Soil needs to be kept moist but not wet. Some drying of the soil can be encouraged in late summer, which will help check active growth and harden off plants for the winter.

Insect and disease control is undertaken only as conditions warrant throughout the growing season. Although some growers still apply preventive sprays on a regular schedule, this procedure is now discouraged. The current view encourages monitoring closely for early pest identification and using spray applications only when damaging pest populations are noticed. During the final growing season, either the second or third year, any damage to foliage will affect plant marketability. It may be necessary to use preventive sprays to stop such damage because the consumer has every reason to expect an insect-

and disease-free product. Chapter 8 presents control methods for various insects and diseases. It is important to know which of these pests are in the local growing area and how to prepare for control.

When azaleas are planted, only the extra long shoots need to be cut back. In about four weeks, after roots are established and before new growth starts, additional pruning can be done. How much to prune depends on how well the plant branched during its first year and what level of compactness is desired. If the plant is already well branched, cut back only to the point where additional branching is desired. New shoots originate downward on the stem at a distance of 1–2 in. (2.5–5 cm). Continue cutting back as necessary to promote additional branching. An alternative method for azaleas is to pinch 0.5 in. (1.3 cm) on the soft tips when new shoots reach about 3–4 in. (7.5–10 cm) in length.

No pruning of any kind should be attempted after August 1. Late pruning forces new growth to develop late in the growing season, and this growth may not harden off before freezing weather. Pruning after August 1 may also prevent flower bud formation. A chemical is available for use as a pruning method for large operations. This chemical works by killing the tender terminal growth. Because plant response varies, the chemical should be used only according to label directions.

If rhododendron liners were properly pruned in the cold frame, the plants will have at least three or four shoots originating within a few inches of the soil level by the time they are moved into the field beds. If improperly pruned, errors need to be addressed at this time. Figure 10.8 shows a rhododendron in need of corrective pruning.

Second-year pruning of rhododendrons is largely accomplished by pinching terminal buds before each flush of growth begins. In fall, at the end of the first growing season in field beds, all terminal buds are pinched out, including any flower buds. This may be all the pruning necessary to produce a well-branched plant. If buds (including flower buds) were pinched out the previous fall, there is no need for additional pruning the final year in the field nursery because most terminals are carrying flower buds for next year's display in the landscape.

Weed control in field beds is partially accomplished through use of 2 in. (5 cm) of fine pine bark mulch or other mulching material. At this depth, it is deep enough to shade the soil and thus prevent weed seed germination. If the soil has been managed to provide good weed control several years prior to use as a nursery bed, few weed problems will be encountered. If weed problems

Figure 10.8. Improperly pruned rhododendron liner ready for transplanting to a field bed. Mary Reiley points to where corrective pruning needs to start. Photograph by H. Edward Reiley

are minimal, hand pulling is a workable control. If the problem is more severe, use herbicides as recommended by your local extension horticulturist.

Wind and sun protection of rhododendrons is important during the winter season in regions where winter winds are strong or temperatures drop below 0°F (–18°C). Snow fencing makes an effective windbreak and also provides shade to plants to the immediate north. A windbreak is necessary every winter. The year before marketing or landscape placement, both a windbreak and winter shade should be provided. This will protect foliage from sun- and windburn and result in dark green, attractive foliage.

If the organic mulch applied at planting time is decomposed, an additional 1 in. (2.5 cm) can be applied in late fall. Mulching at this time will help prevent deep freezing in the soil, thereby improving moisture availability to plant roots. Apply 0.75 lb. (0.3 kg) of urea formaldehyde per 100 sq. ft. (9.3 m^2) prior to mulching. Assuming a fall application of urea formaldehyde has been applied the first year in the field, no fertilizer applications need to be made until active growth starts the following spring. At this time, broadcast 0.75 lb.

(0.3 kg) of urea formaldehyde per 100 sq. ft. (9.3 m²) of bed area. Any fertilizer residue on plant foliage needs to be removed. Ammonium sulfate can be substituted for urea formaldehyde as a surface application, at 1 lb. per 100 sq. ft. (0.4 kg per 9.3 m²). Because this material is a salt, it should not be dug into the soil if the area is to be planted immediately following application. Another application of the same fertilizer at the same rate needs to be made in the fall of the second year in the field. Fertilize either after the first killing frost or after the plants are hardened off for winter.

The soil must be kept moist during the active growing season until midsummer, when soil can be allowed to dry somewhat to harden off plants for winter. Early hardening off should be encouraged the last year in the nursery and before plants go into the landscape.

Container Growing

Container growing is exactly what the term implies: growing plants in containers rather than in a bed in the ground. The result is an entirely different growing environment. Major differences from field growing include a coarser growing medium, a restricted root zone, wider fluctuations in root temperatures, unique water and fertilizer requirements, and more intensive management of cultural factors.

A large and increasing percentage of nursery plants are grown in containers each year by both commercial and hobbyist gardeners. Container growing has the advantage of greater control of the growing medium because it is mixed in exact proportions of medium and fertilizers. Additionally, commercial mixes are available that are ready for use. Plants can be grown from liner to finished product in the same container. This eliminates the costs and labor of digging and transplanting. Root loss in transplanting to the landscape is likely to be reduced, unless the plants are seriously pot-bound, which is often the case. Plants are easier to transport. Weed control is simplified. A greater number of plants can be grown more intensively in a given area, and plants are available for market regardless of wet soils, which prevent digging field-grown plants.

Container growing also has disadvantages. Much more water is required. A 1-gallon pot requires at least 1 pint (400 ml) of water per day because the coarse potting medium drains so rapidly. Plants require daily irrigation during the growing season. Heat from the sun can damage roots growing in the south side of the container. The growing medium is light in weight, so plants can be easily blown or knocked over. Plant roots may become pot-bound.

Close management attention must be paid to fertilizer needs because soilless mixes used in containers essentially contain no nutrients. Plant roots can be damaged when temperatures drop below 20°F (−7°C). Plants transplanted to the landscape from containers require more intensive care the first year.

The commercial grower must select a container that is attractive and has a useful life of one to two years. Injection molded, polyvinyl pots satisfy both these requirements. The home gardener can use anything with sufficient strength and size to hold the root ball. Shallow containers do not drain as well as taller ones because gravitational pull is less on short columns of water. A container depth of at least 6 in. (15 cm) is recommended. The diameter of the pot will not affect drainage, but a pot too small for the plant dries out more quickly because a lower volume of medium is available to hold moisture. Gravel or shards placed in the bottom of pots have traditionally been used to improve drainage but in fact do just the opposite. They reduce the depth of the medium and thus reduce gravitational pull. Containers with holes extending 0.5 in. (1.3 cm) up the side drain more efficiently than those with holes only in the bottom.

Questions regarding container size are determined by how long the plant is to remain in the container and how vigorous the plant is. A proper fit can be determined by the size of the root ball. Roots should reach the edge of the container and may circle the walls but should not become solidly matted around the edges or bottom by the end of the growing cycle. Most nurseries use a 2-gallon container to produce 12- to 15-in. (30- to 38-cm) plants and a 3-gallon container for 15- to 18-in. (38- to 45-cm) plants.

The container medium is made up of three constituents: solids, gases, and liquids. From one-third to one-half the total volume is occupied by solid particles. The remaining volume is pore space and is occupied by water or air in varying percentages over time. A growing medium with small pore spaces retains more water and less air than one with large pore spaces. Shallow containers do not drain as well and therefore will require a coarser mix than tall containers.

A good, well-draining garden soil will remain saturated longer when placed in a container compared to its draining capacity in the garden. This is due to the shallowness of the container, which results in a reduced gravitational pull on the column of water through the soil. The outcome of using even good garden soil in a container is a poorly aerated medium; results are poor root development or root death. Therefore, a satisfactory container medium must be composed of larger particles than those found in even the best garden loam soil.

Nursery stock can be grown in any medium that is nontoxic, provides anchorage, and provides the plant food elements, water, and oxygen. The selection of materials to be used is usually based on cost and availability as well as quality in terms of providing optimum growing conditions. The gardener growing a small number of plants may be best advised to purchase a commercially prepared container mix formulated for ericaceous plants. Any soil and sand used as part of a container medium needs to be sterilized before mixing by heating soil to 160°F (71°C) for 30 minutes to kill any resident disease organisms.

Sand is often included to add weight, thus reducing chances for containers to be blown over by wind. Only coarse sand should be used, and it should not make up more than 10 percent of the total volume because sand fills available pore spaces and can seriously reduce drainage and air space in the medium. Sphagnum peat moss improves moisture retention in a mix, retains plant nutrients well, and lowers the pH of the mixture. If used alone as a container medium, however, it will hold too much moisture.

Conifer bark is probably the most popular container medium in areas where it is readily available. It is quite resistant to decomposition and can be milled and screened to provide a material very uniform in texture or particle size. The best material has 70–80 percent of the particles in the size range of ¼ to ⅜ in. (0.6 to 0.9 cm) in diameter and 20–30 percent of the particles smaller than this. Bark of this particle size can be used alone but dries out quickly when sphagnum peat moss is not added. It will be necessary to add dolomitic limestone to conifer bark, which adjusts pH, as well as plant food elements. Pine bark is naturally acidic with a pH range from 4.0 to 5.5.

I have found that a mixture of pine fines with a ¼ in. (0.6 cm) and smaller particle size mixed with coarse sphagnum peat moss at a ratio of 3:1 provides an excellent medium. This mix does not require watering as often as 100 percent pine bark. Sphagnum moss improves the moisture and nutrient retention qualities of the mix. Another container mix widely recommended is:

3 parts by volume of bark ¼ in. (0.6 cm) and smaller in diameter

1 part by volume of coarse sphagnum peat moss

0.5 part by volume of sand to add weight

Hardwood bark is not recommended due to its high cellulose content, rapid decomposition, and shrinkage. It also has a high pH (6.5–7.5) after decomposition, which is not satisfactory for ericaceous plants.

The frequent watering required by plants grown in rapidly draining containers will also result in fertilizer leaching. Because soilless mixes lack virtually all plant food elements, minor elements also need to be included in the fertil-izer or added separately in fritted form. Slow-release fertilizers mixed into the medium or later sprinkled on the surface will give a consistent level of nutri-ent input. Some soluble plant foods generally recommended for ericaceous plants contain too much sulfate for use in container mixes. One result may be the lowering of the pH below levels best suited to *Rhododendron* growth. If a soluble fertilizer is preferred, it is best applied with irrigation water. Soluble plant food formulations used at half the recommended strength every second or third watering will result in satisfactory plant growth.

The most important considerations in selecting the container growing area are ready accessibility to a water supply, protection from wind, and a gently sloping surface. The reasons for these conditions are quickly apparent. Con-tainer plants require virtually daily watering, so a reliable supply of quality water is a must. Because neither small plants nor containers can withstand winds of any magnitude without being injured or tipped, wind protection is required. Likewise, because root rot can be devastating in container growing, the extra drainage provided by a sloping area is a good preventative measure. Fiber mats or gravel on top of black plastic used for weed control also im-proves drainage.

Fill containers with growing medium to within 1 in. (2.5 cm) of the top to provide the largest volume and deepest root zone possible. Plant liners at the same depth at which they were growing in the flats or small containers. Rhodo-dendrons are planted singly, one liner to each container, yet two or three azalea liners are often planted per pot. This double or triple planting of azaleas re-sults in a finished plant in less time (usually in one year) and requires less pruning. Multiple plants result in a composite, many-branched plant.

Because liners are planted into an organic mix, little if any problem is en-countered with root extension into the soilless mix. However, tightly pot bound root balls need to be broken apart to interrupt the circling growth pattern.

Immediately after planting, containers can be watered thoroughly to settle the medium around the roots (Figure 10.9). Place containers in the growing area as close together as present spread of the foliage allows. Because the sun heats and frosts can cool the growing medium to root-killing temperatures, close spac-ing will moderate temperature fluctuations. Special attention to watering needs is critical especially during the period immediately after transplanting. The coarse, rapidly draining potting medium dries out quickly and will require watering once every two days in early spring and daily as summer heat in-creases. Under conditions of extreme heat (90°F, 32°C and above), water is

Figure 10.9. A rhododendron liner planted to a container that has been pruned properly and displays a good branching pattern. Photograph by H. Edward Reiley

typically required twice a day to maintain a moist growing medium throughout the container.

Pruning and insect and disease control practices are identical to those for field-grown plants. Weed control for container-grown plants is largely a matter of prevention. Because the potting medium is weed-free when made, weed control is a question of preventing weed seeds from blowing into the stored medium or planted containers. Therefore, premixed container medium must be stored inside a windbreak or kept covered. Although some weed seeds can be blown great distances, the area in the immediate vicinity of the weed plant produces the greatest populations. It is imperative to remove all weeds within a radius of 100 ft. (30 m) or more of the medium storage area before they go to seed. After planting, a weed killer can be spread over the surface of the medium in the containers with a cyclone type spreader. Apply only when plant foliage is dry, and remove any residue from the foliage immediately after application. Check with your extension horticulturist for recommendations.

The nurseryman or gardener growing plants in containers or flats must take extra precautions overwintering plants in cold climates. When plants are

Table 10.1. Killing temperatures for some container *Rhododendron*

Species or cultivar	Killing temperature	
	Roots	Flower buds
R. prunifolium	20°F (–7°C)	–15°F (–26°C)
R. 'Hino Crimson'	17°F (–8°C)	0°F (–18°C)
Exbury Hybrids	17°F (–8°C)	–25°F (–32°C)
R. schlippenbachii	15°F (–9°C)	–20°F (–29°C)
R. 'Purple Gem'	15°F (–9°C)	–25°F (–32°C)
R. 'Gibraltar'	10°F (–12°C)	–25°F (–32°C)
R. 'Hinodegiri'	10°F (–12°C)	0°F (–18°C)
R. minus (Carolinianum Group)	0°F (–18°C)	–25°F (–32°C)
R. catawbiense	0°F (–18°C)	–25°F (–32°C)
R. 'P.J.M'	–9°F (–23°C)	–25°F (–32°C)

Adapted from Dr. Francis R. Gouin, University of Maryland Fact Sheet (H.E. 102-76).

grown in the landscape or field, heat continues to rise from the unfrozen soil at deeper levels. Therefore, soil temperatures around the roots do not usually go so low as to cause root damage. Because plants in containers are above ground and are unprotected by warmer soil temperatures, plant roots can be killed at temperatures easily endured by soil-grown plants (see Table 10.1). In addition, when the root balls of container-grown plants are solidly frozen, they are unable to absorb needed moisture. The relatively new pot-in-pot system modifies temperatures in the plant container both summer and winter.

An insulating material such as Microfoam simplifies overwintering container plants where protection of the surface is necessary to help control root temperatures. Plants may be set upright if a frame is used to hold the Microfoam off them, or placed on their sides and closely stacked if the film is to be placed directly on the plants (Figures 10.10, 10.11). All plants should be watered well and sprayed with a fungicide to prevent foliage disease in the moisture-tight enclosure. Place the Microfoam between two sheets of white (not clear) plastic and spread over the plants with all edges extending to the soil, where they are covered with soil to form a moisture-proof seal. Plants should be protected only when night temperatures are below 20°F (–7°C) and removed in spring when the danger of such temperatures for longer than a few hours no longer exists.

For small numbers of plants, a pit dug 3 ft. (0.9 m) deep also works well to overwinter container plants if a well-drained site is available. Cover the pit with any good insulating material, supported so a heavy snow cover does not

Figure 10.10. Container plants laid on their side ready for winter covering with Microfoam and white plastic. Photograph taken at Marshy Point Nursery, zone 7. Average winter low is 0°F (−18°C). Photograph by H. Edward Reiley

Figure 10.11. The same plants as in Figure 10.10, now covered with Microfoam and white plastic. Photograph taken at the end of December. Photograph by H. Edward Reiley

break it. Remove the cover in early spring. Container-grown plants are often wintered in open poly houses. Figure 10.12 shows an example of this system of overwintering. Except in extremely cold areas, no additional heat is needed. Where temperatures are not as severe, plant tops can be protected with a snow fence windbreak. Covering the containers with any mulching material that will adequately insulate and modify temperature extremes in the root zone can protect container plant roots.

At the end of one or two years, the container-grown plant is ready for market or landscape placement. Any plants not sold or moved to the landscape will need to be potted to the next larger size pot to prevent constricting the roots.

In summary, the *Rhododendron* nursery, whether a small hobby venture or of commercial scale, offers many rewards to the grower. The gardener can develop small plants at considerable financial saving, and the nursery person can reap a profit if the business is managed properly. The decision to grow plants in field beds or containers can be made after careful evaluation of the local advantages and disadvantages. A thoughtful decision can then be reached as to which system is best adapted for the resources available. Successful growing of small plants to landscape size requires close attention to details, particularly watering and pruning. Yet, there is every reason to believe that the average gardener can produce plants of professional quality by following the basics of good culture outlined here.

Figure 10.12. Polyethylene house at Marshy Point Nursery used for overwintering container-grown rhododendrons. Photograph by H. Edward Reiley

11

Hybridizing

Earlier I noted that growing rhododendrons can be contagious, and there is no known cure. Hybridizing can be a further symptom of such contagion and a pursuit that injects a kind of mystique and an element of chance. Goals are set, crosses made, seedlings germinated and planted, always with the expectation that something new and outstanding is surely in the genes and about to appear—if not this year, maybe next. Or, one hears about the new superior species just discovered that will add enormously to the genetic material available. This kind of excitement motivates and keeps thousands of hybridizers around the world at work. The results are seen as the newly listed *Rhododendron* cultivar registrations each year, some of which will indeed stand the test of time and improve the variety of first-class rhododendrons available. Many other crosses, equally as good, are not registered. Some may be introduced, yet most will remain unknown.

New and improved cultivars appear only out of the sustained efforts of hybridizers who grow thousands of seedlings. I read years ago that, "All the flowers of all the tomorrows are in the seeds of today." Save for mutants and sports, only seedlings can produce new and exciting plants thanks to the mixing and rearranging of the genes via the mechanism of sexual reproduction.

A bit of counsel to prospective hybridizers is appropriate here. Only a few hybrids will prove to be superior plants. Much patience and a thoroughly disciplined set of judgmental standards are required throughout the long process of evaluation as new crosses are compared to the best available cultivars. Only plants superior to others in existence at the time should be brought forward for registration and introduction. Complete objectivity is a difficult quality to maintain as one evaluates the seedlings, and advice from others is not only wise but also probably necessary. Rhododendron hybridizers are generally friendly, helpful people, ready to assist a new member of the fraternity with hybridizing issues.

The first hybridizers of rhododendrons and azaleas were active in Japan over 300 years ago. Evidence of hybrid plants, among the kurume azaleas in Japanese gardens, dates back at least to the seventeenth century. Beginning in the nineteenth century, extensive hybridizing activity developed in Europe as plant explorers brought back an increasing number of new species. It was not until the early twentieth century, however, that hybridizing started in earnest in North America with such greats as Joe Gable, Guy Nearing, C. O. Dexter, Tony Shammarello, and James Barto. I urge the interested gardener to read some of the detailed accounts of the contributions of early hybridizers before starting to work. Since that time, many more outstanding hybridizers, too numerous to mention, have been at work.

The genus *Rhododendron* is a hybridizer's dream. The tremendous diversity of flower color and size, plant size, foliage, cold hardiness, heat tolerance, disease resistance, and other attributes presents such a huge reservoir of genetic variability that it seems possible to make any number of useful combinations. However, some combinations of characteristics have defied the best efforts of hybridizers. For example, there are no yellow-flowered evergreen azaleas; few heat-tolerant deciduous azalea hybrids; no blue elepidote or red lepidote rhododendrons; few disease-resistant plants; and few ironclad evergreen azaleas. Yet, most of these combinations are within the realm of possibility because the genes are there; it is a matter of cleverly arranging them in the proper order. This is a simple statement, yet for the hybridizer it represents a long, problematic undertaking.

The recent discovery of superior forms of some species offers new potential for the production of superior cultivars. The hybridizer is well advised to search out the best form of each species to use in his or her work. Research at the parent selection stage often makes the difference between achieving hybridizing goals or failing to do so. In any circumstance, parent selection can reduce the time required to meet defined goals.

Probably one of the gravest mistakes a hybridizer can make is to start spreading pollen before thoroughly investigating work already done by others (the best sources for a beginning hybridizer to start his or her research program are Leach 1961; West 1978; Galle 1987; Salley and Greer 1992). Another weakness can be in failing to define goals. A third problem quite often lies in parent selection. It is essential to identify the parent plants most likely to achieve the goals that are set.

The first step in any hybridizing program is to become thoroughly familiar with previous work. Because much hybridizing work has been done and the results are on record with the ARS, it makes no sense to repeat crosses already made, especially those that produced poor results. Such research can also identify parents that consistently pass along certain characteristics to their offspring. Obviously, those cultivars transmitting traits consistent with the goals of the hybridizing program need to be selected for further evaluation and possible use.

In addition, research can often eliminate a step in a hybridizing program by starting with first-generation crosses. It is quite possible that two species, identified by the hybridizer as parents, have already been crossed and seedlings selected that carry the genes for the desired characteristic. Because such primary hybrids represent the first step in a successful breeding program, even if the offspring are of mediocre quality, they carry the genetic potential for better things in the next generation, where the hybridizers' goals are most likely to be met.

The second step is to define goals for the hybridizing program. It is wise to focus on only one or two goals at a time in order to concentrate the focus and make noticeable progress. Because contemporary homes tend to have a low profile, low-growing plants are in increasing demand, while the demand for large plants is declining as vast estates with wooded grounds are decreasing in number. Although many commercial buildings and apartment complexes are of a scale suitable for large plants, there is often little interest in rhododendrons and azaleas in these situations because of their special cultural requirements. The beginning hybridizer might be well advised to aim toward the breeding of low-growing and dwarf forms as one goal. Some other goals might include:

▸ increased disease resistance, particularly mildew resistance in deciduous azaleas;
▸ increased insect resistance;
▸ increased cold hardiness in evergreen azaleas and yellow rhododendrons;
▸ increased heat tolerance in all rhododendrons;
▸ larger flowers with cleaner colors on rhododendrons;
▸ fragrance in rhododendrons and azaleas;

- development of double flowers;
- tightly branched plants;
- increased amounts of persistent foliage on evergreen azaleas;
- improved fall and winter foliage color on evergreen types;
- a yellow-flowered evergreen azalea;
- deciduous azaleas that are easier to root;
- a true blue elepidote rhododendron;
- a true red lepidote rhododendron;
- indumentum on rhododendron leaves; and
- stronger root systems.

The careful selection of parents possessing the characteristics being sought in the cultivar is the third major step toward a promising hybridizing program. Because each generation in the hybridizing program requires from three to seven years, the hybridizer cannot afford to make many mistakes in the selection of parents. Furthermore, if goals are to be met, the parents must be capable of transmitting the characteristics selected by the hybridizer. A thorough knowledge of characteristics most often transmitted by specific parents becomes of utmost importance. This must be researched before the hybridizer can make selections with any degree of accuracy or expectation of success.

Azaleas

Galle's *Azaleas* (1987) contains an excellent chapter on hybridizing azaleas written by Dr. August Kehr. It presents detailed information on hybridizing and offers some wise advice on the selection of parents most likely to transmit specific characteristics to their offspring. Kehr writes, "An informal poll was taken of several azalea breeders and growers [list omitted] to solicit their choices for parents for some of these specific objectives. As might be expected replies were varied, but significant points of agreement developed" (p. 346). Kehr lists some of the plants suggested to realize particular objectives.

Azaleas fall into two broad categories, deciduous and evergreen. It is probably sufficient to note that the single-flowered evergreen species azaleas crossbreed readily, as is also the case among many of the deciduous species. However, the evergreen azaleas do not readily crossbreed with the deciduous species. A handful of hybrids have been produced between an evergreen and a deciduous parent, but they are rare and few of the plants are of much merit.

Most azaleas are self-sterile and cannot pollinate themselves. Below I list evergreen and deciduous azaleas that show the best traits and should be considered by hybridizers for their breeding programs.

Evergreen azaleas:

Most cold hardy: 'Corsage', 'Herbert', *R. kiusianum*, *R. yedoense* var. *poukhanense*

Best winter foliage: 'Glacier', 'Hot Shot', 'Polar Bear'

Reddest color: 'Girard Scarlet', 'Hino Crimson', 'Mother's Day', 'Ward's Ruby'

Yellowest color: 'Cream Cup', 'Frostburg', 'Mizu no Yamabuki'

Fragrance: *R. ripense* var. *mucronatum*, 'Rose Greeley'

Fully double flower: 'Anna Kehr', 'Elsie Lee', 'Hardy Gardenia', 'Louise Gable', 'Rosebud'

Fall-flowering: 'Dorsett', 'Indian Summer', 'Opal'

Compact growth: Beltsville dwarfs, 'Dragon', 'Girard's Border Gem', *R. kiusianum*, 'Myogi'

Lasting quality of flowers: 'Ambrosia', 'Chojuho', 'Jeanne', 'Rosebud', 'Scott Gartrell', 'Vuyk's Scarlet'

Best all-around good doers: 'Corsage', 'Herbert', *R. kiusianum*, 'Martha Hitchcock'

Deciduous azaleas:

Easiest to root: *R. austrinum*, *R. atlanticum*, 'Gibraltar', 'Homebush'

Mildew resistance: 'Coccinea', 'J. Jennings', 'Persil', 'Speciosum'

Compact growth: 'J. Jennings', 'Klondyke', *R. prunifolium*

Red flower color: 'Ilam Red Letter'

Yellow flower color: 'Klondyke'

Most floriferous: 'Gibraltar', 'Knap Hill Red'

Double flowers: 'Homebush', 'Narcissiflorum', 'Norma'

Lasting quality of flowers: 'Homebush', 'Norma'

Best all-around good doer: 'Gibraltar'

Rhododendrons

Rhododendrons also fall into two major groups: the lepidote, or scaly species, which generally also produce small leaves, and the elepidote, or nonscaly, large-leaved species. Lepidotes and elepidotes are cross-sterile, that is, successful crosses are confined to species or cultivars within each group. The following plants are suggested as parents with a proven ability to transmit various desirable traits to offspring:

Large flower size: elepidote—*R. discolor*, *R. fortunei*, 'King George'

Cold hardiness: elepidote—'Clark's White', *R. maximum*; lepidote—*R. dauricum*, *R. minus*, *R. mucronulatum*

Heat and sun tolerance: elepidote—*R. catawbiense*, *R. insularis*, *R. decorum*, *R. fortunei*, *R. hyperythrum*, *R. maximum*, *R. degronianum*; lepidote—*R. minus*, *R. minus* var. *chapmanii*

Disease resistance: elepidote—'Caroline', *R. decorum*, *R. degronianum*, *R. pseudochrysanthum*, *R. yakushimanum*; lepidote—*R. aureum* 'Wada', *R. keiskei*, *R. racemosum*

Compact size: elepidote—*R. williamsianum*, *R. yakushimanum*; lepidote—*R. keiskei* 'Yaku Fairy'

Late-flowering: elepidote—*R. haematodes*, *R. maximum*

Early-flowering: elepidote—*R. fortunei*, *R. vernicosum* '18139'; lepidote—*R. dauricum*, *R. mucronulatum*

Fragrance: elepidote—*R. fortunei*

Red flower color: elepidote—'Captain Jack', 'Essex Scarlet', *R. griersonianum*, *R. haematodes*, *R. strigillosum*, 'Vulcan'

Yellow flower color: elepidote—*R. campylocarpum*, 'Gold Mohur', *R. wardii*; lepidote—*R. keiskei*

White flower color (usually masked in the first generation and recovered in the second): elepidote—'Clark's White', *R. yakushimanum*; lepidote—*R. dauricum* var. *album*

Pink flower color: nearly all red × white crosses

Perhaps one way to demonstrate the process of selecting suitable parents is to present an example. Let's say the goal is to develop a compact, large-leaved rhododendron with large, fragrant flowers. The search begins with research to identify parents with a record of transmitting these characteristics to their offspring. The first observation is that typically the less complex or heterogeneous a plant is genetically, the better the prospect of transmitting the desired traits without passing undesirable traits that would require subsequent crosses to eliminate. In other words, a species or primary hybrid possessing the desired characteristics is a better choice than a complex hybrid. A careful search reveals that *R. fortunei* has both large flowers and fragrance plus good foliage and resistance to lace bug. Similar research reveals that the species capable of dwarfing or developing compact offspring among the nonscaly rhododendrons include *R. yakushimanum*, *R. degronianum*, and *R. williamsianum*. By carrying crosses of these plants through two or more generations and crossing or backcrossing after each generation (depending on those characteristics needing reinforcing or reducing), the hybridizing goal might possibly be met.

Here is another example. The goal is to develop a compact plant with a dark red flower. *Rhododendron williamsianum* has a dwarfing effect and also has outstanding foliage. *Rhododendron yakushimanum* also has a dwarfing effect but masks red flower color so completely that the chance of producing a red offspring is very limited. In this case *R. williamsianum* is the better choice for the parent contributing a dwarfing effect. 'Mars' and 'Essex Scarlet' are cultivars that reliably pass red on to their offspring, as does the species *R. haemotodes*; any one of the three is a candidate for obtaining a red flower.

Making a Cross

After the prospective parents have been researched and carefully selected, it is a good idea to start a record book in which the crosses made, subsequent outcomes, further crosses and outcomes, and other data are meticulously recorded. Any cross should be recorded before it is actually made. The female parent or pod parent is always listed first and the pollen parent second. For example, in the cross 'Mars' × 'America', 'Mars' is the female parent. This record book must be carefully maintained so that all significant events and observations are recorded at the time of their occurrence.

If both parent plants are growing in the same garden and flower at the same time, the actual process of cross-pollinating is very simple. The flowers of both rhododendrons and azaleas are fortunately large enough that the male and female flower parts are easy to identify and work with. See Figure 11.1 for an illustration of male and female flower parts.

Hand pollination requires the following steps:

Identify three or four flower buds on two or more stems. More than one bud should be pollinated to insure against loss through physical damage. Flowers should be just ready to open but not yet accessible to insect pollinators. Next, on the plant to be used as the female parent, reduce the attractiveness of the immediate vicinity to pollinating insects by removing any other flowers within 1 ft. (30 cm) of the selected buds.

Pollen from the anthers must be prevented from reaching the stigma. Carefully remove the flower petals (corolla) of the selected flower buds; separate the flower petals with the fingers and pull or cut them free from their base around the ovary.

With a tweezers or small scissors, remove the anthers of the selected flowers one at a time and discard.

When the top surface of the stigma of the prepared flower exudes a sticky substance, it is receptive and can be pollinated immediately. If it is not sticky, cover the stigma with a small paper bag fastened to the stem to prevent

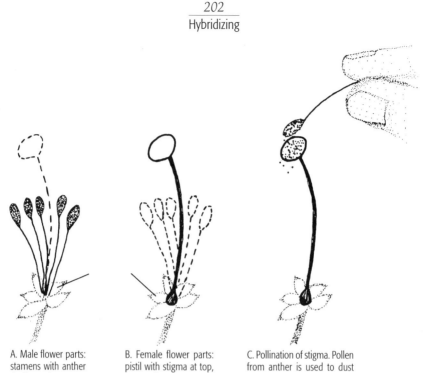

A. Male flower parts: stamens with anther (pollen sac).

B. Female flower parts: pistil with stigma at top, ovary at base.

C. Pollination of stigma. Pollen from anther is used to dust stigma of female parent.

Figure 11.1. Hand-pollination: cutaway view of flower parts.

accidental pollination. Check the stigma daily to determine when it is sticky and thus receptive to pollen. (Many hybridizers do not think such stigma protection is necessary because rhododendron pollen is not wind-borne and the emasculated flowers are not attractive to insects.)

When the stigma of the female plant is receptive, remove the corollas to expose anthers on several unopened buds from the male parent plant. Collect the entire flower stem intact and transfer pollen from the anthers to the stigma immediately. If pollen must be held until later, clip the anthers off and place them in a gelatin capsule (no. 0 or no. 1). Store the capsule containing the male pollen parts in a refrigerator with a desiccant such as silica gel for drying until the female plant is ready.

Apply the pollen from the end of the anther to the sticky surface of the stigma. Because rhododendron pollen is not dusty and does not shake out easily, touch the pollen sac to the surface of the stigma to transfer the pollen. The total surface of the stigma needs to be covered with pollen.

Some hybridizers next cover the pollinated flower with a small brown paper bag to protect the fertilized stigma. Others consider such protection unnecessary for the same reasons mentioned above.

Label the female parent to show the cross, again listing the name of the female parent first.

Check the record book to confirm recording and date the cross.

If the selected parents do not flower at the same time, label and store the pollen. Pollen may be air dried and stored in the open for up to two weeks at 50°F (10°C). If the male parent flowers after the female flowers, the pollen may be stored in the freezer at 0°F (–18°C) for a year after it is dried or about a week at 50°F (10°C). If stored for an extended period, enclose the capsule in a sealed jar containing calcium chloride or silica gel as a drying agent. Place the drying agent in the bottom of the jar and cover with a layer of cotton on which the capsules are placed. Be certain the capsule is labeled with the parent name.

Prior to use, warm frozen pollen to ambient temperatures by setting the jar with the capsules in warm water. When pollinating with stored pollen, insert the receptive stigma into the capsule to transfer the pollen, as the pollen frequently sticks to the sides of the capsule. Unused pollen may be refrozen for later use.

Alternatively, off-season flowering of the female parent can be induced. Transplanting the female parent into a container the previous fall and placing it in a greenhouse or transplanting into a greenhouse bed most commonly do this. By controlling temperature and day length, the time of flowering can be made to coincide with the flowering time of the pollen parent. If a choice can be made, it is easier to store pollen than to alter flowering dates.

If pollination was successful, the ovaries of the female parent will expand rapidly and produce the seedpod containing the new hybrid seed. Seed usually matures about the end of September, at which time the pod can be removed. There is no need to wait until the seedpod turns brown because the seeds are mature and are capable of germinating a month before changes in pod color. Seedpods must be collected no later than the first killing frost, as frost accelerates pod splitting and subsequent seed loss.

Place the pods collected from one plant in a separate small envelope or cup that has been labeled to identify the cross. Place the seed container in a warm, dry location to dry the pods so they will release the seeds. To remove seeds from pods that have failed to open by drying, crush the pods. Next, separate the pod and other plant material from the seeds. Because the seeds are extremely small, it is necessary to take great care not to lose them. Seeds may be sown immediately or stored in a cool, dry place for up to a year. Follow the instructions on propagation given in chapter 9.

The success or failure of the cross (noted when the seeds are recovered), the disposition of the seed, sowing dates, and other information must all be noted in the record book together with any observations that might prove useful later. For example, the amount of seed set would indicate the degree of compatibility or success in technique.

The accepted method of ultimately combining in a single cultivar the most desirable characteristics existing separately in the two parent plants is to then cross-pollinate two first-generation seedlings that most closely exhibit the desired characteristics. Intended results are most often obtained in the resulting second generation, the grandchildren of the original parents. It is best to grow as many seedlings of this second generation as possible. This will exploit the maximum number of genetic combinations to find the one closest to the desired plant.

If the hybridizing goal is to improve only one or two traits of an otherwise outstanding plant, for instance, tightening the truss or increasing disease resistance, backcrossing is undertaken. Backcrossing may require a large number of seedlings to produce the desired results because it is open to the expression of undesirable qualities. The steps in backcrossing are given below.

Cross the rhododendron needing improvement with a rhododendron having a proven reputation for transmitting the desired trait.

Backcross the first-generation seedling that best exhibits the trait desired to the pod parent needing improvement.

If the desired result is not obtained in the resulting second generation, then proceed to cross two sister seedlings of the second generation.

A single gene seldom controls any physical characteristic. Rather, a number of genes are involved, some of which may work in opposition to others. This fact is one of the reasons that breeding results are difficult to predict. Furthermore, some characteristics are linked on a single gene. A good example is color and fragrance in rhododendrons. I know of no fragrant red rhododendron, and to my knowledge fragrance only occurs in white or light-colored flowers. These two characteristics are probably located on the same gene, in which case a breeding goal of producing a fragrant red rhododendron may be close to impossible to reach.

Sometimes crosses will not produce seeds. This outcome occurs when the two plants selected as parents are too genetically different. For example, an elepidote × lepidote rhododendron cross or a deciduous × evergreen azalea cross usually will not produce seed. In addition, polyploids (that is, plants bearing two or three times the normal number of 26 chromosomes) are usually incompatible with plants containing 26 chromosomes. In such cases, any seed produced is sterile or weak and yields unthrifty or sterile offspring.

The Seedlings

The genetic purity and potential of the parents in terms of their ability to transmit the genetic characteristics being sought determines how many seedlings need to be grown. Fewer seedlings are needed with inbred lines, such as species, while more are needed with hybrid parents. The greater the heterogeneity of the parents, the greater the variety of possible results. Accordingly, a greater number of seedlings must be grown to increase the likelihood of arriving at the desired characteristic.

The following are guidelines as to the optimal number of seedlings to be grown for various crosses. (These numbers are estimates. In practice, the greater the number of seedlings grown, the better the chance of reaching the goals set.) As the list progresses, the parents are increasingly more heterogeneous or variable in genetic makeup, so a greater number of seedlings must be grown.

> Cross between two different species: As few as twenty seedlings are adequate if resulting seedlings are to be used as primary hybrid parents in a second cross. The expectation is to reach the goal in the second generation.
>
> Cross between a species and a hybrid: A minimum of fifty seedlings is needed if the offspring are to be used as intermediate parents to be crossed again. If the expectation is to meet the hybridizing goal in this first generation, several hundred seedlings are a minimum.
>
> Cross between two hybrids: Because both parents are hybrids and more heterogeneous than species plants, a minimum of 500 seedlings must be grown for evaluation.
>
> Backcrossing: The number of seedlings required depends upon the number of characteristics one is attempting to recombine in the progeny. When seeking to recombine two characteristics, 100 seedlings are probably adequate. If more than two characteristics are sought, more seedlings should be grown.

Recognize that the first generation of seedlings rarely produce the desired results and usually present a group of mediocre plants. Due to the uncertain blending of parental characteristics, efforts must usually be carried on to at least a second generation. Desired characteristics in selected parents (especially if controlled by recessive genes) are often absent in the first generation yet will appear in future generations, hopefully in the combination desired.

Plants not meeting the hybridizer's goals must be eliminated from the breeding program as soon as it is clear that any of them fall short of the goals. All such roguing needs to be recorded in the record book. Any seedlings selected for growing on should also be recorded.

All hybridizers could use assistance in the selection process because it is impossible to be objective about one's own work. Some suggested evaluation practices include:

Evaluate any new hybrid over a period of at least ten years.

Make comparisons by planting the seedlings thought to be better in a test garden beside plants widely agreed to be superior.

Share the seedlings with other gardeners in different geographic locations for evaluation under different conditions.

Introduce and register only plants that prove superior to existing cultivars after these practices have been completed.

There are far too many new rhododendron and azalea cultivars registered each year simply because many hybridizers fail to reach an objective assessment of their work. This assertion is not meant to criticize the registration system. The registrar is, after all, only doing the job required by the international code—registering the cultivars submitted. The registrar is not expected to judge the garden worthiness of the cultivars submitted. The issue of selection rests with the hybridizer. This can be a difficult position if a hybridizer lacks knowledge of existing cultivars or understands the plant's performance only under limited conditions. It is for these reasons that objective assistance in determining if a new cultivar is worthy of registration and introduction is warranted. Yet, there is some advantage in having too many cultivars registered rather than losing a truly great plant when an amateur hybridizer fails to test it adequately before registration.

Superior selections need to be propagated and shared with other growers, both to make sure they are not lost to cultivation and to test them as widely as possible. Plant sharing is a critical part of the evaluation process. If the new cultivar is judged to be superior in a diverse set of gardens, registration may be justified.

Registration forms, available from the ARS, require the registrant to provide considerable detail so that the cultivar can be well identified. Precise measurements of leaf and flower, precise flower color, truss size and shape, and parentage are among the details requested. Contact a local hybridizer or the ARS for more information.

Hybridizing requires considerable patience, the ability to sustain disappointment, a strong back to transplant thousands of seedlings, and some good, honest gardening friends to help maintain the proper perspective and objectivity for evaluating new hybrids. On the other hand, hybridizing does add an additional level of satisfaction to gardening. Even if the amateur hybridizer never registers or introduces a single plant, the enjoyment of the undertaking can make it all worth the effort.

12

The Flower Show

Rhododendron flower shows are one of the most rewarding activities an ARS chapter can undertake. Such a show provides members an opportunity to work together and encourages the formation of rewarding relationships within the membership. In addition, it is a multifaceted educational undertaking in which *Rhododendron*, in all its diversity, can be presented to gardeners unacquainted with the plants. A flower show also nurtures future show judges. It provides an opportunity to reach a more profound understanding of the finer points of the species. Finally, if a plant sale is made part of the event, it can become not only a source of income for the chapter but a community resource for the acquisition of well-adapted plants.

Organizing

A flower show requires considerable work and planning and therefore a significant time commitment by a large number of members. However, when properly organized and conducted, this potentially daunting task can become a satisfying common undertaking leading to an unparalleled closeness among the club members.

Rhododendron flower shows take many forms, yet, in general, can be described as either competitive or noncompetitive. If the objective of the show is to recruit new members or educate the public by acquainting them with a wide range of *Rhododendron* well suited to the local landscape, a noncompetitive show is the wisest choice. If, however, the show is intended principally for members, a competitive show may be best because committed growers are generally more greatly stimulated by a competitive show. It is, of course, both possible and often desirable to mount a show that combines features of both.

Because there are no winners or losers at a noncompetitive show, there is little potential for injured feelings. Flowers may be arranged in more attractive and diverse ways than that called for by the formal classes required for judging. The need for judges, ribbons, judging regulations, record keeping, and other formalities is eliminated, which makes the show easier to prepare and conduct. Finally, the flowers are labeled for educational objectives and grouped in ways better suited for use in the landscape. The public has more interest in landscape use than in competitive judging and formal plant classification.

A competitive show also has advantages. It provides a forceful incentive to improve plant selection and cultivation. If the reasons winning trusses were selected are posted following judging, the show becomes a powerful educational tool. The required formal grouping of plants leads to a clearer understanding of plant classification.

The choice of show type must be made early in the planning stages because the requirements are very different. For example, competitive shows limited to ARS members can be mounted in quite informal settings. To launch a large public show, however, a chairperson should form committees, each with a head, to perform the following functions.

Site selection—This committee would be charged with locating and renting a facility suited to the show objectives. When a large public show is conducted, including a plant sale and a display garden to be built on site (Plate 109), the location must have good access, visibility, parking facilities, and a substantial display area. Shopping malls are ideal for such a show, if security is available. Schools with a large cafeteria or gymnasium are also excellent as are some large nurseries with covered display areas. The owners of most facilities require a renter to provide liability insurance to cover any damage to the facility and to protect the owners against any liability arising from injury to any participant or visitor. The chances for securing any facility are greatly improved if the show committee guarantees the proprietor that provision will be made to prevent dirt and water damage to the facility and that everything related to show activities will be promptly and thoroughly cleaned following the close of the show. These guarantees must be faithfully met, particularly if the chapter ever expects to use that facility or neighboring facilities again.

After the facility is secured, the space must be allocated to the layouts for display purposes, considering ease of moving plants and equipment in and out and ensuring smooth traffic flow both vehicular and pedestrian. Lighting requirements for displaying the true color of flowers and water to maintain plants and flowers must also be considered.

Property—This committee would be responsible for obtaining the tables, containers, entry cards, and other necessary show props.

Publicity—The responsibilities of this committee are to advertise the events, targeting groups within the public with most possible interest.

Judging—This committee is responsible for lining up the judges, clerks, and other staff. It also is responsible for providing the materials such as entry forms and class listings to all prospective exhibitors.

Plant sale—If a plant sale is included, this committee is charged with establishing the rules and conducting the sale. The committee must decide whether members only or local nurseries as well be encouraged to sell, as well as what percentage of sales will be given to the sponsoring chapter. Personnel to handle the sales, provide advice on how to plant and care for plants purchased, and perform other essential duties need to be secured (Plate 108).

Education—Because the principal objective of most shows is educational, considerable time needs to be devoted to providing first-class exhibits. The responsibility of the education committee would be to arrange any such exhibits and/or provide take-home materials.

Display—This committee is responsible for managing all plants and flowers in the display areas set up for educational and decorative purposes. Plate 106 illustrates some of the displays and flower arrangements at a recent Mason-Dixon Chapter ARS Show held in Westminster, Maryland. It seems best to undertake the creation of only as many displays as can be done well. A few outstanding exhibits are more effective than numerous poorly mounted ones.

Clean-up—The condition in which the facility is left following the show will largely determine whether this facility or similar facilities will be available again.

Preparing Trusses for Judging

The goals of a competitive show are to teach exhibitors how to grow, select, and prepare flower trusses and sprays and to broaden their understanding of

Rhododendron classification. The following observations are offered to assist exhibitors in cultivating and selecting trusses and sprays that will meet the demands of a well-judged show. These recommendations reiterate in brief form the cultural practices required to produce a healthy, attractive plant in the landscape as described earlier.

Deadhead plants the previous year to assure good flower bud formation.

Water as needed to maintain unstressed growth.

Fertilize as necessary to produce healthy, green foliage and vigorous growth.

Screen the foliage in the winter to prevent wind- and sunburn. Plants growing in the shade produce better foliage and fewer but larger flower trusses. Plants grown in the sun produce a greater number of trusses on compact plants and are best suited for display plants.

Limit insect and disease damage with an adequate prevention program, especially when leaves are young and tender and easily damaged.

For best appearance, trusses or sprays should be selected either the evening before or the morning of the show date. If necessary, they may be stored in a refrigerator up to a week and still remain in good condition. If stored in a frost-free refrigerator, protect from drying by placing in a plastic bag. Guidelines for selection are as follows.

Identify the truss or spray on which the greatest numbers of flowers are fully open. One or two unopened flowers are not counted against the display when judged. Flower buds just opening usually open fully the following day. Reject any truss or spray on which flowers are starting to fade or have developed brown discoloration around the edges.

The stem should preferably be straight. It is especially important that a rhododendron truss sit vertically on top of the stem. Such a truss typically develops on a branch at the top of the plant that can grow straight up; side branches seldom produce winning trusses. The stem needs to be cut sufficiently long that it will fit well down in the display container.

Trusses that have been grown in the shade are often larger because fewer trusses are produced. This reduces competition for nutrients, which in turn results in each truss being larger. In addition, the foliage on plants grown in shade is usually a darker green. For these reasons a preponderance of winning trusses come from plants grown in shade.

Consider the number of buds. Elepidote (large-leaved, nonscaly) trusses should have a single bud, as multiple buds are disqualified in most shows. By contrast, multiple bud trusses and sprays are allowed for lepidote rhododendrons and azaleas.

Select a truss uniformly surrounded by dark green leaves having no insect or disease damage. The leaves need to frame the truss evenly. Remove all dirt and other foreign material from the display. Bud scales and any pips or dead flowers should also be removed. Grooming is a must and can make the difference between a blue ribbon and no ribbon at all. Plate 110 illustrates a winning truss.

Azalea or lepidote rhododendron sprays must conform to show rules governing overall size, usually a maximum of 12–15 in. (30–38 cm) tall and wide. Sprays are most attractive when balanced with good foliage and flowers at their peak of freshness. Faded flowers with brown edges are not acceptable and can usually be removed without damaging the display. Typically, sprays bearing a few unopened flowers are at the best stage for display.

Deciduous azaleas are usually entered as a single truss, and the same grooming suggestions apply. The foliage may be removed if it obscures the truss. Sometimes the foliage is used to frame it.

Some classes in every show have few entries. It may be a good idea to enter trusses or sprays in these classes. Not only is it easier to win a blue ribbon, but it helps to enlarge the scope of entries.

Care of the display truss after it is severed from the plant and before it is entered in the show is critical. At no time should the flower be exposed to heat or drying conditions, and the stem must be kept in water at all times. Transporting to the show must be done carefully to prevent bruising or crushing the delicate flowers.

Show Classes and Entry Rules

Here, I outline the show classes and entry rules used by several ARS chapters. They are sufficiently inclusive to be used in conducting regional shows. National shows must necessarily provide more classes because a wider variety of species and cultivars are regularly entered.

Show Classes
Class 1.0. Rhododendron species
Section 1.1. Elepidotes (nonscaly series)
Section 1.2. Lepidotes (scaly series)
Class 2.0. Rhododendron hybrids—elepidote
Section 2.1. White
Section 2.2. White with prominent blotch
Section 2.3. Pink, light
Section 2.4. Pink, deep
Section 2.5. Pink with prominent blotch
Section 2.6. Red, scarlet (orange-red)
Section 2.7. Red, rose-red, or crimson

Section 2.8. Red, vermilion, or blackish
Section 2.9. Red with prominent blotch
Section 2.10. Blue-purple, lavender-blue
Section 2.11. Blue-purple, strong purple
Section 2.12. Blue purple, with prominent blotch
Section 2.13. Yellow, light shades
Section 2.14. Yellow, deeper shades
Section 2.15. Yellow-orange, any shade

Class 3.0. Rhododendron hybrids—lepidote
Section 3.1. White
Section 3.2. Pink
Section 3.3. Salmon
Section 3.4. Lavender shades

Class 4.0. New rhododendron introductions[1]
Section 4.1. Rhododendron species
Section 4.2. Elepidote hybrids
Section 4.3. Lepidote hybrids

Class 5.0. Azalea species
Section 5.1. Deciduous
Section 5.2. Evergreen

Class 6.0. Azalea hybrids—deciduous
Section 6.1. White
Section 6.2. Yellow
Section 6.3. Orange
Section 6.4. Pink
Section 6.5. Red
Section 6.6. Bicolored or tricolored

Class 7.0. Azalea hybrids—evergreen
Section 7.1. White, single
Section 7.2. White, hose-in-hose or double
Section 7.3. White with colored blotch, stripe, or border
Section 7.4. Orange-pink, single
Section 7.5. Orange-pink, hose-in-hose or double
Section 7.6. Lavender-pink, single
Section 7.7. Lavender-pink, hose-in-hose or double
Section 7.8. Rose-red, single
Section 7.9. Rose-red, hose-in-hose or double
Section 7.10. Orange-red, single
Section 7.11. Orange-red, hose-in-hose or double
Section 7.12. Lavender-purple, single

Section 7.13. Lavender-purple, hose-in-hose or double

Section 7.14. Pink, single

Section 7.15. Pink, hose-in-hose or double

Class 8.0. New azalea introductions[1]

Section 8.1. Deciduous

Section 8.2. Evergreen

Class 9.0. Specimen plants—azalea or rhododendron plants of any size

Section 9.1. Plant in bloom

Section 9.2. Foliage only (interest and quality; may be budded or in bloom)

---

[1]A special award may be given for the best new rhododendron or azalea not previously exhibited, seed grown from ARS Seed Exchange.

Entry Rules

Only ARS members may exhibit. No fee.

Only one entry per species or cultivar may be made in each section by an entrant. However, any number of different species and cultivars may be entered in a section.

Entries must have been grown and wintered outdoors under ordinary garden conditions.

Entries must have been in the possession of the exhibitor for at least six months.

Lepidote rhododendrons and azalea entries shall be a single stem spray not longer than 15 in. (38 cm) in height or width above the container. Sprays may not be artificially constrained in any way.

Elepidote rhododendron and deciduous azalea entries shall be a single truss from a single bud, which need not be fully open.

A sweepstakes award shall be made to the exhibitor with the most cumulative points determined as follows: best azalea in show (8 points), best rhododendron in show (8 points), best in a class (5 points), blue ribbon in a section (3 points), red ribbon in a section (2 points), white ribbon in a section (1 point), special award (5 points).

All exhibits must be received between 9:00 and 11:30 A.M. on the day of the show. Late entries will not be judged. The judging committee will make classification and placement.

Judging will start at 12:00 P.M. No exhibitors may be present during judging. All judges' decisions are final.

Judging must be as objective as possible, employing rules established before the show. There is no room for personal preferences; only the quality and typical form for the species or cultivar being judged are valid considerations. A truss or spray must be judged as it is seen on the day of judging. Thus, a truss on which half the buds are unopened cannot be evaluated in terms of how it will look in a few days. Conversely, a truss with brown edges on flowers or dropped flowers cannot be judged on how it might have looked yesterday. Points to consider in judging rhododendron and deciduous azalea trusses include:

- truss is held upright on a straight stem;
- truss is framed by a uniform rosette of leaves;
- truss is fresh with no damaged flowers or missing pips (most judges prefer tight over loose trusses);
- truss is typical of the size or larger for the species or cultivar;
- foliage is a healthy color and free of insect and disease damage;
- foliage does not obscure the floral display;
- truss is clean and properly groomed; and
- no more than two or three unopened buds are present in the truss.

Points to consider in judging an azalea or lepidote rhododendron spray include:

- spray is no larger than 15 in. (38 cm) wide or tall;
- shape is pleasing to the eye (spray may be centered on the stem and balanced or may drift to one side);
- foliage is a healthy color and free of insect and disease damage;
- spray is clean and properly groomed;
- flowers are fresh, clean, and undamaged.

To make judging more objective, it is best to use a point system based on numeric values assigned to each judging consideration listed above.

Members can be encouraged to take a leisurely walk through the exhibits after judging, observing which trusses won ribbons and comparing winning entries to others. Such an exercise is a valuable lesson in what to look for in growing winning trusses. An even better way to learn is by revolving the job of clerk among the members. The clerk's duties are to record show results, which provides first-hand experience with winning entries.

Immediately after the show's closing, the chairperson and committee heads need to meet to evaluate the show and determine if show objectives were met. This evaluation should be written up by one of the organizers and reviewed with the entire membership at the earliest possible date. Feedback from the public as well as members is necessary to accurately assess the need for future changes. One way to obtain public feedback is by distributing survey sheets to all show visitors. Forms could be collected at the show or mailed in after completion. The chairperson would be in charge of collecting, reviewing, and sharing these results with members. All summary evaluations need to be subsequently discussed with the entire membership. This provides a learning experience as well as a foundation for the development of future shows. Such sharing can also encourage member participation in following years.

Show development can be an ongoing process for an ARS chapter. If a positive yet sensitive orientation is maintained, the show will consistently improve and prove more effective each year. This progress will, in turn, lead to greater community awareness and encourage a larger portion of the community to improve the appearance of the gardens through familiarity with *Rhododendron*.

A

Good Doer Tables

The following tables outline detailed information for nearly all good doer rhododendrons and azaleas mentioned in chapter 3. The tables divide plants into eight groups:

Table A1. Rhododendron Species: Elepidote
Table A2. Rhododendron Species: Lepidote
Table A3. Rhododendron Hybrids: Elepidote
Table A4. Rhododendron Hybrids: Lepidote
Table A5. Evergreen Azalea Species
Table A6. Evergreen Azalea Hybrids
Table A7. Deciduous Azalea Species
Table A8. Deciduous Azalea Hybrids

NAME is the registered name for the particular species and/or cultivar.

COLD HARDINESS ZONES refers to the zone or zones to which the plant is adapted. This is a general guide, and the plant may not be adapted to all specific microclimates within that zone. Both cold and heat limits are provided for azaleas. Hardiness zone data for deciduous azalea hybrids is given by hybrid group. All Knap Hill Hybrids, for example, are cold hardy to zone 5a and heat tolerant to 8a unless otherwise indicated. The Mollis Hybrids as a group are more heat tolerant than the Knap Hill Hybrids. Only cold hardiness data is presented for rhododendrons. Also mentioned in this column, for those rhododendrons for which data is available, is the lowest temperature tolerable to flower buds. Plant foliage is usually more cold hardy than flower buds. Cold and heat tolerance data is not absolute, yet it can be valuable as a guide.

HEIGHT IN 10 YEARS is the height the plant, grown under favorable conditions in the landscape, will be after 10 years. In some cases mature height is given instead and is so indicated. Some species, due to natural variation, will diverge somewhat from the measurement given.

QUALITY RATING refers to the numerical rating assigned by judges using the American Rhododendron Society rating system, with 1 being lowest and 5 highest. The first number is an evaluation of the flower and the second the plant. A plant evaluated 5/3 has an excellent flower on an average plant. In some cases a third number rates plant performance in the landscape. Not all species and cultivars have been evaluated, so quality ratings are not always available. (Note that the azalea tables do not include a quality rating because this information is not available.)

FLOWER COLOR is given in general color terms such as *pink*, *red*, or *white* with no reference to a color chart.

FLOWERING SEASON is presented as very early (VE), early (E), midseason (M), late midseason (LM), late season (L), and very late (VL). The designations are relative; no specific dates are given because weather conditions, primarily temperature, vary from place to place and year to year, which in turn advances or delays time of flowering.

COMMENTS include miscellaneous information that may assist in the selection process.

Table A1. Rhododendron species: elepidote

NAME	COLD HARDINESS	HEIGHT IN 10 YEARS	QUALITY RATING	FLOWER COLOR	FLOWERING SEASON	COMMENTS
R. adenogynum (Adenophorum Group)	−10°F (−23°C)	4 ft. (1.2 m)	3/4/3	rose	EM-M	dark green foliage; thick indumentum below
R. adenopodum	−10°F (−23°C)	5 ft. (1.5 m)	3-4/4/3	rose	EM-M	large, long, narrow leaf; fawn-colored indumentum
R. arboreum	5°F (−15°C)	6 ft. (1.8 m)	3/4/3	red	E	name means treelike; white indumentum under leaves
R. arboreum sp. *zeylanicum*	10°F (−12°C)	5 ft. (1.5 m)	3/3/3	red and pink	EM	open, growth habit; excellent foliage
R. auriculatum	−5°F (−21°C)	6 ft. (1.8 m)	4/4/4	white	VL	treelike, upright grower; large leaves
R. brachycarpum	−10°F (−23°C)	4 ft. (1.2 m)	3/5/3	white	M	dark green leaves; beautiful indumentum; needs good drainage
R. bureavii	−10°F (−23°C)	4 ft. (1.2 m)	3/5/3	white	M	beautiful foliage; needs excellent drainage
R. callimorphum	−5°F (−21°C)	3 ft. (0.9 m)	3/4/3	pink	M	bell-shaped flower; shiny dark green leaves
R. calophytum	−15°F (−26°C)	5 ft. (1.5 m)	4/4/3	pink	E	very beautiful plant and flower
R. campanulatum	−5°F (−21°C)	4 ft. (1.2 m)	3/5	lilac to white	EM	superior foliage, cinnamon indumentum on underside of leaf
R. campylocarpum	0°F (−18°C)	4 ft. (1.2 m)	3-4/4/3	pale yellow	EM	round leaf shape
R. catawbiense	−25°F (−32°C)	6 ft. (1.8 m)	2/2/4	lilac to pink	ML	widely adapted plant
R. citriniflorum	0°F (−18°C)	3 ft. (0.9 m)	3/3/3	yellow to crimson	M	fawn indumentum
R. clementinae	−5°F (−21°C)	3 ft. (0.9 m)	4/5/3	white	E-M	silky indumentum; crimson spotting on flowers
R. decorum	0°F (−18°C)	5 ft. (1.5 m)	4/3/4	white to pink	EM	compact grower; fragrant flowers
R. degronianum	−5°F (−21°C)	3 ft. (0.9 m)	3-4/3-4/3-4	pink	EM	compact grower; reddish indumentum
R. degronianum ssp. *heptamerum*	−15°F (−26°C)	3 ft. (0.9 m)	4/4/3	light pink	EM	compact, rounded growth habit; light indumentum on underside of leaf
R. degronianum ssp. *yakushimanum*	−20°F (−29°C)	1-4 ft. (0.3-1.2 m)	5/5/4	pink to white	EM	excellent growth habit; indumentum on underside of leaf
R. dichroanthum ssp. *scyphocalyx*	−10°F (−23°C)	4 ft. (1.2 m)	3/3/3	orange	ML	open, spreading growth habit

Table A1. Rhododendron species: elepidote (continued)

NAME	COLD HARDINESS	HEIGHT IN 10 YEARS	QUALITY RATING	FLOWER COLOR	FLOWERING SEASON	COMMENTS
R. discolor	−5°F (−21°C)	6 ft. (1.8 m)	3/3/4	white to pink	VL	upright growth habit; fragrant flowers
R. elegantulum	0°F (−18°C)	4 ft. (1.2 m)	3/5/3	pale purplish pink	M	brownish red indumentum
R. falconeri	10°F (−12°C)	5 ft. (1.5 m)	3/3/2	white to cream	EM	red-brown flaking bark; rusty indumentum
R. fortunei	−15°F (−26°C)	6 ft. (1.8 m)	4/4/4−5	pink to white	EM	treelike growth habit, beautiful, fragrant flowers
R. fortunei ssp. discolor (Houlstonii Group)	−5°F (−21°C)	5 ft. (1.5 m)	2−3/3/3	pink	M	upright, open growth habit, to 20 ft. (6 m) wide
R. fulgens	5°F (−15°C)	4 ft. (1.2 m)	3/4/2	scarlet	E-EM	tubular bell-shaped flowers; reddish brown indumentum
R. fulvum	0°F (−18°C)	4 ft. (1.2 m)	3/5/2	white	EM	bright cinnamon indumentum
R. griersonianum	10°F (−12°C)	3 ft. (0.9 m)	3/3/4	scarlet	L	narrow leaves; whitish indumentum
R. haematodes	−5°F (−21°C)	3 ft. (0.9 m)	3−4/4−5/4	crimson	EM	compact, excellent shrub; brown indumentum
R. hyperythrum (Creech's Narrowleaf Form)	−15°F (−26°C)	3 ft. (0.9 m)	3/4/3−4	white	EM	long, narrow leaf
R. insigne	0°F (−18°C)	3 ft. (0.9 m)	4/5/3	pinkish white	ML	slow growing; bell-shaped flowers
R. irroratum ssp. aberconwayi	0°F (−18°C)	3 ft. (0.9 m)	4/3/3	white	EM	open, upright growth habit
R. lacteum	−5°F (−21°C)	5 ft. (1.5 m)	4/3/2	pale yellow	EM	handsome foliage; best grafted
R. macabeanum	10°F (−12°C)	5 ft. (1.5 m)	5/5/3	creamy yellow	E	enormous foliage; woody; white indumentum
R. maximum	−25°F (−32°C)	5 ft. (1.5 m)	2/3/3−4	white	L-VL	large, open, upright growth habit
R. morii	−5°F (−21°C)	4 ft. (1.2 m)	3−4/4/3	white	EM	upright, open growth habit; bell-shaped flowers
R. neriiflorum	5°F (−15°C)	1.5 ft. (0.5 m)	3/3/3	scarlet	EM	dark green leaves; bell-shaped, fleshy flowers
R. orbiculare	5°F (−15°C)	3 ft. (0.9 m)	3/4/3	rose	EM	compact, well-shaped plant
R. oreodoxa	−5°F (−21°C)	5 ft. (1.5 m)	2−3/2−3/3	pink	E	open, upright growth habit
R. oreodoxa var. fargesii	−10°F (−23°C)	5 ft. (1.5 m)	3/3/3	white to pink	E	heavy bloomer; open, upright growth habit

Table A1. Rhododendron species: elepidote (continued)

NAME	COLD HARDINESS	HEIGHT IN 10 YEARS	QUALITY RATING	FLOWER COLOR	FLOWERING SEASON	COMMENTS
R. ovatum	5°F (−15°C)	3 ft. (0.9 m)	3/3/3	white to pink or purple	ML	dense growth habit; new growth red; gable form hardy to −10°F (−23°C) and superior
R. pachysanthum	−5°F (−21°C)	2.5 ft. (0.75 m)	3–4/5/3–4	light pink	EM	beautiful foliage plant; indumentum on underside of leaf
R. ponticum	−15°F (−26°C)	4 ft. (1.2 m)	2–4/4/4–5	purple to white	L	open, upright growth habit; excellent foliage
R. pseudo-chrysanthum (Nelson's Form)	−10°F (−23°C)	2 ft. (0.6 m)	3/4–5/4–5	pink	EM	compact grower; several forms available
R. roxieanum	−10°F (−23°C)	3 ft. (0.9 m)	3/5/4	white	EM	compact growth habit; heavy, cinnamon indumentum on underside
R. smirnowii	−15°F (−26°C)	3 ft. (0.9 m)	3/3–4/2–3	rose-purple	ML	open growth habit; beautiful tomentum and indumentum on leaf
R. smithii	5°F (−15°C)	4 ft. (1.2 m)	4/4/3	red	E	good plant habit; white indumentum on underside of leaf
R. souliei	5°F (−15°C)	5 ft. (1.5 m)	4/3/3	cream or pink	M	compact, upright growth habit
R. strigillosum	5°F (−15°C)	4 ft. (1.2 m)	5/4/4	blood red	E	red new growth indumentum
R. sutchuenense	−10°F (−23°C)	5 ft. (1.5 m)	4/3/3	lilac to rose	VE	open, upright growth habit
R. temenium	−5°F (−21°C)	1.5 ft. (0.5 m)	3/3	red crimson	EM	very compact growth habit; highly variable
R. thayerianum	0°F (−18°C)	5 ft. (1.5 m)	3/3/3	white or pink	VL	compact, upright
R. thomsonii	5°F (−15°C)	5 ft. (1.5 m)	3/2–4/3–4	blood red	EM	open, upright growth habit
R. vernicosum	−5°F (−21°C)	5 ft. (1.5 m)	2–3/2–3/3	pink	E-M	upright growth habit; 'Vernicosum 18139' is a good selection
R. wardii	0°F (−18°C)	4 ft. (1.2 m)	4/3–4/3–4	yellow	M	open growth habit; difficult to grow in some areas
R. wasonii	−5°F (−21°C)	4 ft. (1.2 m)	3/3/3	white, pink, or yellow	EM	dark shiny leaves; dark brown indumentum
R. williamsianum	−5°F (−21°C)	1.5 ft. (0.5 m)	3/4/4	pink	EM	compact growth habit; very lovely plant

Table A2. Rhododendron species: lepidote

NAME	COLD HARDINESS	HEIGHT IN 10 YEARS	QUALITY RATING	FLOWER COLOR	FLOWERING SEASON	COMMENTS
R. ambiguum	−5°F (−21°C)	5 ft. (1.5 m)	3/3/3	pale yellow	E-M	compact, upright habit
R. anthopogon	−5°F (−21°C)	1 ft. (0.3 m)	3/3/2	pink	E-EM	small, aromatic foliage; narrow tubular flowers
R. augustinii var. chasmanthum	−5°F (−21°C)	4 ft. (1.2 m)	4/3/3−4	purple or lavender	M	compact growth habit; long, narrow leaf
R. burmanicum	15°F (−9°C)	4 ft. (1.2 m)	4/3/4	yellow	EM	open, upright growth habit; fragrant flowers
R. calostrotum	−5°F (−21°C)	2 ft. (0.6 m)	4/4/2	purple crimson	M	saucer-shaped flowers; aromatic leaves
R. calostrotum ssp. keleticum	−15°F (−26°C)	1 ft. (0.3 m)	4/4/4	purplish crimson	M	semi-prostrate growth habit; good bonsai plant
R. calostrotum ssp. radicans	−10°F (−23°C)	3−6 ft. (0.9−1.8 m)	3/4/3	purple	EM	prostrate, creeping
R. campylogynum	−15°F (−26°C)	1 ft. (0.3 m)	3/3/3	white to red	EM	compact upright growth; bell-shaped flowers
R. cephalanthum	−5°F (−21°C)	2 ft. (0.6 m)	4/3/1−2	white, pink, or yellow	E-M	low spreading habit; small, aromatic leaves
R. ciliatum	5°F (−15°C)	3 ft. (0.9 m)	4/4/3−4	white and pink	EM	cinnamon-colored bark
R. cinnabarinum	5°F (−15°C)	5 ft. (1.5 m)	4/4/2−3	pink, red, or yellow	EM-VL	aromatic foliage
R. concinnum	−5°F (−21°C)	5 ft. (1.5 m)	4/3/3−4	white, purple	M	widely funnel-shaped flowers; treelike growth
R. dauricum	−25°F (−32°C)	4 ft. (1.2 m)	4/3/3	rose, purple, or white	VE	upright growth habit; also white form (album)
R. davidsonianum	0°F (−18°C)	6 ft. (1.8 m)	4/3/3	white, pink	EM	upright and open; trusses two to six flowers
R. fastigiatum	−15°F (−26°C)	1.5 ft. (0.5 m)	4/4/3−4	purple	M	many forms, some of which are excellent
R. ferrugineum	−15°F (−26°C)	2 ft. (0.6 m)	3/4/3	rose, pink, or white	M	requires excellent drainage; very attractive foliage
R. fletcherianum	5°F (−15°C)	30 in. (0.8 m)	4/4/4	lemon yellow	EM	bristly, hairy foliage; bronze leaves in winter
R. glaucophyllum	0°F (−18°C)	3 ft. (0.9 m)	3/2/3	white, pink	EM	dwarf, open habit; bell-shaped flowers
R. hippophaeoides	−25°F (−32°C)	3 ft. (0.9 m)	4/2−3/4	lavender-blue	E	best of the blues; tolerates sun
R. impeditum (syn. R. litangense)	−15°F (−26°C)	0.5−1 ft. (0.2−0.3 m)	4/4/3−4	purple	EM	compact growth habit; good groundcover

Table A2. Rhododendron species: lepidote

NAME	COLD HARDINESS	HEIGHT IN 10 YEARS	QUALITY RATING	FLOWER COLOR	FLOWERING SEASON	COMMENTS
R. johnstoneanum	15°F (−9°C)	4–12 ft. (1.2–3.6 m)	—	yellow to white	E-L	varies widely in bloom date
R. keiskei	−10°F (−23°C)	1–5 ft. (0.3–1.5 m)	4/3–4/4	yellow	EM	many forms, from the dwarf 'Yaku Fairy' to tall forms
R. lutescens	5°F (−15°C)	6 ft. (1.8 m)	4/3/3–4	yellow	EM	upright, open growth habit; new growth red
R. minus	−15°F (−26°C)	4 ft. (1.2 m)	2–3/2/2–3	white or pink	M-L	varies widely in growth habit
R. minus (Carolinianum Group)	−25°F (−32°C)	4 ft. (1.2 m)	3/3/2–3	rose, pink, or white	M	many-branched plant; sun tolerant
R. minus var. *chapmanii*	−5°F (−21°C)	4 ft. (1.2 m)	3/3/2–3	pink	EM	rounded growth habit; heat tolerant
R. moupinense	0°F (−18°C)	2 ft. (0.6 m)	4/3/3	white	VE	open growth habit; new growth is bronze-red
R. mucronulatum	−15°F (−26°C)	5 ft. (1.5 m)	3–4/3/3	pink to rose-purple	VE	upright growth habit; deciduous in cold areas
R. oreotrephes	0°F (−18°C)	5 ft. (1.5 m)	3/4/4	pink to lavender	EM	upright, tight grower; variable species
R. racemosum	−5°F (−21°C)	2–5 ft. (0.6–1.5 m)	4/3/4–5	rose or white	E-EM	upright, open growth habit; best in sun; variable in size
R. rigidum	−5°F (−21°C)	6 ft. (1.8 m)	4/3/4	white to pink	EM	funnel-shaped flowers; beautiful in flower
R. rubiginosum	0°F (−18°C)	6 ft. (1.8 m)	3/2–3/3–4	pink or rose	EM	open, upright growth habit; purplish new growth
R. russatum	−15°F (−26°C)	3 ft. (0.9 m)	4/3/4	purple, blue, or pink	EM	open, upright growth habit; variable in form
R. saluenense	−5°F (−21°C)	1.5 ft. (0.5 m)	4/3/4	purple	EM	small, mound shape; aromatic leaves
R. sargentianum 'Maricee'	−5°F (−21°C)	2 ft. (0.6 m)	4/3/2	white	M	easier, faster growing selection of *R. sargentianum*
R. triflorum	5°F (−15°C)	6 ft. (1.8 m)	2/2/3	yellow	ML	open, upright habit; beautiful peeling bark
R. veitchianum	20°F (−7°C)	4 ft. (1.2 m)	4/3/3	white	M-L	compact growth habit; fragrant flowers
R. yungningense	−15°F (−26°C)	2 ft. (0.6 m)	3/3/4	purple	EM	open, upright growth habit; tiny leaf, scaly on both sides
R. yunnanense	0°F (−18°C)	6 ft. (1.8 m)	4/2–3/3–4	white to pink	EM-M	open, upright growth habit; extremely variable

Table A3. Rhododendron hybrids: elepidote

NAME	COLD HARDINESS	HEIGHT IN 10 YEARS	QUALITY RATING	FLOWER COLOR	FLOWERING SEASON	COMMENTS
'A. Bedford'	–5°F (–21°C)	6 ft. (1.8 m)	4/3/5	mauve to lavender	ML	upright growth habit; sun tolerant
'Acclaim'	–5°F (–21°C)	5 ft. (1.5 m)	3/3	red	M	ball-shaped truss; flowers of good substance
'Albert Close'	–10°F (–23°C)	5 ft. (1.5 m)	3/2/3	rose	L	open growth habit; sun and heat tolerant
'Album Elegans'	–20°F (–29°C)	6 ft. (1.8 m)	2/2–3/4	white	L	open growth habit; good foliage
'Alice'	–5°F (–21°C)	6 ft. (1.8 m)	4/3–4/4–5	pink	M	upright growth habit; easy to grow; sun tolerant
'America'	–20°F (–29°C)	5 ft. (1.5 m)	3/2–3/3–4	red	ML	better plant habit in full sun
'Anah Kruschke'	–15°F (–26°C)	6 ft. (1.8 m)	3–4/4/4	lavender	ML-L	compact growth habit; does well in full sun
Anita Gehnrich'	–5°F (–21°C)	3.5 ft. (1.1 m)	—	deep pink	M	domed truss of 14 flowers
'Anna H. Hall'	–25°F (–32°C)	3 ft. (0.9 m)	3/3/4	white	M	semi-dwarf; good foliage
'Anna Rose Whitney'	–5°F (–21°C)	6 ft. (1.8 m)	4/3/5	pink	ML	vigorous, upright grower; well-shaped plant
'Antoon van Welie'	–5°F (–21°C)	6 ft. (1.8 m)	4/3–4/4	deep pink	ML	vigorous grower; attractive plant
'Apple Blossom' ('Sandwich Apple Blossom', 'Dexter's Pink')	–10°F (–23°C)	5 ft. (1.5 m)	—	pink	EM	floriferous
'Atroflo'	–5°F (–21°C)	5 ft. (1.5 m)	3/3–4/4	bright rose	M	fawn colored indumentum on underside of leaf
'Aunt Martha'	–10°F (–23°C)	5 ft. (1.5 m)	4/3	red	ML	dense foliage; purple, sun tolerant
'Autumn Gold'	–5°F (–21°C)	5 ft. (1.5 m)	3–4/3–4/4	salmon	ML	tolerates heat
'Avondale'	–5°F (–21°C)	5 ft. (1.5 m)	3/3	strong red	M	flowers of heavy substance; fragrant
'Baden Baden'	–15°F (–26°C)	2 ft. (0.6 m)	3–4/4/3–4	red	M	low growth habit; good foliage
'Ballad'	–15°F (–26°C)	3 ft. (0.9 m)	3/3	pale purple	ML	pyramidal trusses of 15 flowers
'Barmstedt'	–15°F (–26°C)	3 ft. (0.9 m)	—	rose red	M	very floriferous; silvery new growth
'Beaufort'	–20°F (–29°C)	5 ft. (1.5 m)	2–3/3–4/3	white	M	compact growth habit
'Beauty Master'	–10°F (–23°C)	6–8 ft. (1.8–2.4 m)	—	purplish red	M	star-shaped center in flower
'Beauty of Littleworth'	–5°F (–21°C)	6 ft. (1.8 m)	4/3	pink	M	vigorous, upright growth habit; large flowers

Table A3. Rhododendron hybrids: elepidote (continued)

NAME	COLD HARDINESS	HEIGHT IN 10 YEARS	QUALITY RATING	FLOWER COLOR	FLOWERING SEASON	COMMENTS
'Belle Heller'	−10°F (−23°C)	5 ft. (1.5 m)	4/3	white	M	good foliage plant; sun tolerant; sometimes flowers in the fall
'Bell Ringer'	0°F (−18°C)	3 ft. (0.9 m)	—	creamy white	M	well formed plant; floriferous
'Bellrose'	−15°F (−26°C)	5 ft. (1.5 m)	—	rose pink	M	tall, upright truss
'Ben Moseley'	−15°F (−26°C)	5 ft. (1.5 m)	—	purplish pink	ML	*R. fortunei* hybrid
'Besse Howells'	−15°F (−26°C)	3 ft. (0.9 m)	3−4/3−4/4	wine red	EM	compact, low-growing plant; frilled flowers
'Betty Hume'	−5°F (−21°C)	6 ft. (1.8 m)	4/3/3	pink	ML	frilled, scented flowers
'Big Deal'	−20°F (−29°C)	2 ft. (0.6 m)	—	pale ivory	ML	large ball trusses
'Blewbury'	0°F (−18°C)	2 ft. (0.6 m)	3/4/3	white	M	pale brown indumentum
'Blue Ensign'	−15°F (−26°C)	4 ft. (1.2 m)	4/3/4	lilac blue	M	well-shaped plant; sun tolerant
'Blue Peter'	−10°F (−23°C)	5 ft. (1.5 m)	4/2−3/4	lavender blue	M	spreading growth habit; heat and sun tolerant
'Bonfire'	−5°F (−21°C)	5 ft. (1.5 m)	3/3/4	orange red	ML	long, narrow leaves; loose truss
'Bonnie Maid'	−10°F (−23°C)	5 ft. (1.5 m)	—	pink	M	saucer-shaped flowers
'Bosley-Dexter 1009'	−25°F (−32°C)	7 ft. (2.1 m)	3/3	pink	M	very hardy Dexter Hybrid selection
'Boule de Neige'	−25°F (−32°C)	5 ft. (1.5 m)	4/4/3	white	M	well-shaped plant; heat and sun tolerant
'Bow Bells'	−5°F (−21°C)	3 ft. (0.9 m)	3/4/3	pink	EM	mound-shaped plant; needs afternoon shade
'Bravo'	−15°F (−26°C)	5 ft. (1.5 m)	—	purplish pink	ML	compact growth habit
'Britannia'	−5°F (−21°C)	4 ft. (1.2 m)	4/3−4/3	scarlet	ML	First Class Certificate 1937, RHS; large pendulous leaf
'Broughtonii Aureum'	−5°F (−21°C)	4 ft. (1.2 m)	3−4/2/4	yellow	ML	yellow azaleadron; sun and heat tolerant
'Brown Eyes'	−15°F (−26°C)	6 ft. (1.8 m)	—	pink	ML	prominent brown blotch in flowers
'Bruce Brechtbill'	0°F (−18°C)	4 ft. (1.2 m)	3/5/4	pink	EM	mounded plant habit
'Bud Flanagan'	−5°F (−21°C)	6 ft. (1.8 m)	—	mauve	ML	large conical trusses
'Burma'	−20°F (−29°C)	5 ft. (1.5 m)	4/4/4	red	ML	grows wider than tall
'Buttermint'	−5°F (−21°C)	3 ft. (0.9 m)	3−4/4/4	yellow	M	dense growing; thick leathery leaf; large flowers
'Cadis'	−15°F (−26°C)	5 ft. (1.5 m)	3/4/5	pink	ML	Award of Excellence, 1959; fragrant flowers
'Calsap'	−25°F (−32°C)	5 ft. (1.5 m)	—	white	L	dark purple blotch like 'Sappho', but a better plant habit

Table A3. Rhododendron hybrids: elepidote (continued)

NAME	COLD HARDINESS	HEIGHT IN 10 YEARS	QUALITY RATING	FLOWER COLOR	FLOWERING SEASON	COMMENTS
'Capistrano'	−20°F (−29°C)	5 ft. (1.5 m)	—	yellow	—	appears to be the best hardy yellow
'Carmen'	−5°F (−21°C)	1 ft. (0.3 m)	4/5/4	dark red	EM	very attractive plant
'Caroline'	−15°F (−26°C)	6 ft. (1.8 m)	3/4/4	orchid	ML	compact growth habit; easy to grow; fragrant flowers
'Casanova'	−25°F (−32°C)	4 ft. (1.2 m)	4/5/4	yellow	M	flowers have an orange flair
'Catawbiense Album'	−25°F (−32°C)	6 ft. (1.8 m)	3/3/4	white	ML-L	very vigorous and extremely cold hardy
'Catawbiense Boursault'	−20°F (−29°C)	6 ft. (1.8 m)	2/3	rose-lilac	ML-L	selection of *R. catawbiense*
'Chesterland'	−25°F (−32°C)	6 ft. (1.8 m)	—	pink	E	
'Chocheco Bright Star'	−25°F (−32°C)	5 ft. (1.8 m)	—	red	M	white star-shaped center in flower
'Chionoides'	−10°F (−23°C)	4 ft. (1.2 m)	3/4/4	white	ML	compact growth habit; tolerates sun and cold
'Christmas Cheer'	−10°F (−23°C)	4 ft. (1.2 m)	3/4/4	pink	VE-E	well-shaped plant; tight growth habit
'Countess of Athlone'	−10°F (−23°C)	6 ft. (1.8 m)	3/3/4	mauve	ML	dense, verticle trusses
'County of York'	−15°F (−26°C)	6 ft. (1.8 m)	3–4/3/4–5	white	M	vigorous growth habit; large leaves, especially in shade
'Crest' ('Hawk Crest')	−5°F (−21°C)	6 ft. (1.8 m)	4–5/3/3	yellow	M	open growth habit, exposing limbs as the plant gets older
'Cynthia'	−15°F (−26°C)	6 ft. (1.8 m)	4/3/4	rose	M	tall; excellent grower; sun and heat tolerant
'Daphnoides'	−15°F (−26°C)	4 ft. (1.2 m)	3/4/4	deep purple	ML	rolled glossy leaves
'David Gable'	−15°F (−26°C)	5 ft. (1.5 m)	4/4/3–4	pink	EM-M	large flowers with strawberry throat; good growth habit
'Day Dream'	5°F (−15°C)	5 ft. (1.5 m)	3/3/3	orange pink	ML	open growth habit
'Delp's Quest'	−10°F (−23°C)	3 ft. (0.9 m)	—	yellow	L	medium green foliage
'Desert Gold'	0°F (−18°C)	5 ft. (1.5 m)	5/4/4	golden	M	well-shaped plant
'Dexter 974'	−15°F (−26°C)	5 ft. (1.5 m)	4/4	deep pink	ML	outstanding plant; dependable bloomer
'Dexter's Champayne'	—	—	—	creamy apricot	M	medium to tall grower, wider than tall
'Dexter's Giant Red'	−5°F (−21°C)	6 ft. (1.8 m)	4/3/4	pink	L	dark red throat in flowers; large truss
'Dexter's Pink' see 'Apple Blossom'						
'Disca'	−10°F (−23°C)	6 ft. (1.8 m)	3/3/4	white	ML	compact growth habit; fragrant; best grown in afternoon shade
'Dolly Madison'	−20°F (−29°C)	5 ft. (1.5 m)	4/4/4	white	M	large foliage and flowers

ble A3. Rhododendron hybrids: elepidote (continued)

ME	COLD HARDINESS	HEIGHT IN 10 YEARS	QUALITY RATING	FLOWER COLOR	FLOWERING SEASON	COMMENTS
r. Edward Lufton'	−15°F (−26°C)	4 ft. (1.2 m)	—	white	M	excellent foliage; indumentum on underside of leaf; Pride Hybrid
r. H. C. Dresselhuys'	−15°F (−26°C)	6 ft. (1.8 m)	2/3	aniline red	M	upright growth habit; scant foliage
lith Pride'	−25°F (−32°C)	5 ft. (1.5 m)	2/4	pink	ML	well-branched plant; leaves hold three years
dmond Amateis'	−15°F (−26°C)	6 ft. (1.8 m)	4/4/4	white	M	red dorsal blotch
izabeth'	−20°F (−29°C)	3 ft. (0.9 m)	3–4/4/5	red	EM	outstanding plant, Award of Merit, First Class Certificate, ARS
izabeth Hobbie'	−5°F (−21°C)	2.5 ft. (0.8 m)	4/4–5/3	scarlet	EM	very compact and heavily foliaged plant
speth'	0°F (−18°C)	4 ft. (1.2 m)	3/4/3	scarlet to pink	EM	compact, upright plant
nglish Roseum'	−25°F (−32°C)	6 ft. (1.8 m)	2–3/3/3–4	rose	ML	compact plant habit; easy to grow under most conditions
ta Burrows'	5°F (−15°C)	6 ft. (1.8 m)	4/4/4	blood red	E	sensational foliage
verestianum'	−15°F (−26°C)	6 ft. (1.8 m)	2/3	lilac	ML	vigorous, full plant habit; widely adapted
bia'	5°F (−15°C)	3 ft. (0.9 m)	3/4/4	orange	M	a grex, so many forms and colors exist
aggetter's Favorite'	−5°F (−21°C)	6 ft. (1.8 m)	5/4/3	white and pink	M	outstanding plant
antastica'	−5°F (−21°C)	3 ft. (0.9 m)	4/4	rose red	ML	one of Hackman's best
istuosum Flore Pleno'	−15°F (−26°C)	6 ft. (1.8 m)	3/3	lavender blue	ML	semi-double flowers; sun tolerant
asher'	−10°F (−23°C)	6–8 ft. (1.8–2.4 m)	—	strong red	M	greenish yellow throat in flower
ancesca'	−10°F (−23°C)	6 ft. (1.8 m)	—	deep red	ML	open growth habit
angrantissimum'	15°F (−9°C)	3 ft. (0.9 m)	4/2/4	white E	M	tender, leggy plant
host'	−10°F (−23°C)	4–5 ft. (1.2–1.5 m)	—	white	M	outstanding foliage
igi'	−5°F (−21°C)	5 ft. (1.5 m)	4/3	rose red	ML	compact growth habit; red spotting on flowers
ilbert Myers'	−10°F (−23°C)	4 ft. (1.2 m)	—	light purple	EM	dense, good foliage
ladys' ('Gladys Rose', ary Swathling')	0°F (−18°C)	6 ft. (1.8 m)	3/3	cream	EM	tall, open plant
olden Gate'	−5°F (−21°C)	3 ft. (0.9 m)	3/4/4	orange	M	compact growth habit
olden Star'	0°F (−18°C)	5 ft. (1.5 m)	4/3–4/3–4	deep yellow	ML	
oldsworth Orange'	−5°F (−21°C)	5 ft. (1.5 m)	3/2	pale orange	L	open, spreading plant; heat tolerant

Table A3. Rhododendron hybrids: elepidote (continued)

NAME	COLD HARDINESS	HEIGHT IN 10 YEARS	QUALITY RATING	FLOWER COLOR	FLOWERING SEASON	COMMENTS
'Goldsworth Yellow'	−15°F (−26°C)	5 ft. (1.5 m)	3/3/3	yellow	ML	dense growth habit
'Golfer'	−15°F (−26°C)	1 ft. (0.3 m)	4/5	pink	M	twice as wide as high; good indumentum on underside of leaf
'Gomer Waterer'	−15°F (−26°C)	6 ft. (1.8 m)	3/4–5/4–5	white	ML	good foliage plant; sun tolerant
'Grace Seabrook'	−5°F (−21°C)	4 ft. (1.2 m)	4–5/4/4	red	E-EM	excellent foliage; good plant habit
'Great Eastern'	−15°F (−26°C)	5 ft. (1.5 m)	3/4	pink	ML	free-flowering R. fortunei hybrid; fragrant
'Great Smokey'	−15°F (−26°C)	6 ft. (1.8 m)	−	mauve pink	LM	tall, vigorous grower
'Gretsel'	−5°F (−21°C)	3 ft. (0.9 m)	4/4/3	pastel pink	M	dark green foliage; salmon edge on flowers
'Grierosplendour'	−5°F (−21°C)	4 ft. (1.2 m)	3/3/4	reddish purple	ML	upright grower when young; spreads as it gets older
'Grumpy'	−10°F (−23°C)	3 ft. (0.9 m)	4/4/4	yellow	M	dark green foliage
'Halfdan Lem'	−5°F (−21°C)	5 ft. (1.5 m)	4–5/4/4–5	red	M	fast grower; good plant habit
'Hallelujah'	−15°F (−26°C)	4 ft. (1.2 m)	4–5/5/4–5	rose red	M	excellent foliage; compact growth habit
'Hansel'	−5°F (−21°C)	3 ft. (0.9 m)	4/4/3	salmon	M	good foliage with buff-colored indumentum
'Hardy Giant'	−5°F (−21°C)	6 ft. (1.8 m)	−	white	ML	large leaves
'Helene Schiffner'	−5°F (−21°C)	4 ft. (1.2 m)	4/4/3–4	white	M	plant heavily clothed with narrow leaves and red stem
'Hello Dolly'	−10°F (−23°C)	3 ft. (0.9 m)	3–4/3/3–4	yellow and orange	EM	well-branched plant; light indumentum on underside of leaf
'Henry's Red'	−25°F (−32°C)	5 ft. (1.5 m)	3/3/4	dark red	M	open habit
'Hong Kong'	−20°F (−29°C)	5 ft. (1.5 m)	3/3/3	yellow	ML	glossy green leaves
'Hotei'	5°F (−15°C)	3 ft. (0.9 m)	5/4/3	canary yellow	M	compact growth habit; prone to root rot
'Ice Cube'	−20°F (−29°C)	5 ft. (1.5 m)	4/3/4	white	ML	good growth habit; reliable and easy grower
'Jan Dekens'	−5°F (−21°C)	5 ft. (1.5 m)	3–4/3–4/3	bright pink	ML	vigorous grower; frilled flowers
'Janet Blair'	−15°F (−26°C)	6 ft. (1.8 m)	4/3/4	light pink	ML	excellent growth habit; easy to grow, widely adapted
'Jean Marie de Montague'	−5°F (−21°C)	5 ft. (1.5 m)	4/4/4	bright red	M	good foliage plant; sun tolerant
'Jock'	−5°F (−21°C)	3 ft. (0.9 m)	3/3/4	rosy pink	EM	low mounding habit

able A3. Rhododendron hybrids: elepidote (continued)

AME	COLD HARDINESS	HEIGHT IN 10 YEARS	QUALITY RATING	FLOWER COLOR	FLOWERING SEASON	COMMENTS
oe Paterno'	–35°F (–37°C)	4 ft. (1.2 m)	—	white	LM	compact growth habit; extremely cold hardy
ate Waterer'	–10°F (–23°C)	5 ft. (1.5 m)	2/3/3	pink	ML	compact upright grower; bright yellow eye in flowers
atherine Dalton'	–15°F (–26°C)	5 ft. (1.5 m)	3/4/3	light pink	M	a good Gable Hybrid
en Janeck'	–15°F (–26°C)	3 ft. (0.9 m)	5/5/4	pink	M	probably a *yakushimanum* × *smirnowii* cross
avender Girl'	–5°F (–21°C)	5 ft. (1.5 m)	3/4/4	orchid	M	glossy foliage on a good plant habit
avender Princess'	–15°F (–21°C)	4 ft. (1.2 m)	3/4/5	lavender pink	ML	compact plant; dark leaves
ee's Dark Purple'	–15°F (–26°C)	6 ft. (1.8 m)	2–3/3–4/4	purple	ML	outstanding foliage plant; reliable grower
emon Ice', see 'Chionoides'						
em's Cameo'	5°F (–15°C)	5 ft. (1.5 m)	5/3/3	apricot	M	outstanding foliage; Superior Plant Award, 1971
em's Monarch'	–5°F (–21°C)	6 ft. (1.8 m)	4/4/4	pink	M	outstanding flower truss
em's Storm Cloud'	–15°F (–26°C)	5 ft. (1.5 m)	—	glossy red	ML	perfect truss; paler in center
etty Edwards'	0°F (–18°C)	5 ft. (1.5 m)	3/3/3	pale yellow	M	medium to large leaves; rounded truss
Loderi King George'	5°F (–15°C)	6 ft. (1.8 m)	4/4/4	white	M	fragrant; becomes huge
oder's White'	0°F (–18°C)	5 ft. (1.5 m)	4/3–4/3–4	white	M	large, upright truss; Award of Merit, Award of Garden Merit, ARS
odestar'	–20°F (–29°C)	5 ft. (1.5 m)	3/3/4	white	ML	large, vigorous grower; flower buds open pale lilac
Madame Masson'	–15°F (–26°C)	5 ft. (1.5 m)	3/3/4	white	M	large growing, well-shaped plant; golden eye in flowers
Marcia'	0°F (–18°C)	4 ft. (1.2 m)	4/3/2	yellow	M	slow, upright grower; needs afternoon shade
Mardi Gras'	0°F (–18°C)	30 in. (0.8 m)	4/4/4	pink white	M	large leaves; 3-in. (7.5-cm) flowers
Marinus Koster'	–5°F (–21°C)	6 ft. (1.8 m)	4/3/4	deep pink	M	upright, large plant
Markeeta's Flame'	–5°F (–21°C)	5 ft. (1.5 m)	4/4/4	rose red	M	vigorous grower, good plant form; red leaf stems
Markeeta's Prize'	–5°F (–21°C)	5 ft. (1.5 m)	5/4/4	bright red	M	vigorous grower, good plant form; huge flower truss
Mary Belle'	–15°F (–26°C)	5 ft. (1.5 m)	3–4/3–4/4	pink to peach	M	more yellow than most yellow-flowered forms of similar hardiness
Masterblend'	–10°F (–23°C)	6–8 ft. (1.8–2.4 m)	—	pink with darker throat	M	long blooming period

Table A3. Rhododendron hybrids: elepidote (continued)

NAME	COLD HARDINESS	HEIGHT IN 10 YEARS	QUALITY RATING	FLOWER COLOR	FLOWERING SEASON	COMMENTS
'Maxecat'	−25°F (−32°C)	6 ft. (1.8 m)	—	pink	L	good woodland plant
'Maximum Roseum'	−25°F (−32°C)	6 ft. (1.8 m)	—	pinkish lilac	L-M	long, narrow leaf
'May Day'	5°F (−15°C)	3 ft. (0.9 m)	3/3/4	orange scarlet	EM	vigorous with attractive foliage
'Medusa'	−5°F (−21°C)	3 ft. (0.9 m)	3/3/3	orange	M	light indumentum on underside of leaf
'Mist Maiden'	−25°F (−32°C)	4 ft. (1.2 m)	5/5/4	pink to white	EM	one of the best *yakushimanum* cultivars; drought tolerant
'Moonstone'	−5°F (−21°C)	3 ft. (0.9 m)	3–4/4/3	cream	EM	compact growth habit
'Moser's Maroon'	−10°F (−23°C)	5 ft. (1.5 m)	2/3/4	wine red	ML	small trusses
'Mrs. A. T. de la Mare'	−15°F (−26°C)	5 ft. (1.5 m)	3/3	white	M	large flower truss; tolerates exposure
'Mrs. Betty Robertson'	−5°F (−21°C)	4 ft. (1.2 m)	3/3/3	cream	M	compact growth habit; red blotch in flowers
'Mrs. Charles S. Sargent'	−25°F (−32°C)	6 ft. (1.8 m)	3/3/4	rose pink	ML	easy to grow
'Mrs. E. C. Sterling'	−5°F (−21°C)	6 ft. (1.8 m)	4/3/3–4	white	L	upright grower; long, narrow foliage
'Mrs. Furnivall'	−15°F (−26°C)	4 ft. (1.2 m)	5/3–4/3–4	light pink	M	prominent, deep pink blotch in flowers
'Mrs. G. W. Leak'	0°F (−18°C)	6 ft. (1.8 m)	4/3/4	light pink	EM	tall, vigorous growth habit
'Mrs. J. G. Millais'	−5°F (−21°C)	6 ft. (1.8 m)	5/3/4	white	ML	magnificent flowers, gold blotch
'Mrs. Tom H. Lowinsky'	−15°F (−26°C)	5 ft. (1.5 m)	4/3/4	white	L	compact plant, vigorous growth; striking orange blotch in flowers
'Mrs. W. C. Slocock'	−5°F (−21°C)	—	—	apricot pink	M	Award of Merit, 1929, RHS
'Mrs. W. R. Coe'	−5°F (−21°C)	6 ft. (1.8 m)	3/4/3	pink	ML	shiny dark green foliage; huge truss
'Nancy Evans'	5°F (−15°C)	3 ft. (0.9 m)	5/4/3	yellow	M	free-flowering; beautiful flowers
'Nepal'	−25°F (−32°C)	6 ft. (1.8 m)	4/4/4	white	M	outstanding plant and flower
'Newburyport Belle'	−20°F (−29°C)	4 ft. (1.2 m)	—	pink	E	
'Nova Zembla'	−25°F (−32°C)	5 ft. (1.5 m)	3/3/4	red	M	good growth habit for a red rhododendron; requires good soil drainage
'Odee Wright'	−5°F (−21°C)	4 ft. (1.2 m)	4/4/3–4	yellow	M	compact grower; dark green shiny leaves; large trusses
'Old Copper'	−5°F (−21°C)	5 ft. (1.5 m)	4/4/4	orange	L	good foliage; heat tolerant
'Old Port'	−15°F (−26°C)	5 ft. (1.5 m)	3/3–4/4	purple	M	vigorous grower

Table A3. Rhododendron hybrids: elepidote (continued)

NAME	COLD HARDINESS	HEIGHT IN 10 YEARS	QUALITY RATING	FLOWER COLOR	FLOWERING SEASON	COMMENTS
'Olin O. Dobbs'	−15°F (−26°C)	4 ft. (1.2 m)	5/3/3–4	reddish purple	M	flowers heavy and displayed in large, cone-shaped truss
'Olympic Lady'	−5°F (−21°C)	3 ft. (0.9 m)	3–4/4/4	white	EM	compact growth habit; very floriferous
'Pana'	−15°F (−26°C)	4 ft. (1.2 m)	—	red pink	L	flowers have a white throat
'Parker's Pink'	−15°F (−26°C)	5 ft. (1.5 m)	4/3/3	pink	ML	fragrant flowers, fade to white in center
'Parson's Gloriosum'	−25°F (−32°C)	5 ft. (1.5 m)	2/2/3	lavender	ML	hardy, vigorous, compact plant
'Party Pink'	−20°F (−29°C)	5 ft. (1.5 m)	5/5/4	pink	ML	one of the very few with a 5/5 rating
'Pearce's American Beauty'	−15°F (−26°C)	6 ft. (1.8 m)	4/4	deep red	VL	ball-shaped trusses; very showy flowers
'Percy Wiseman'	5°F (−15°C)	3 ft. (0.9 m)	—	peach	M	compact grower; vigorous and floriferous
'Persia'	−20°F (−29°C)	5 ft. (1.5 m)	4/4	light pink	ML	conical spreading plant
'Peter Vermeulen'	−25°F (−32°C)	4 ft. (1.2 m)	—	pink	M	shiny, deep green foliage
'Phyllis Korn'	−10°F (−23°C)	5 ft. (1.5 m)	—	white	M	nice foliage
'Pink Fondant'	−15°F (−26°C)	5 ft. (1.5 m)	—	pink	ML	very good foliage; flowers of heavy substance
'Pink Pearl'	−5°F (−21°C)	6 ft. (1.8 m)	3/3/3	pink	M	one of best pinks; has won many awards
'Pink Scallop'	—	—	—	—	—	striking pink blotch on upper lobe
'Pink Walloper'	−5°F (−21°C)	6 ft. (1.8 m)	4–5/4–5/4	pink	M	huge trusses; reddish leaf stem; may be same as 'Lem's Monarch'
'Platinum Pearl'	−10°F (−23°C)	6 ft. (1.8 m)	4/4/4	pink	ML	strong grower with huge trusses; grows in shade
'Polar Bear'	−5°F (−21°C)	6 ft. (1.8 m)	3/3/4	white	L-VL	large fragrant flowers with green throat
'Purple Splendor'	−5°F (−21°C)	5 ft. (1.5 m)	4/3/3	purple	ML	good growth habit; excellent foliage; Award of Merit winner
'Purpureum Elegans'	−25°F (−32°C)	5 ft. (1.5 m)	2/3	bluish purple	ML	old ironclad; good plant
'Queen Nefertite'	0°F (−18°C)	5 ft. (1.5 m)	3/4	neyron rose	M	ball-shaped truss
'Redder Yet'	−25°F (−32°C)	5 ft. (1.5 m)	—	red	ML	introduced about 1988; not widely distributed
'Red Hot Mamma'	−15°F (−26°C)	8 ft. (2.4 m)	—	bright cerise	L	good plant habit
'Red River'	−20°F (−29°C)	5 ft. (1.5 m)	—	bright red	L	flowers have a white throat

Table A3. Rhododendron hybrids: elepidote (continued)

NAME	COLD HARDINESS	HEIGHT IN 10 YEARS	QUALITY RATING	FLOWER COLOR	FLOWERING SEASON	COMMENTS
'Rhody Romance'	−10°F (−23°C)	8 ft. (2.4 m)	—	pink and white	M	outstanding foliage
'Ring of Fire'	0°F (−18°C)	4 ft. (1.2 m)	4/4	yellow ringed in red	M-ML	vigorous, compact plant
'Rochelle'	−10°F (−23°C)	4 ft. (1.2 m)	4/4/4	rose	ML	outstanding truss
'Rocket'	−15°F (−26°C)	5 ft. (1.5 m)	3/4–5/5	pink	M	full foliage
'Roseum Elegans'	−25°F (−32°C)	6 ft. (1.8 m)	2/3/4	rosy lilac	ML	dependable in heat or cold
'Roseum Pink'	−25°F (−32°C)	6 ft. (1.8 m)	2/3/3	pink	ML	dependable in heat or cold
'Roseum Superbrum'	−20°F (−29°C)	6 ft. (1.8 m)	2/3	pink	ML	good plant habit
'Rothenburg'	−10°F (−23°C)	4 ft. (1.2 m)	3/4	light yellow	EM	glossy, green foliage
'Ruby Bowman'	−5°F (−21°C)	5 ft. (1.5 m)	4/4/4	rose pink	M	formal habit
'Ruby Hart'	0°F (−18°C)	2 ft. (0.6 m)	4–5/4–5/5	red	EM	compact, tightly foliaged plant
'Russell Harmon'	−25°F (−32°C)	6 ft. (1.8 m)	4/3	pink	L	large, vigorous grower
'Sappho'	−20°F (−29°C)	6 ft. (1.8 m)	3/2/4	white	M	open growth habit; prominent purple blotch in flowers
'Scarlet Romance'	−25°F (−32°C)	4 ft. (1.2 m)	—	red	L	spreading habit
'Scarlet Wonder'	−15°F (−26°C)	2 ft. (0.6 m)	4/4–5/4	red	M	low, compact plant; outstanding foliage; prefers sun
'Scintillation'	−15°F (−26°C)	5 ft. (1.5 m)	4/4/4–5	pink	M	outstanding foliage plant; beautiful flower
'Scintillation' (Melquist Form)	−25°F (−32°C)	6 ft. (1.8 m)	4/4/4	deep pink	M	more cold hardy than the other 'Scintillation'
'September Song'	0°F (−18°C)	4 ft. (1.2 m)	4–5/4	orange	M	beautiful flowers for milder climates
'Sham's Candy'	−20°F (−29°C)	5 ft. (1.5 m)	3/3/3	deep pink	ML	tight, conical truss
'Sham's Ruby'	−20°F (−29°C)	3 ft. (0.9 m)	3/3/3	red	ML	upright, semi-dwarf
'Shawme Lake'	−5°F (−21°C)	6 ft. (1.8 m)	—	rosy lavender	M	open truss, lovely flower; Dexter Hybrid
'Shaazam'	−10°F (−23°C)	4 ft. (1.2 m)	—	neyron rose	M	ball-shaped truss
'Shrimp Girl'	0°F (−18°C)	3 ft. (0.9 m)	3/3/3	rose	M	good foliage; compact plant habit
'Sir Charles Lemon'	5°F (−15°C)	5 ft. (1.5 m)	4/5/3	white	EM	outstanding foliage; cinnamon-brown indumentum on underside of leaf
'Sir Robert Peel'	5°F (−15°C)	5 ft. (1.5 m)	—	crimson	VE	vigorous plant; heat tolerant
'Solidarity'	−15°F (−26°C)	3 ft. (0.9 m)	4/4	pink	M	large trusses; dense plant
'Spring Parade'	−20°F (−29°C)	4 ft. (1.2 m)	3/2/3–4	scarlet	M	recurved, dark green leaf; upright grower

Table A3. Rhododendron hybrids: elepidote (continued)

NAME	COLD HARDINESS	HEIGHT IN 10 YEARS	QUALITY RATING	FLOWER COLOR	FLOWERING SEASON	COMMENTS
'Summer Summit'	−20°F (−29°C)	11 ft. (3.3 m) in 20 years	—	pink to white	VL	dense foliage
'Susan'	−5°F (−21°C)	6 ft. (1.8 m)	4/4–5/4	violet blue	M	excellent plant habit; fast grower
'Taurus'	−5°F (−21°C)	6 ft. (1.8 m)	4–5/4/4	red	EM	vigorous, fully clothed plant; leaves hold three years
'Teddy Bear'	0°F (−18°C)	3 ft. (0.9 m)	4/5/4	pink	EM	compact grower; shiny, dark green foliage
'Temple Belle'	−5°F (−21°C)	3 ft. (0.9 m)	3/4/3	pink	M	loose truss
'Terrific'	−25°F (−32°C)	—	—	deep pink	M	good foliage; very floriferous and reliable; Pride Hybrid
'Tiana'	−5°F (−21°C)	4 ft. (1.2 m)	—	white	M	burgundy blotch
'Tidbit'	5°F (−15°C)	5 ft. (1.5 m)	3/4	red to yellow	M	vigorous plant; free-flowering
'Todmorden'	−10°F (−23°C)	5 ft. (1.5 m)	3–4/3/3–4	pink	ML	vigorous plant; bicolor flower, pink fading to nearly white in center
'Tom Everett'	−5°F (−21°C)	4 ft. (1.2 m)	—	pink	M	large, dark green foliage and a huge, perfect truss
'Tony'	−15°F (−26°C)	4 ft. (1.2 m)	3/4/4	red	M	low-growing, attractive plant
'Tortoiseshell Wonder'	−5°F (−21°C)	4 ft. (1.2 m)	4/3/3	salmon	ML	salmon-pink blend in flowers
'Trilby'	−15°F (−26°C)	5 ft. (1.5 m)	3/4/4	crimson	ML	red stems add to an already beautiful plant
'Trinity'	−25°F (−32°C)	2.5 ft. (0.8 m)	4/4	white	ML	uniform growth habit; leaves hold three years
'Trojan Warrior'	−15°F (−26°C)	4 ft. (1.2 m)	—	red	ML	low, compact grower
'Trude Webster'	−10°F (−23°C)	5 ft. (1.5 m)	5/4/4–5	pink	M	huge trusses and attractive foliage; ARS Superior Plant Award, 1971
'Unique'	−5°F (−21°C)	4 ft. (1.2 m)	3/4–5/4	pink to cream	EM	rounded plant habit
'Van'	−5°F (−21°C)	6 ft. (1.8 m)	3–4/4/4	deep pink	ML	excellent foliage plant; very floriferous
'Vanessa'	5°F (−15°C)	5 ft. (1.5 m)	3/3/3	pink	ML	handsome lax trusses
'Vanessa Pastel'	5°F (−15°C)	5 ft. (1.5 m)	3/3/3	cream pink	ML	deeper pink in throat
'Vernus'	−25°F (−32°C)	5 ft. (1.5 m)	3/3/4	pale pink	VE	one of the earliest large-leaved rhododendrons to flower
'Virginia Richards'	0°F (−18°C)	4 ft. (1.2 m)	4/4/4	pink to yellow	M	compact growth habit
'Vulcan'	−15°F (−26°C)	5 ft. (1.5 m)	4/4/4	red	ML	several forms available

Table A3. Rhododendron hybrids: elepidote (continued)

NAME	COLD HARDINESS	HEIGHT IN 10 YEARS	QUALITY RATING	FLOWER COLOR	FLOWERING SEASON	COMMENTS
'Vulcan's Flame'	−15°F (−26°C)	5 ft. (1.5 m)	4/4/4	bright red	ML	the reverse cross of 'Vulcan' and nearly identical
'Westbury'	−10°F (−23°C)	4 ft. (1.2 m)	—	purplish pink	M	slow growing; spreading; fragrant flowers
'Wheatley'	−15°F (−26°C)	6 ft. (1.8 m)	3–4/4/4	pink	M	outstanding plant and flower
'White Pearl'	5°F (−15°C)	6 ft. (1.8 m)	3/3–4/4–5	white	M	vigorous, upright growth habit
'White Peter'	−25°F (−32°C)	4 ft. (1.2 m)	—	white	M	compact; glossy dark green foliage
'Willard'	−10°F (−23°C)	4 ft. (1.2 m)	—	purplish red	M	wider than tall
'Winsome'	0°F (−18°C)	3 ft. (0.9 m)	3–4/4/4	rose	EM	compact plant
'Wojnar's Purple'	−20°F (−29°C)	3 ft. (0.9 m)	—	reddish purple	ML	compact plant
'Wyandanch Pink'	−15°F (−26°C)	6 ft. (1.8 m)	—	vivid pink	M	excellent foliage; sun tolerant; Dexter Hybrid
'Yaku King'	−10°F (−23°C)	3 ft. (0.9 m)	—	deep pink	ML	semi-dwarf *R. yakushimanum* hybrid; good landscape plant
'Yaku Prince'	−10°F (−23°C)	3 ft. (0.9 m)	—	pink	ML	semi-dwarf *R. yakushimanum* hybrid; good landscape plant
'Yaku Queen'	−10°F (−23°C)	3 ft. (0.9 m)	—	pink	ML	semi-dwarf *R. yakushimanum* hybrid; good landscape plant; pink flowers fade to white; glossy foliage; larger than 'Yaku Duchess', 'Yaku King', or 'Yaku Prince'
'Years of Peace'	−15°F (−26°C)	5 ft. (1.5 m)	2/4/4	clear pink	M	vigorous grower; sun tolerant flowers

Table A4. Rhododendron hybrids: lepidote

NAME	COLD HARDINESS	HEIGHT IN 10 YEARS	QUALITY RATING	FLOWER COLOR	FLOWERING SEASON	COMMENTS
'Aglo'	−25°F (−32°C)	4 ft. (1.2 m)	—	bright pink	E	good plant habit; sun tolerant
'Airy Fairy'	0°F (−18°C)	4 ft. (1.2 m)	3/3/3	pink	E	pink flowers spotted red in the throat
'Alfred Wiacek'	−20°F (−29°C)	2.5 ft. (0.8 m)	4/3	lavender pink	EM	rivals 'P.J.M.' in growth habit and flower
'Alice Swift'	−15°F (−26°C)	3 ft. (0.9 m)	—	pink	EM	upright plant habit; very floriferous
'Alison Johnstone'	0°F (−18°C)	5 ft. (1.5 m)	4/3/3	golden amber	EM	keep roots cool; Award of Merit, 1945
'Ambie'	−20°F (−29°C)	3 ft. (0.9 m)	—	white and pink	M	white flowers, one lobe pink
'Anna Baldsiefen'	−20°F (−29°C)	3 ft. (0.9 m)	3/3	phlox pink	E	very free-flowering
'April Blush'	−25°F (−32°C)	2 ft. (0.6 m)	—	pink	E	frequently deciduous
'April Gem'	−20°F (−29°C)	4 ft. (1.2 m)	4/4/4	white	E	double flower; Mehlquist Hybrid
'April Rose'	−25°F (−32°C)	3 ft. (0.9 m)	4/4/4	rose	VE	abundant double flowers
'April Snow'	−18°F (−28°C)	3 ft. (0.9 m)	4/3–4	white	EM	double white flowers
'April White'	−25°F (−32°C)	3 ft. (0.9 m)	4/4/4	white	EM	semi-double flowers; compact plant
'Balta'	−25°F (−32°C)	3 ft. (0.9 m)	—	pink to white	E	very floriferous
'Barto Alpine'	−10°F (−23°C)	3ft. (0.9 m)	3/4/3	rose	EM	dense, upright growth habit; needs good drainage and moisture
'Blaney's Blue'	−5°F (−21°C)	4 ft. (1.2 m)	4/4/4	blue	EM	vigorous grower and very floriferous
'Blue Bird' ('Bluebird')	0°F (−18°C)	3 ft. (0.9 m)	4/3	blue	EM	finely textured; performs best in full sun
'Blue Diamond'	−5°F (−21°C)	3 ft. (0.9 m)	4/4/4	blue	EM	well shaped and dense; best in sun
'Blue Ridge'	−12°F (−24°C)	2 ft. (0.6 m)	— v	iolet	M	well-branched, rounded plant; fragrant foliage
'Blue Tit'	−5°F (−21°C)	3 ft. (0.9 m)	3/4/4	gray blue	EM	very compact plant
'Bo-Peep'	5°F (−15°C)	4 ft. (1.2 m)	3/3/3	yellow	E	low, open growing
'Bric-a-brac'	0°F (−18°C)	2.5 ft. (0.8 m)	3/3/3	pink and white	VE	fuzzy, attractive leaves
'California Blue'	−5°F (−21°C)	4 ft. (1.2 m)	4/4	blue	EM	flowers heavily
'Carita'	5°F (−15°C)	4–5 ft. (1.2–1.5 m)	4/4/3	yellow	M	good plant habit
'Carolina Rose'	−10°F (−23°C)	3 ft. (0.9 m)	—	pink	M	well-branched azaleadron
'Checkmate' ('P.J.M. Checkmate')	−25°F (−32°C)	3 ft. (0.9 m)	—	lavender pink	E	the most dwarf 'P.J.M.'

Table A4. Rhododendron hybrids: lepidote (continued)

NAME	COLD HARDINESS	HEIGHT IN 10 YEARS	QUALITY RATING	FLOWER COLOR	FLOWERING SEASON	COMMENTS
'Chick'	−5°F (−21°C)	3 ft. (0.9 m)	3/−/−	pale yellow	EM	loses most of its leaves in winter
'Chikor'	0°F (−18°C)	1.5 ft. (0.5 m)	4–5/4/3	yellow	EM	requires light and well-drained soil
'Conewago'	−25°F (−32°C)	5 ft. (1.5 m)	3/2/3	rose	E	open growth habit; a reliable grower
'Cornell Pink', see *R. mucronulatum* 'Cornell Pink'						
'Crater Lake'	−5°F (−21°C)	4 ft. (1.2 m)	4/4/4	violet blue	EM	upright growth habit; new growth yellow
'Cream Crest'	0°F (−18°C)	3 ft. (0.9 m)	3/4/3	cream	EM	compact growth habit; does well in full sun
'Curlew'	−5°F (−21°C)	1.5 ft. (0.5 m)	4/5/3	bright yellow	EM	beautiful flowers; fertilize sparingly
'Donna Totten'	−5°F (−21°C)	4 ft. (1.2 m)	3/4/3	pink	EM	attractive foliage
'Dora Amateis'	−15°F (−26°C)	3 ft. (0.9 m)	4/4/4	white	EM	excellent growth habit, Award of Excellence, ARS; Award of Merit, RHS, 1976; First Class Certificate, RHS 1981
'Early Bird'	−10°F (−23°C)	5 ft. (1.5 m)	—	lavender	E	spreading growth habit
'Elsie Frye'	15°F (−9°C)	4 ft. (1.2 m)	5/3	white	E	good foliage; fragrant
'Epoch'	−10°F (−23°C)	3 ft. (0.9 m)	3/3/2–3	white	M	flowers have strong substance
'Ethel Mae'	−10°F (−23°C)	4 ft. (1.2 m)	—	lavender pink	E	bell-shaped flowers held in large groups
'Fairy Mary'	−15°F (−26°C)	2 ft. (0.6 m)	—	white and pink	EM	excellent plant; hardiest of the 'Yaku Fairy' hybrids
'Fasia'	−15°F (−26°C)	3 ft. (0.9 m)	—	lavender	E	Delp Hybrid
'Forsterianum'	20°F (−7°C)	5 ft. (1.5 m)	4/4/4	white	EM	upright growth habit; large flowers
'Fragrantissimum'	15°F (−9°C)	3 ft. (0.9 m)	4/2–3/4	white	EM	leggy growth habit; very fragrant flowers
'Ginny Gee'	−15°F (−26°C)	2 ft. (0.6 m)	—	pink	EM	very tight, compact grower
'Goldstrike'	0°F (−18°C)	4 ft. (1.2 m)	4/4/3	yellow	M	outstanding plant; tubular flowers of heavy substance
'Hudson Bay'	−20°F (−29°C)	3 ft. (0.9 m)	—	white	E	well-branched, rounded plant
'Gristedi'	−5°F (−21°C)	3 ft. (0.9 m)	3/3/3	bluish lavender	M	excellent plant habit
'Jenny' ('Creeping Jenny')	−5°F (−21°C)	2 ft. (0.6 m)	3/4	bright red	EM	small leaves
'Ivory Coast'	−25°F (−29°C)	4 ft. (1.2 m)	3/3/3	ivory to white	VE	compact, upright grower

able A4. Rhododendron hybrids: lepidote (continued)

AME	COLD HARDINESS	HEIGHT IN 10 YEARS	QUALITY RATING	FLOWER COLOR	FLOWERING SEASON	COMMENTS
ady Chamberlain'	10°F (–12°C)	5 ft. (1.5 m)	4/3/2–3	salmon	ML	upright growth habit; flowers of heavy substance
anny's Pride'	–15°F (–26°C)	5 ft. (1.5 m)	—	purple	EM	vigorous, upright growth habit; easily pruned
aurie'	–20°F (–29°C)	2 ft. (0.6 m)	—	pink to white	EM	slow-growing, spreading plant
emon Mist'	10°F (–12°C)	3 ft. (0.9 m)	3/4/4	greenish yellow	EM	compact growth habit; Award of Excellence, ARS, 1969
ittle Olga'	–24°F (–31°C)	3 ft. (0.9 m)	—	clear pink	E	blooms just after 'P.J.M.'
lenroc'	–15°F (–26°C)	4 ft. (1.2 m)	—	light pink	E	upright growth habit
Malta'	–25°F (–32°C)	4 ft. (1.2 m)	—	light purple	EM	Leach Hybrid; twiggy; red stems
Manitou'	–25°F (–32°C)	3 ft. (0.9 m)	4/3	white to pink	EM	similar to 'Windbeam'
Marisee', see *R. sargentianum* 'Maricee'						
Mary Fleming'	–15°F (–26°C)	3 ft. (0.9 m)	4/3/4	salmon and pink	EM	attractive plant and flower; Award of Excellence, ARS, 1973
Mi Amor'	–15°F (–26°C)	6 ft. (1.8 m)	5/3/4	white	M	bell-shaped flowers are 6 in. (15 cm) wide
Midnight Ruby'	–20°F (–29°C)	1.5 ft. (0.5 m)	—	reddish purple	M	frilled flowers
Milestone'	–15°F (–26°C)	3 ft. (0.9 m)	3/3/3	purplish red	EM	dense growth habit
Molly Fordham'	–18°F (–27°C)	4 ft. (1.2 m)	—	white	E	closest to a white 'P.J.M.'; compact growth habit
Mother Greer'	–10°F (–23°C)	1.5 ft. (0.5 m)	3–4/4/4	blue	M-ML	compact plant with brilliant blue flowers
Mrs. J. A. Withington III'	–25°F (–32°C)	4 ft. (1.2 m)	—	lavender	E	double flowers; compact plant
My Lady'	15°F (–9°C)	3 ft. (0.9 m)	4/3/3	white	E	compact growth habit
Myrtifolium'	–15°F (–26°C)	3 ft. (0.9 m)	3/5/4	pink	L	excellent growth habit; tolerates heat and sun
New Patriot'	–25°F (–32°C)	3 ft. (0.9 m)	—	purplish red	EM	deep red buds; red stems
Olga Mezitt'	–15°F (–26°C)	3 ft. (0.9 m)	—	phlox pink	EM	well-branched, upright plant
Olive'	–15°F (–26°C)	4 ft. (1.2 m)	3/3/3	orchid pink	VE	vigorous plant; Award of Merit, RHS, 1942
Patty Bee'	–5°F (–21°C)	1.5 ft. (0.5 m)	—	clear yellow	EM	small leaves; good growth habit
Penheale Blue'	0°F (–18°C)	4 ft. (1.2 m)	—	violet blue	EM	vigorous grower
Pink Diamond', see 'Weston's Pink Diamond'						
Pink Drift'	–10°F (–23°C)	1.5 ft. (0.5 m)	4/4/3	pinkish plum	EM	cinnamon-colored foliage; very floriferous

Table A4. Rhododendron hybrids: lepidote (continued)

NAME	COLD HARDINESS	HEIGHT IN 10 YEARS	QUALITY RATING	FLOWER COLOR	FLOWERING SEASON	COMMENTS
'Pink Snowflakes'	0°F (–18°C)	2 ft. (0.6 m)	4/4/3	pink to white	E	very attractive plant; new foliage bronze-red
'Pioneer'	–25°F (–32°C)	4 ft. (1.2 m)	4/3/4	rose-pink	VE	semi-deciduous; upright grower; very floriferous
'Pioneer Silvery Pink'	–25°F (–32°C)	4 ft. (1.2 m)	—	clear pink	E	blooms two weeks later than 'Pioneer'
'Pipit'	0°F (–18°C)	1 ft. (0.3 m)	3/3/1	reamy pink	EM	difficult to grow
'P.J.M.'	–25°F (–32°C)	4 ft. (1.2 m)	4/4/4	lavender pink	E	very easy to grow; tolerates sun and cold
'P.J.M. Elite'	—	—	—	—	—	selected form of 'P.J.M'
'Praecox'	–5°F (–21°C)	4 ft. (1.2 m)	3/3/3	lilac	E	upright growth habit; Award of Garden Merit, RHS, 1926; First Class Certification, RHS, 1978
'Princess Anne'	–10°F (–23°C)	2 ft. (0.6 m)	4/4	yellow	EM	compact growth habit; very floriferous
'Purple Gem'	–25°F (–32°C)	2 ft. (0.6 m)	3/4/3	purple	EM	new foliage blue
'Ramapo'	–20°F (–29°C)	2 ft. (0.6 m)	3/4/4	pinkish violet	EM	good foliage plant; more compact in sun
'Red Quest'	–10°F (–23°C)	2–3 ft. (0.6–0.9 m)	—	light red	E	compact grower
'Rose Elf'	5°F (–15°C)	1.5 ft. (0.5 m)	3/4/3–4	orchid pink	E	well-clothed dwarf; extremely floriferous
'Rose Marie'	5°F (–15°C)	4 ft. (1.2 m)	—	purple	M	very floriferous
'Saffron Queen'	20°F (–7°C)	4.5 ft. (1.4 m)	4/3	yellow	EM	upright growth habit
'Sapphire'	–5°F (–21°C)	2.5 ft. (0.8 m)	3/3/3–4	light blue	EM	dwarf; bushy, round plant; small flowers
'Senora Meldon'	0°F (–18°C)	5 ft. (1.5 m)	—	blue	E	upright growth habit; fragrant flowers
'Seta'	0°F (–18°C)	5 ft. (1.5 m)	4/3/3	light pink	E	deeper pink stripe on back of flowers; Award of Merit, RHS, 1933; First Class Certificate, RHS 1960
'Shrimp Pink' ('Shrimp Girl')	0°F (–18°C)	3 ft. (0.9 m)	2/3	rose	M	compact, slow grower
'Small Gem'	–5°F (–21°C)	1.5 ft. (0.5 m)	3/3/4	white	E	very floriferous
'Snow Lady'	0°F (–18°C)	2.5 ft. (0.8 m)	3/4/4	white	E	floriferous even in shade
'Southland'	–10°F (–23°C)	1.5 ft. (0.5 m)	—	salmon	M	flowers tolerant to heat
'Spring Delight'	–20°F (–29°C)	2 ft. (0.6 m)	—	purplish pink	EM	well-branched plant; broader than tall

ble A4. Rhododendron hybrids: lepidote (continued)

ME	COLD HARDINESS	HEIGHT IN 10 YEARS	QUALITY RATING	FLOWER COLOR	FLOWERING SEASON	COMMENTS
ring Song'	−10°F (−23°C)	2 ft. (0.6 m)	—	light yellow	E-EM	
Judy'	−10°F (−23°C)	2 ft. (0.6 m)	4/4	yellow	EM	compact growth habit; very floriferous
fany'	−15°F (−26°C)	2.5 ft. (0.8 m)	3−4/3/4	pink	M	apricot and yellow in flower throat; good foliage
m Koenig'	−10°F (−23°C)	2.5 ft. (0.8 m)	3/3	pink	EM	
whead' ('Tow Head')	−15°F (−26°C)	1 ft. (0.3 m)	3/4/3	greenish yellow	EM	small, almost round leaves
alley'	−25°F (−32°C)	5 ft. (1.5 m)	3/3/3	shrimp	E	vigorous, upright grower
altham'	−18°F (−27°C)	1 ft. (0.3 m)	—	pink	M	low-growing, compact plant, wider than tall; grow in shade
ee Bee'	5°F (−15°C)	1 ft. (0.3 m)	4/4/4	red	EM	well branched; wider than tall
eston's Pink amond'	−10°F (−23°C)	5 ft. (1.5 m)	—	light fuchsia-purple	E	upright growth habit; double flowers
igeon'	0°F (−18°C)	3 ft. (0.9 m)	—	pink	M	saucer-shaped flowers; Award of Merit, RHS, 1982
ilsonii'	−15°F (−26°C)	3 ft. (0.9 m)	3/3/4	rosy pink	L	spreading growth habit; sun tolerant
indbeam'	−25°F (−32°C)	4 ft. (1.2 m)	4/3/4	light pink	EM	very hardy; easy to grow
yanoki'	−15°F (−26°C)	3 ft. (0.9 m)	3/3−4/4	white	M	very floriferous
llow Eye'	−20°F (−29°C)	3 ft. (0.9 m)	—	white	EM	upright, vigorous growth habit
llow Hammer'	0°F (−18°C)	4 ft. (1.2 m)	4/3/4	deep yellow	EM	upright growth habit; tolerates sun

Azalea Hybrid Groups: A Brief Description

Back Acres Hybrids—B. Y. Morrison, of Pass Christian, Mississippi, developed the Back Acres Hybrids after his retirement from the USDA. Largely an extension of his work with the Glenn Dale Hybrids, Morrison's purpose was to develop late-blooming, bordered, and double-flowering clones. Most of the 370 clones selected for testing bloom mid to late midseason, tolerate high temperatures, and are bud hardy in zone 7b.

Belgian Indian Hybrids—Developed as indoor or greenhouse plants, these hybrids are generally tender. The principal parent is *R. simsii*, usually incorrectly identified as 'Indica'. Hardiness is listed as zones 9–10, and some clones are more cold hardy.

The Rutherford Hybrids originated in Rutherford, New Jersey, during the 1920s as an extension of the Belgian Indian Hybrid line. Plants are spreading, compact, medium in height (6–8 ft., 1.8–2.4 m) and very floriferous, blooming from early to late midseason. Most are hardy to zone 9 and a few to zone 7a.

Beltsville Hybrids—Developed and introduced by Guy E. Yerkes and Robert L. Pryor of the USDA, Beltsville, Maryland, Station. Parents include *R. kaempferi*, 'Firefly', 'Indicum Album', 'Maxwell', and 'Snow'. The objective was to produce greenhouse azaleas as well as hardy outdoor types. All Beltsville Hybrids are hardy in zones 7a–8b.

Brooks Hybrids—Leonard L. Brooks of Modesto, California, developed these hybrids using Belgian and Southern Indian Hybrids crossed on 'Ledifolium Album' and various Kurume Hybrids. Most flower midseason, are medium in height (4–6 ft., 1.2–1.8 m), and are cold hardy in zone 8.

Carla Hybrids—The Carla Hybrids were developed at North Carolina State University and Louisiana State University. Program objectives are cold hardiness, the development of resistance to root rot diseases, floriferousness, and drought resistance. Seventeen clones have been introduced to date, and the program continues at North Carolina State University. Carla Hybrids are hardy in zones 7b–9a.

Carlson Hybrids—Hybrids of *R. ripense* var. *mucronatum* selected by Bob and Jan Carlson of South Salem, New York. The Carlson Hybrids were selected for their low, spreading habit and reach 2–3 ft. (0.6–0.9 m) tall in 10 years. Plants are hardy in zone 7a.

Chisolm-Merritt Hybrids—Developed in 1934 by the late Julian J. Chisolm and later introduced by the late Dr. E. I. Merritt. These hybrids were derived using *R. yedoense* var. *poukhanense* and 'Cleopatra' as seed parents and crossed by numerous pollen parents. Plants bloom early to midseason and are of compact growth habit. All plants are hardy in zones 7a–9.

Eden Hybrids—The Eden Hybrids were developed by the late W. David Smith at Spring Grove, Pennsylvania. His goals were to produce large flower size, a wide color range, and plants cold hardy in zone 6. Most are still under observation, and cold hardiness has not been established.

Encore Hybrids—Mr. Robert "Buddy" Lee of Independence, Louisiana, developed the Encore Hybrids. The azaleas differ by forming flower buds on new wood as well as on mature wood. This feature changes their bloom sequence, so that they bloom heavily in spring and again in the fall, with scattered blooms throughout the summer. Most Encore cultivars flower heaviest in the fall, when an extended flowering period occurs. The Encore azaleas are cold hardy to about 0°F (–18°C), zone 7, and will survive in zone 6 with protection. Plants have dense, dark green foliage, making a good appearance in the landscape.

Gable Hybrids—These plants were developed and introduced by the late Joseph B. Gable of Stewartstown, Pennsylvania. His objective was to improve quality and cold hardiness in evergreen azaleas. The species *R. yedoense* var. *poukhanense* and *R. kaempferi* were used for hardiness, and other parents, including the Kurume Hybrids, were used for other characteristics. The resulting clones are among the hardiest, most widely adapted evergreen azaleas and are widely used in the landscape and as parents in other hybridizing programs. Plants are of medium size and hardy in zones 6b–8b.

Girard Hybrids—Starting with Gable Hybrids and later using his own seedlings, the late Peter Girard Sr. of Geneva, Ohio, began a hybridizing program in the late 1940s. His efforts resulted in the development of some of the most cold hardy evergreen azaleas available today. Plants are medium growers, 4–6 ft. (1.2–1.8 m) in height, and are hardy in zones 6a–9b. See also deciduous Girard Hybrids.

Glenn Dale Hybrids—Developed by the late B. Y. Morrison, former chief of the Plant Introduction Section and Director of the National Arboretum, USDA. The Glenn Dale Hybrids represent an extensive and diverse breeding program.

Nine principal species and clones were used as parents, and more than 70,000 seedlings were grown. From this group 454 clones were selected.

The plants exhibit wide diversity in flower color, bloom from early to late season, and vary in height from 3 to 8 ft. (0.9 to 2.5 m). Breeding objectives were to develop plants with large flowers, cold hardiness, and an extended bloom period. The objectives were met because the Glenn Dale Hybrids have large flowers and are hardy in zones 6b–9a. A few clones are hardy to –10°F (–23°C).

Harris Hybrids—Hybridized by James Harris of Lawrenceville, Georgia, most of the Harris Hybrids bloom late midseason and have large flowers. Parents include hybrids of the Kaempferi, Satsuki, and Glenn Dale series. Plants are cold hardy in zones 7b–9a.

Hershey Hybrids—Hybridized and introduced by Ralph Hershey and his son Everett Hershey, these represent an extension of the Kurume Hybrids and have similar characteristics. Hershey Hybrids are hardy in zones 6b–9b.

H. R. Schroeder Hybrids—Developed by the late Dr. H. R. Schroeder of Evansville, Indiana, in the early 1970s. The goal was to develop compact, evergreen azaleas adapted to the cold, harsh climate of the American Midwest. Plants flower midseason and are hardy in zone 5b.

Kaempferi Hybrids—The species *R. kaempferi* and the azalea clone 'Malvatica' are the principal parents of this hybrid group originally developed in The Netherlands. *Rhododendron kaempferi* was introduced into the United States in 1892 by Prof. C. S. Sargent of the Arnold Arboretum, where it was later used in hybridizing. Plants are medium to tall (4–10 ft., 1.2–3.0 m) and bloom early to midseason with large flowers. *Rhododendron kaempferi* and its hybrids are often used to transmit cold hardiness. These hybrids are hardy in zones 5b–9a.

Kehr Hybrids—Developed by a retired plant geneticist from the USDA, Dr. August Kehr, of Hendersonville, North Carolina. He introduced four outstanding azalea clones. They are medium size plants. Cold hardiness varies from 10 to 0°F (–12 to –18°C), zones 6a–7a.

Kerrigan Hybrids—Developed by Howard Kerrigan of Hayward, California, using Belgian Indian and Kurume Hybrids as parents. Plants are upright, 3–5 ft. (0.9–1.5 m) high, and are hardy in zones 8b–10.

Kurume Hybrids—Originating near the city of Kurume on the Island of Kyushu, Japan, this is one of the oldest hybrid groups. There is some confusion regarding parentage, but Fred C. Galle states in *Azaleas* (1987), "They were probably crosses of R. *sataense* and R. *kiusianum*." The Kurume Hybrids represent one of the largest hybrid groups and are widely used in the landscape. Plants grow slowly yet ultimately reach heights up to 6 ft. (1.8 m). Flowers are single or hose-in-hose. Kurume Hybrids are adapted in zones 6b–9a.

Linwood Hardy Hybrids—Dr. Charles Fisher, Jr., of Linwood, New Jersey, began developing evergreen azaleas for greenhouse forcing in 1950, and in 1953 G. Albert Reid took over the program and focused on development of hardy varieties. Parentage is very diverse, including Kurume and Kaempferi Hybrids as well as Indian greenhouse cultivars. Most plants are hardy in zones 7 and 8, with a few hardy to zone 6a.

Mossholder-Bristow Hybrids—The Gold Cup Hybrids were developed by Owen R. Bristow of San Bernardino, California, as greenhouse forcing azaleas. Parents used were Belgian Indian and Rutherford Hybrids. Plants are medium in size, 4–6 ft. (1.2–1.8 m) tall, and are hardy in zone 8.

North Tisbury Hybrids—Selected by Mrs. Julian (Polly) Hill of Martha's Vineyard, Massachusetts, from seed and cuttings sent by Dr. Tsuneshige Rokujo, Tokyo, Japan. The North Tisbury Hybrids are generally low-growing, groundcover hybrids of R. *nakaharae*. Others are developed from seed of 'Gumpo' collected in a friend's garden in Tokyo, Japan. Most are hardy in zones 6b–9a.

Pericat Hybrids—Developed by Alphonse Pericat of Collingdale, Pennsylvania, as greenhouse forcing plants. Parentage is unknown. Plants are of medium height, 3–5 ft. (0.9–1.5 m) tall, and have a dense growth habit. Flowers show much variation, including single, hose-in-hose, semi-double, and petaloid. Pericat Hybrids are hardy in zones 7a–9b.

Pride Hybrids—Orlando Pride started hybridizing in 1928 using a seedling plant obtained from Joe Gable. Most of his azalea selections came from this seedling, which was later named 'Nadine'. Plants are medium to tall, 6–8 ft. (1.8–2.5 m), and hardy in zones 6a–8b.

Robinhill Hybrids—Robert Gartrell of Wyckoff, New Jersey, had as his goal to produce hardy, late-blooming azaleas with flower size comparable to the Satsuki Hybrids. Most Robinhill Hybrids bloom mid to late midseason, are 3–5 ft. (0.9–1.5 m) high, and are hardy in zones 6b–9b.

Satsuki Hybrids—Highly revered by the Japanese, the Satsuki Hybrids were developed using principally R. *indicum* and R. *eriocarpum* (syn. R. *tamurae*) as parents. They are among the most diverse group of hybrids, presenting a wide range of flower color and growth habit. The first hybrids occurred naturally in the wild and were used along with other species in development. The Satsuki Hybrids were widely used as parents in hybridizing the Glenn Dale, Robinhill, and Harris Hybrids. Blooming period is late, and flowers are generally single with widely variable color patterns even on the same plant. Satsuki Hybrids are hardy in zones 7a–9b, and a few are hardy in zone 6.

Shammarello Hybrids—Developed and introduced by the late A. M. (Tony) Shammarello. These hybrids were tested in the harsh climate of South Euclid, Ohio, are among the hardiest of evergreen azaleas. *Rhododendron yedoense* var. *poukhanense* and *R. kaempferi* were widely used as parents. Plants are hardy in zones 5a–9b.

Southern Indian Hybrids—The Belgian Indian Hybrids were highly prized in the southern United States, and local hybridizing and selection gave birth to the Southern Indian Hybrids. Though not all plants are hybrids, they are all similar to the earlier Belgian Indian Hybrids.

Southern Indian Hybrids can be assigned to two groups based on size and blooming period: an early-blooming group that is faster growing, up to 10 ft. (3.0 m) tall, and a later-blooming, more compact group ultimately reaching 8 ft. (2.5 m) tall. The Southern Indian Hybrids are more cold hardy than the Belgian Indian Hybrids, being hardy in zones 8a–10a.

Vuyk Hybrids—Developed in the Netherlands by Aart Vuyk using principally *R. kaempferi* in an effort to produce hardier evergreen azaleas. The Vuyk Hybrids have large flowers, bloom early to midseason, and are adapted in zones 5b–9a.

Table A5. Evergreen azalea species

NAME	USDA HARDINESS ZONES	HEIGHT IN 10 YEARS	FLOWER COLOR	FLOWERING SEASON	COMMENTS
indicum (formerly *macranthum*)	7a–10a	1–4 ft. (0.3–1.2 m)	pink, red, orange, or white	L	commonly sold as 'Macranthum' and 'Balsaminiflorum'; many forms in trade
kaempferi	5b–9a	6–8 ft. (1.8–2.4 m)	red to yellowish pink	M-L	many forms available; widely used in hybridizing
kiusianum	7a–8b	1–2 ft. (0.3–0.6 m)	purple, red, or pink	M	requires good soil drainage; white form also available
ripense var. *mucronatum*	7a–9b	6–8 ft. (1.8–2.4 m)	white	EM	cultured in Japan for more than 300 years; not found in the wild
nakaharae	6b–9a	1–2 ft. (0.3–0.6 m)	reddish orange	L	excellent ground cover
oldhamii	8a–9a	6–10 ft. (1.8–3.0 m)	reddish orange	M-L	recommended for summer flowers in warm climates
serpyllifolium	6a–8b	3 ft. (0.9 m)	light pink	—	requires well-drained soil; white form also available
simsii	8a–9a	6 ft. (1.8 m)	pink to red	—	parent of the Belgian Indian Hybrids
stenopetalum	7a–8b	3–4 ft. (0.9–1.2 m)	purple	EM	requires well-drained soil; fragrant flowers
yedoense	6a–9b	4–6 ft. (1.2–1.8 m)	light purple	—	deciduous in colder climates; fragrant flowers; double flowering forms also available
yedoense var. *poukhanense*	6a–9b	5–6 ft. (1.5–1.8 m)	purple	E	flowers single; excellent for cold climates; pink form also available

Table A6. Evergreen azalea hybrids

NAME	USDA HARDINESS ZONES	HEIGHT IN 10 YEARS	FLOWER COLOR	FLOWERING SEASON	COMMENTS
'Addy Wery'	6a–8a	4 ft. (1.2 m)	—	EM	upright habit; Kurume Hybrid
'Adelaine Pope'	7a–8a 5°F (–15°C)	4–5 ft. (1.2–1.5 m)	purplish red	—	dense, upright grower; Carla Hybrid
'Adonis'	—	—	white	E	hose-in-hose, frilled; Kurume Hybrid
'Aladdin'	—	—	vivid red	E	Kurume Hybrid
'Alexander'	6a–8a –10°F (–23°C)	3 ft. (0.9 m)	reddish orange	VL	ground-cover plant; North Tisbury Hybrid
'Ambrosia'	7–9a	ultimate height 8 ft. (2.4 m)	yellowish pink	E	spreading habit
'Amoenum'	6b–9a 0°F (–18°C)	6–8 ft. (1.8–2.4 m)	purplish red	EM	spreads up to 15 ft. (4.5 m); *R. obtusum* group

Table A6. Evergreen azalea hybrids (continued)

NAME	USDA HARDINESS ZONES	HEIGHT IN 10 YEARS	FLOWER COLOR	FLOWERING SEASON	COMMENTS
'Amy'	—	—	pink	—	compact grower; glossy foliage; flower double; Kurume Hybrid
'Anna Kehr'	6b–8a 0°F (–18°C)	2 ft. (0.6 m)	pink	M	easy to grow, compact plant; Kehr Hybrid
'Atlanta'	—	2–3 ft. (0.6–0.9 m)	reddish purple	—	Kaempferi Hybrid
'Azuma Kagami' ('Pink Pearl')	6b–8a	—	strong pink	E	hose-in-hose; Kurume Hybrid
'Beni Kirishima'	6b–8a –5°F (–21°C)	4 ft. (1.2 m)	orange-red	—	excellent azalea; flower double; Satsuki Hybrid
'Ben Morrison'	7a–9a 5°F (–15°C)	5 ft. (1.5 m)	scarlet and white	EM	beautiful bicolor scarlet; USDA Hybrid
'Big Joe'	6b–8b	4 ft. (1.2 m)	purplish pink	EM	spreading habit; Gable Hybrid
'Bixby'	6a–8a	2 ft. (0.6 m)	vivid red	LM	spreading habit; semi-evergreen
'Blaauw's Pink'	6a–8a	5 ft. (1.5 m)	yellowish pink	E	hose-in-hose flower; Kurume Hybrid
'Blue Danube'	6b–8a	4 ft. (1.2 m)	violet	M	easy to grow; excellent foliage; Vuyk Hybrid
'Boudoir'	6b–8a	—	purplish red	—	introduced by Old Kent Nursery; Gable Hybrid
'Buccaneer'	6b–9a	5 ft. (1.5 m)	orange-red	E	erect; best in afternoon shade; Glenn Dale Hybrid
'Cameo'	—	—	light pink	L	hose-in-hose; Gable Hybrid
'Caroline Gable'	6b–8a	4 ft. (1.2 m)	vivid red	LM	hose-in-hose; Gable Hybrid
'Carrie Amanda'	5a–8a –15°F (–26°C)	2 ft. (0.6 m)	white	M	purplish pink border; very compact
'Cascade' (Glenn Dale Hybrid)	—	4 ft. (1.2 m)	white	E	upright grower; hose-in-hose; Glenn Dale Hybrid
'Cascade' (Shammarello Hybrid)	6a–8b –10°F (–23°C)	2 ft. (0.6 m)	white	M	R. yedoense var. poukhanense hybrid; Shammarello Hybrid
'Cavalier'	6b–9a	6 ft. (1.8 m)	yellowish pink	E	dense, bushy plant; Glenn Dale Hybrid
'Cloud Nine'	8b	4 ft. (1.2 m)	white	—	flowers double; Kerrigan Hybrid
'Conversation Piece'	6b–8a 0°F (–18°C)	2 ft. (0.6 m)	light pink	M	flowers vary in color, Robinhill Hybrid
'Corsage'	5b–8a –15°F (–26°C)	5 ft. (1.5 m)	purple	E	fragrant, very floriferous; Gable Hybrid
'Daphne'	6b–8a	—	white with purple edge	E	Kurume Hybrid
'Dayspring'	6b–9a –5°F (–21°C)	6 ft. (1.8 m)	white center, purple edge	M	striking floral display; Glenn Dale Hybrid
'Debonnaire'	6a–8a	3 ft. (0.9 m)	vivid pink	LM	flower petal edge deeper pink; Back Acres Hybrid

Table A6. Evergreen azalea hybrids (continued)

NAME	USDA HARDINESS ZONES	HEIGHT IN 10 YEARS	FLOWER COLOR	FLOWERING SEASON	COMMENTS
'Delaware Valley White'	6b–8b −5°F (−21°C)	3 ft. (0.9 m)	white	EM	hardier form of *R. indicum* f. *album*
'Delos'	6b–9a	ultimate height 7 ft. (2.1 m)	purplish pink	M	heavy texture; double flowers
'Desiree'	6a–8b −10°F (−23°C)	5 ft. (1.5 m)	white	EM	flowers frilled; Shammarello Hybrid
'Diana'	6b–8a	5 ft. (1.5 m)	yellowish pink	EM	hose-in-hose; Kurume Hybrid
'Dorothy Clark'	7a–9a 0°F (−18°C)	3 ft. (0.9 m)	light pink	—	light red border on flowers; Harris Hybrid
'Dream'	7a–9a 0°F (−18°C)	6 ft. (1.8 m)	purplish pink	E	spreading habit; frilled flowers; Glenn Dale Hybrid
'Easter Parade'	8a–10a	4 ft. (1.2 m)	light pink	M	semi-double hose-in-hose flower; Mossholder-Bristow Hybrid
'Edna'	6b–8a	—	pink	E	large flowers; Yavorsky Hybrid
'Eikan'	7a–9b	3 ft. (0.9 m)	white with pink stripe	ML	vigorous, spreading habit; Satsuki Hybrid
'Elizabeth Gable'	6b–8b −5°F (−21°C)	4 ft. (1.2 m)	red	L	flowers frilled; Gable Hybrid
'Eliza Hyatt'	5b–8a −15°F (−26°C)	2 ft. (0.6 m)	light pink	M	flowers double; H. R. Schroeder Hybrid
'Elsie Lee'	5b–8a −15°F (−26°C)	3 ft. (0.9 m)	orchid	LM	flowers semi-double; Shammarello Hybrid
'Eureka'	7a–8b 0°F (−18°C)	3 ft. (0.9 m)	light purplish pink	—	hose-in-hose; spreading habit; Beltsville Hybrid
'Everest'	7a–9a	4 ft. (1.2 m)	white	M	broad, spreading habit; Glenn Dale Hybrid
'Fascination'	7a–9a	4 ft. (1.2 m)	light pink with red edge	EM	Harris Hybrid
'Fashion'	7a–9a	5 ft. (1.5 m)	pink	E	purple blotch in flower, hose-in-hose; Glenn Dale Hybrid
'Fedora'	6b–9a	5 ft. (1.5 m)	purplish pink	M	Kaempferi Hybrid
'Festive'	6b–9a	5 ft. (1.5 m)	white	E	flowers striped purplish red; Glenn Dale Hybrid
'Flamingo'	—	5 ft. (1.5 m)	deep pink	LM	hose-in-hose; Brooks Hybrid
'Forest Fire'	6b–8b	4 ft. (1.2 m)	deep pink	—	hose-in-hose; Gable Hybrid
'Gaiety'	7a–9a	ft. (1.2 m)	purplish pink	EM	flowers single with darker blotch; Glenn Dale Hybrid
'Gay Paree'	8b–10	3 ft. (0.9 m)	white	—	dark red edge on flower petals; Kerrigan Hybrid
'George Lindley Tabor'	8a–10a	3 ft. (0.9 m)	white to purple	M	Southern India Hybrid

Table A6. Evergreen azalea hybrids (continued)

NAME	USDA HARDINESS ZONES	HEIGHT IN 10 YEARS	FLOWER COLOR	FLOWERING SEASON	COMMENTS
'Girard's Border Gem'	6a–9a −10°F (−23°C)	2 ft. (0.6 m)	deep pink	E	dwarf; dense growth habit; Girard Hybrid
'Girard's Chiara'	5b–9a −15°F (−26°C)	3 ft. (0.9 m)	purplish pink	EM	hose-in-hose, flowers ruffled; Girard Hybrid
'Girard's Fuchsia'	6a–9a −10°F (−23°C)	3 ft. (0.9 m)	deep reddish purple	EM	wavy lobes on flowers; Girard Hybrid
'Girard's Hot Shot'	6b–9a −5°F (−21°C)	2 ft. (0.6 m)	reddish orange	EM	wavy lobes on flowers; Girard Hybrid
'Girard's Pleasant White'	6a–8a	3 ft. (0.9 m)	white	L	upright grower
'Girard's Rose'	6a–9a 0°F (−18°C)	2 ft. (0.6 m)	deep pink	EM	wavy lobes on flowers; Girard Hybrid
'Girard's Scarlet'	5b–9 −15°F (−26°C)	2 ft. (0.6 m)	strong red	EM	deep red blotch on flower; Girard Hybrid
'Glacier'	6b–9a	5 ft. (1.5 m)	white	E	dark green foliage; Glenn Dale Hybrid
'Glamour'	6b–9a	5 ft. (1.5 m)	rose red	E	beautiful, dark green leaves; Glenn Dale Hybrid
'Gumpo'	6b–9b	1 ft. (0.3 m)	pink, red, or white	L	various color selections; Satsuki Hybrid
'Guy Yerkes'	7a–8b	5 ft. (1.5 m)	pink	—	hose-in-hose; Beltsville Hybrid
'Hampton Beauty'	7a–9b	5 ft. (1.5 m)	deep pink	EM	partially petaloid sepals; Pericat Hybrid
'Hardy Gardenia'	7a–9b	5 ft. (1.5 m)	white	ML	double, gardenia-like flowers; Linwood Hybrid
'Helen Curtis'	5b–9 −15°F (−26°C)	3 ft. (0.9 m)	white	ML	semi-double flowers; Shammarello Hybrid
'Helena'	—	4 ft. (1.2 m)	yellowish pink	—	vivid red blotch; Eden Hybrid
'Herbert'	6a–8b −10°F (−23°C)	4 ft. (1.2 m)	reddish purple	EM	hose-in-hose, frilled flowers; Gable Hybrid
'Hershey's Red'	6b–9b −5°F (−21°C)	2 ft. (0.6 m)	red	EM	outstanding grower; Hershey Hybrid, Kurume type
'H. H. Hume'	7a–8b	—	white	—	hose-in-hose, 2-in. (5-cm) flowers; Beltsville Hybrid
'Hilda Niblett'	6b–9b	1 ft. (0.3 m)	pink	M	low, spreading habit; different color on individual flowers
'Hino Crimson'	7b–9a −5°F (−21°C)	2 ft. (0.6 m)	bright crimson	E	sun tolerant; excellent plant
'Hinode giri'	6b–8a −5°F (−21°C)	3 ft. (0.9 m)	rose-crimson	E	easy to grow; Kurume Hybrid
'Hinomayo'	6b–8a	5 ft. (1.5 m)	purplish pink	EM	Kurume Hybrid
'Hino Pink'	6a–8b −10°F (−23°C)	3 ft. (0.9 m)	purplish pink	EM	Shammarello Hybrid

Table A6. Evergreen azalea hybrids (continued)

NAME	USDA HARDINESS ZONES	HEIGHT IN 10 YEARS	FLOWER COLOR	FLOWERING SEASON	COMMENTS
'Hino Red'	5b–8b −15°F (−26°C)	1.5 ft. (0.5 m)	medium red	EM	very hardy; Shammarello Hybrid
'Ima Shojo' ('Christmas Cheer')	—	5 ft. (1.5 m)	rose red	E	hose-in-hose; Kurume Hybrid
'Irohayama'	6b–8a	2 ft. (0.6 m)	white	—	Kurume Hybrid
'Iveryana'	8a–10a	2 ft. (0.6 m)	white	L	deep red flecks in flower petals; Southern Indian Hybrid
'James Gable'	6a–8b −10°F (−23°C)	2 ft. (0.6 m)	strong red	EM	hose-in-hose; darker blotch; Gable Hybrid
'Jean Haerens'	—	—	white	M	purplish red edge on flower petals; Belgian Indian Hybrid
'John Cairns'	5b–9a	4 ft. (1.2 m)	vivid red	EM	hybridized at Exbury; Kaempferi Hybrid
'Karens'	4b–8a −25°F (−32°C)	4 ft. (1.2 m)	reddish purple	E	wavy, fragrant flowers; tolerates pH 7; Kurume Hybrid
'Kathleen' (Gable Hybrid)	—	—	light pink	—	
'Kathleen' (Glenn Dale Hybrid)	6b–9a −5°F (−21°C)	4 ft. (1.2 m)	yellowish pink	L	spreading habit
'Kirin' ('Coral Bells')	6b–8a	2 ft. (0.6 m)	strong pink	E	Kurume Hybrid
'Koromo Shikibu'	—	—	purplish pink	—	straplike flower petals
'Leo'	6b–8a	2 ft. (0.6 m)	vivid orange	LM	Exbury Hybrid
'Lorna'	6b–8a −5°F (−21°C)	3 ft. (0.9 m)	pink	L-M	beautiful, double flowers; reliable; Gable Hybrid
'Louise Gable'	6a–8a −5°F (−21°C)	5 ft. (1.5 m)	salmon	M	very dependable; large, semi-double flowers; Gable Hybrid
'Madame Butterfly'	—	6 ft. (1.8 m)	light purple	M	tall; strong grower
'Margaret Douglas'	7a–8a	4 ft. (1.2 m)	light pink	M-L	deep, yellowish pink edge on flower petals; Back Acres Hybrid
'Marion Lee'	—	—	red and white	M	Glenn Dale; bicolor
'Marjorie'	6a–8a −10°F (−23°C)	4 ft. (1.2 m)	reddish purple	M	Pride Hybrid
'Marjorie Ann'	7a–9b 0°F (−18°C)	3 ft. (0.9 m)	salmon	EM	Pericat; hose-in-hose
'Martha Hitchcock'	6b–9a −5°F (−21°C)	4 ft. (1.2 m)	white	EM	reddish purple edge on flower petals; Glenn Dale Hybrid
'Mary Dalton'	6b–8b −5°F (−21°C)	6 ft. (1.8 m)	reddish orange	EM	hose-in-hose; Gable Hybrid
'May Belle'	6a–8b −10°F (−23°C)	1.5 ft. (0.5 m)	deep pink	LM	semi-double flowers; Shammarello Hybrid

Table A6. Evergreen azalea hybrids (continued)

NAME	USDA HARDINESS ZONES	HEIGHT IN 10 YEARS	FLOWER COLOR	FLOWERING SEASON	COMMENTS
'Midnight Flair'	—	—	dark red	—	vigorous growth habit
'Mildred Mae'	6b–8b −5°F (−21°C)	4 ft. (1.2 m)	reddish purple	EM	spreading, large grower; Gable Hybrid
'Misty Plum'	—	—	white	—	purple margins; funnel-shaped flowers
'Modesty'	6b–9a	5 ft. (1.5 m)	purplish red	E	flowers flushed purplish pink from center; Glenn Dale Hybrid
'Moonbeam'	6b–9a	5 ft. (1.5 m)	white	M	frilled flower margins; Glenn Dale Hybrid
'Mother's Day'	6b–8a	2.5 ft. (0.8 m)	vivid red	EM	hose-in-hose to semi-double flowers; Kurume Hybrid
'Mrs. G. G. Gerbing'	8a–10a	5 ft. (1.5 m)	white	M	large flowers; Southern Indian Hybrid
'Mrs. Henry Schroeder'	6b–7a	1.5 ft. (0.5 m)	purplish pink	M	very double flowers
'Mrs. Nancy Dipple'	5b–7a	2 ft. (0.6 m)	pale pink	ML	double flowers; H.R. Schroeder Hybrid
'Nadine'	6a–8b	6 ft. (1.8 m)	light pink	—	not widely distributed; Pride Hybrid
'Nancy of Robinhill'	6b–9b	2 ft. (0.6 m)	light pink	ML	semi-double flowers; Robinhill Hybrid
'Naomi'	6b–8a	5 ft. (1.5 m)	strong pink	LM	Exbury/Kaempferi Hybrid
'Olga Niblett'	6b–9b	4 ft. (1.2 m)	white	LM	flowers have a yellow cast; vigorous grower
'Orange Beauty'	5b–9a	4 ft. (1.2 m)	light orange	EM	Kaempferi Hybrid; Kurume Hybrid by the same name
'Palestrina'	6a–9a −10°F (−23°C)	5 ft. (1.5 m)	white	E	syn. 'Wilhelmina Vuyk'; Vuyk Hybrid
'Parfait'	7a–9a −10°F (−23°C)	3.5 ft. (0.9 m)	pink	LM	slight fragrance; hose-in-hose, ruffled flowers; Kaempferi Hybrid
'Phyllis Moore'	7a–9a −5°F (−21°C)	—	white	—	upright, spreading habit; hose-in-hose
'Pink Ruffles'	9a–10a	6 ft. (1.8 m)	deep pink	M	semi-double, hose-in-hose; Rutherford Hybrid
'Polaris'	6b–8a	2.5 ft. (0.8 m)	white	LM	hose-in-hose; Gable Hybrid
'Pride's Pink'	6a–8a	—	pink	L	introduced shortly before 1990, not widely distributed; Pride Hybrid
'Pure Perfection'	7–8a	2 ft. (0.6 m)	white	L	hose-in-hose; wavy flowers
'Purple Splendor'	6a–8a	3 ft. (0.9 m)	reddish purple	EM	similar to 'Herbert'; Gable Hybrid
'Red Red'	5b–8b	3 ft. (0.9 m)	strong, deep red	EM	Shammarello Hybrid
'Red Ruffles'	9a–10a	6 ft. (1.8 m)	strong red	M	semi-double, hose-in-hose; Rutherford Hybrid
'Refrain'	6b–9a	6 ft. (1.8 m)	white and purplish pink	E	hose-in-hose; Glenn Dale Hybrid
'Renee Michelle'	6a–8a	3 ft. (0.9 m)	deep pink	ML	red spotting in flowers

ble A6. Evergreen azalea hybrids (continued)

ME	USDA HARDINESS ZONES	HEIGHT IN 10 YEARS	FLOWER COLOR	FLOWERING SEASON	COMMENTS
ɔbinhill Gillie'	6b–9b	2–3 ft. (0.6–0.9 m)	reddish orange	M	dwarf; broad; rounded
ɔehr's Peggy Ann'	6b–9a	—	white	L	purplish pink petal edge; Kaempferi Hybrid
ɔsebud'	6a–8a	2 ft. (0.6 m)	pink	M-L	double, hose-in-hose; Gable Hybrid
ɔse Greeley'	6a–8a	3 ft. (0.9 m)	white	E	hose-in-hose, fragrant; Gable Hybrid
ɑkata Red'	6b–9a	2.5 ft. (0.8 m)	vivid red	E	Kurume Hybrid
chroeder's ɑvender Rose'	5a–8a −15°F (−26°C)	2 ft. (0.6 m)	purplish pink	M	semi-double flowers
chroeder's ɑn Ray'	5a–8a	2 ft. (0.6 m)	purplish pink	M	compact habit
eneca'	6b–9a	5 ft. (1.5 m)	strong purple	E	ascending branches; Glenn Dale Hybrid
herwoodii' ɕherwood Orchid')	6b–8a	4 ft. (1.2 m)	reddish purple	EM	darker blotch in flower; Kurume Hybrid
herwood Red'	6b–8a	2 ft. (0.6 m)	vivid red	E	heavy bloomer; Kurume Hybrid
ɪr Robert'	6b–9b	1.5 ft. (0.5 m)	light purplish pink	—	dwarf Robinhill Hybrid; flowers with sectoring and stripes
ʰow'	6b–8a	2 ft. (0.6 m)	white	E	hose-in-hose; Kurume Hybrid
ɔringtime'	6a–8a	4 ft. (1.2 m)	purplish red, purplish pink	EM	one of the best pinks; Gable Hybrid
ɕtarlight' ɕerrigan Hybrid)	8b–10a	4 ft. (1.2 m)	yellowish pink	—	semi-double; Kerrigan Hybrid
ɕtarlight' ɕarlson Hybrid)	4a–8a	2–3 ft. (0.6–0.9 m)	yellowish pink	M	Carlson Hybrid
tewartstonian'	5b–8a	5 ft. (1.5 m)	vivid red	EM	reddish winter foliage; Gable Hybrid
ɕunglow'	7b–9b	4 ft. (1.2 m)	purplish red	—	rounded, upright grower; Carla Hybrid
ɕurprise'	6b–9a	3 ft. (0.9 m)	medium red	—	flower margins irregular white; Glenn Dale Hybrid
ɕusan Camille'	—	2 ft. (0.6 m)	pale pink	—	semi-double flowers
ɕadition'	7a–9a −5°F (−21°C)	3 ft. (0.9 m)	pink	M	hose-in-hose
ɕwenty Grand'	7a–9b −5°F (−21°C)	2–3 ft. (0.6–0.9 m)	reddish violet, salmon	E	spreading habit
ɕespers'	6b–9a	5 ft. (1.5 m)	white	M	purplish red stripes in flowers; Glenn Dale Hybrid
ʰuyk's Rosyred'	6b–8a	3 ft. (0.9 m)	deep pink	EM	2.5- to 3-in. (6.3- to 7.6-cm) flowers; Vuyk Hybrid
ʰuyk's Scarlet'	5a–8a	4 ft. (1.2 m)	deep red	EM	2.5- to 3-in. (6.3- to 7.6-cm) flowers; Vuyk Hybrid

Table A6. Evergreen azalea hybrids (continued)

NAME	USDA HARDINESS ZONES	HEIGHT IN 10 YEARS	FLOWER COLOR	FLOWERING SEASON	COMMENTS
'Wakaebisu'	7a–8a	1.5 ft. (0.5 m)	medium red	—	very pale throat, dark blotch in flower Kurume Hybrid
'Ward's Ruby'	7a–8a	—	strong red	E	one of the best reds; Kurume Hybrid
'White Rosebud'	6a–8b	4 ft. (1.2 m)	white	M	double flower, fragrant; Kehr Hybrid
'Williamsburg'	7a–8a	3 ft. (0.9 m)	white	—	flowers mixed with pink; hose-in-hose
'Yankee Doodle'	5b–9a	—	pink	M	introduced by Abbott; Kaempferi Hybrid

Deciduous Azalea Hybrids

Most deciduous azaleas are very cold hardy (from zone 5b) and heat tolerant (through zones 7–8).

Beasley Hybrids—Developed and introduced by George, Mary, and Jeffrey Beasley of Lavonia, Georgia. The Beasley Hybrids are derived from the following North American species: *R. arborescens*, *R. atlanticum*, *R. calendulaceum*, *R. cumberlandense*, *R. periclymenoides*, and *R. viscosum*. Most plants are hardy to zone 5b.

Carlson Hybrids—Clones of the North American species were selected by Bob and Jan Carlson in an effort to extend the blooming season into summer. All plants are hardy to zone 4b.

Ghent Hybrids—These hybrids were developed in Ghent, Belgium, using *R. calendulaceum*, *R. luteum*, *R. molle* ssp. *japonicum*, *R. molle* ssp. *molle*, *R. periclymenoides*, and *R. viscosum*. Flower color is white, pale yellow, and red. Ghent Hybrids grow up to 8–10 ft. (2.5–3.0 m) high and 6–8 ft. (1.8–2.5 m) wide. Plants are hardy in zones 4b–8a.

Girard Hybrids—These hybrids were developed at Girard Nurseries principally from Knap Hill Hybrids. The goal was to establish mildew resistance, ease of propagation, and heat resistance. Flower color runs the full color range for deciduous azaleas, and some clones have double flowers. Plants are hardy in zones 5a–8a. See also evergreen Girard Hybrids.

Knap Hill Hybrids—Developed by Anthony Waterer in England in 1870 at the Knap Hill Nursery, Knap Hill, Woking, England. Knap Hill Hybrids have been used extensively in further hybridizing. The goal has been to improve the Ghent Hybrids by crossing with the Chinese azalea *R. molle* ssp. *molle* and several other species. Knap Hill Hybrids are generally medium to large, 4–10 ft. (1.2–3.0 m) high and 4–6 ft. (1.2–1.8 m) wide. Flower colors are white, yellow, orange, pink, and red. Plants bloom mid to late midseason and are hardy in zones 5a–8a.

There are five subgroups of Knap Hill Azaleas: the Knap Hill, Exbury, Ilam, Slocock, and Windsor. The Exbury Hybrids are an extension of the Knap Hill Hybrids selected by Lionel de Rothschild of Exbury, Southampton, England. The Ilam Hybrids are an extension of the Knap Hill Hybrids by Edgar Stead of Ilam Estate, Christchurch, New Zealand. Ilam Hybrids have slightly larger flowers.

Leach Hybrids—Developed by David G. Leach of North Madison, Ohio, from cold hardy species and hybrids of North American deciduous azaleas. The Leach Hybrids are cold hardy to zone 4b. Plants are medium to tall, 6–8 ft. (1.8–2.5 m) high and 4–6 ft. (1.2–1.8 m) wide.

Mollis Hybrids—Originating in Belgium, the Mollis Hybrids are derived and selected from the Japanese azalea *R. molle* ssp. *japonicum* and the Chinese azalea *R. molle* ssp. *molle*. Plants bloom mid to late season in colors of white, yellow, orange, pink, and red. Most plants are tall and upright to 8 ft. (2.5 m) and 6 ft. (1.8 m) wide. Mollis Hybrids are hardy in zones 5b–8a.

Occidentale Hybrids—These hybrids of the western azalea, *R. occidentale*, native to the west coast of North America, first originated in England and Belgium and later in Tacoma, Washington. Occidentale Hybrids are tall plants, 8–10 ft. (2.5–3.0 m) in height. Flowers are fragrant, light in color with a yellow blotch, and appear in mid to late summer. Plants are hardy in zones 7a–8b.

Rustica Flora Pleno Hybrids—Originating in Belgium; parentage of these hybrids is unknown. Plants are tall and upright, 6–8 ft. (1.8–2.5 m) high, and 5 ft. (1.5 m) wide. Plants are hardy in zones 6b–8.

Slonecker Hybrids—Developed by Howard Slonecker from Knap Hill Hybrids. The goal was to produce deciduous azaleas adapted to the west coast of North America. Plants are 4–8 ft. (1.2–2.5 m) high and 3–5 ft. (0.9–1.5 m) wide. Slonecker Hybrids are hardy to zones 5b–8a.

Weston Hybrids—Developed at Weston Nurseries of Hopkinton, Massachusetts, with the goal of improving cold hardiness. Plants are 6–8 ft. (1.8–2.5 m) high and 4–6 ft. (1.2–1.8 m) wide. Weston Hybrids are adapted to zones 4b–8a.

Table A7. Deciduous azalea species

NAME	USDA HARDINESS ZONES	HEIGHT IN 10 YEARS	FLOWER COLOR	FLOWERING SEASON	COMMENTS
R. alabamense	6b–9a	2–6 ft. (0.6–1.8 m)	white	LM	stoloniferous; yellow blotch in flower
R. albrechtii	6b–8a	6–8 ft. (1.8–2.4 m)	purplish red	E	bell-shaped flowers; prefers woodlands
R. arborescens	5a–9a	to 15 ft. (4.5 m)	white	ML	yellow blotch in flower; fragrant
R. atlanticum	6a–9a	1–2 ft. (0.3–0.6 m)	white	M	known as the coast azalea; flowers fragrant
R. austrinum	6b–10a	to 15 ft. (4.5 m)	pink and yellow	E	flowers fragrant; probably the yellow form is the original
R. calendulaceum	5b–8b	6–12 ft. (1.8–3.6 m)	yellow to red	L	known as the flame azalea; wide color range; a tetraploid
R. canadense	3b–7a	3–4 ft. (0.9–1.2 m)	purplish pink	E	stoloniferous; prefers soils of low pH (4.5)
R. canescens	6b–10a	to 15 ft. (4.5 m)	white	M	sometimes stoloniferous; prefers moist woodlands
R. cumberlandense	5b–8b	2–18 ft. (0.6–5.4 m)	red and orange	L	small, deep green leaves; 'Camp's Red' is a selected clone
R. cumberlandense 'Camp's Red'		5 ft. (1.5 m)	strong red	L	species selection of *R. cumberlandense*
R. flammeum (formerly *speciosum*)	6b–9a	2–10 ft. (0.6–3.0 m)	orange to red	E-M	stoloniferous
R. luteum	6b–8a	to 12 ft. (3.6 m)	yellow	M	flowers fragrant; not widely grown in North America
R. mariesii	–	8 ft. (2.4 m)	pale reddish purple	E	upright; not common
R. molle	6b–8a	4–6 ft. (1.2–1.8 m)	yellow	E	erect; less cold hardy than *R. japonicum*
R. molle ssp. *japonicum*	5a–8b	4–6 ft. (1.2–1.8 m)	yellow, orange, and red	E-M	often confused with *R. molle*
R. occidentale	7a–9b	6–15 ft. (1.8–4.5 m)	white, yellow, or pink	M	flowers fragrant; not heat tolerant
R. pentaphyllum	6b–8b	4 ft. (1.2 m)	strong pink	E	slow to flower; white form also available
R. periclymenoides (formerly *nudiflorum*)	4b–9a	4–6 ft. (1.2–1.8 m)	pale to deep pink	E-M	white form also available
R. prinophyllum (formerly *roseum*)	4b–9a	6–15 ft. (1.8–4.5 m)	pink	M	known as the pinkshell azalea; clove-scented flowers
R. prunifolium	7a–9b	6–15 ft. (1.8–4.5 m)	orange to red	VL	prefers partial shade
R. quinquefolium	6a–8b	3 ft. (0.9 m)	white	E	five-whorled leaves often have reddish margin

Table A7. Deciduous azalea species (continued)

NAME	USDA HARDINESS ZONES	HEIGHT IN 10 YEARS	FLOWER COLOR	FLOWERING SEASON	COMMENTS
R. reticulatum	6b–8a	—	strong purple	E	
R. schlippenbachii	5a–9a	10–15 ft. (3.0–4.5 m)	light purplish pink	VE	known as the royal azalea; prefers a slightly acid soil (pH 6.5)
R. serrulatum	7a–10a	to 15 ft. (4.5 m)	white	L	clove-scented flowers; not included in *R. viscosum*
R. vaseyi	5a–9a	to 15 ft. (4.5 m)	pink	E	white form also available
R. viscosum	4b–9a	3–15 ft. (0.9–4.5 m)	white	M-L	stoloniferous; flowers have a spicy fragrance
R. wadanum	6–9	5 ft. (1.5 m)	deep purple	EM	listed with *R. reticulatum*

Table A8. Deciduous azalea hybrids

NAME	USDA HARDINESS ZONES	HEIGHT IN 10 YEARS	FLOWER COLOR	FLOWERING SEASON	COMMENTS
'Admiral Semmes'	—	—	yellow	—	Confederate Series; heat tolerant; mildew resistant
'Annabella'	5a–8a	—	strong orange-yellow	—	Exbury Hybrid
'Arneson Gem'	—	—	yellow-orange	EM	outside of flowers red
'Aurora'	5b–8a	to 8 ft. (2.4 m)	orange	EM	Mollis Hybrid; more heat tolerant than Knap Hill Hybrids
'Balzac'	—	—	reddish orange	—	fragrant; Knap Hill Hybrid
'Beaulieu'	5a–8a	—	cream	M	orange blotch in flower; Knap Hill Hybrid
'Berryrose'	5a–8a	4 ft. (1.2 m)	vivid yellow	M	fragrant; Exbury Hybrid
'Bouquet de Flore'	5b–8a	to 10 ft. (3.0 m)	vivid red	L	yellow blotch, frilled flowers; Ghent Hybrid
'Brazil'	5a–8a	5 ft. (1.5 m)	reddish orange	M	frilled flowers; very dependable; Knap Hill Hybrid
'Bullfinch'	5a–8a	5 ft. (1.5 m)	deep red	LM	Knap Hill Hybrid
'Buttercup'	5a–8a	—	yellow	LM	Knap Hill Hybrid
'Buzzard'	5a–8a	—	pale yellow	M	flowers tinged pink, fragrant; Knap Hill Hybrid
'Cannon's Double'	5a–8a	—	yellowish white	M	double flowers, pink lobes; Exbury Hybrid
'Cecile'	5a–8a	5 ft. (1.5 m)	salmon, pink, and yellow	LM	orange-yellow blotch in flower; Exbury Hybrid

Table A8. Deciduous azalea hybrids (continued)

NAME	USDA HARDINESS ZONES	HEIGHT IN 10 YEARS	FLOWER COLOR	FLOWERING SEASON	COMMENTS
'Cheerful Giant'	5b –8a	4 ft. (1.2 m)	bright yellow	M	
'Chetco'	6a–8a	4 ft. (1.2 m)	vivid yellow	M	Slonecker Hybrid
'Chicago'	5b–8a	to 10 ft. (3.0 m)	light reddish orange	M	Mollis Hybrid
'Christopher Wren'	5b–8a	3 ft. (0.9 m)	bright yellow		Mollis Hybrid
'Coccinea Speciosa'	5b–8a	—	yellowish pink	LM	strong orange blotch in flower; Ghent Hybrid
'Corneille'	5b–8a −15°F (−26°C)	—	pink	LM	Ghent Hybrid; double flowers
'Corringe'	5b–8a	6–10 ft. (1.8–3.0 m)	pink	LM	flowers double; Ghent Hybrid
'Crimson Tide'	6b–8a	—	red	—	flowers double; Girard Hybrid
'Daviesii'	5b–8a	6–10 ft. (1.8–3.0 m)	pale yellow	L	Ghent Hybrid
'Delicatissima'	7a–9	—	yellowish white	M-L	yellow blotch in flower; Occidentale Hybrid
'Evening Glow'	—	—	deep red	—	Mollis Hybrid
'Fanny'	5b–8a	6 ft. (1.8 m)	purplish pink	EM	upright grower; Ghent Hybrid
'Fireball'	5a–8a	—	fiery red	M	upright growth habit; Knap Hill Hybrid
'Fraseri'	—	3 ft. (0.9 m)	purplish pink	E	twiggy growth habit
'George Reynolds'	5a–8a	—	yellow	EM	Knap Hill Hybrid
'Gibraltar'	5a–8a	4 ft. (1.2 m)	vivid orange	M	very popular and easy to grow; Exbury Hybrid
'Ginger'	5a–8a	—	strong orange	—	Exbury Hybrid
'Girard's Yellow Pom Pom'	5b–8a	3 ft. (0.9 m)	vivid yellow	—	hose-in-hose
'Golden Crest'	5a–8a	—	brilliant yellow	—	orange blotch in flower; Knap Hill Hybrid
'Golden Eagle'	5b–8a		tall reddish orange	M	Knap Hill Hybrid
'Golden Flair'	5b–8a		tall yellow	—	Knap Hill Hybrid
'Golden Horn'	—	—	golden yellow	—	Knap Hill Hybrid
'Golden Lights'	3a–8a −35°F (−37°C)	3 ft. (0.9 m)	orange yellow	ML	*R. atlanticum* hybrid; very fragrant
'Golden Oriole'	5a–8a	—	brilliant yellow	EM	deep orange blotch in flower; Knap Hill Hybrid
'Golden Peace'	5a–8a	—	yellow	—	strong orange blotch in flower; Exbury Hybrid
'Golden Sunset'	5a–8a	—	vivid yellow	M	Knap Hill Hybrid
'Goldflakes'	5a–8a	4 ft. (1.2 m)	vivid yellow	EM	strong orange blotch in flower; Bovee–Knap Hill Hybrid

Table A8. Deciduous azalea hybrids (continued)

NAME	USDA HARDINESS ZONES	HEIGHT IN 10 YEARS	FLOWER COLOR	FLOWERING SEASON	COMMENTS
'Homebush'	5a–8a	6 ft. (1.8 m)	rose pink	LM	semi-double flowers; Knap Hill Hybrid
'Ilam Copper Cloud'	5a–8a	—	orange	—	flowers frilled; Leach Hybrid
'Ilam Peachy Keen'	—	low	light pink	—	dwarf; compact habit; Leach Hybrid
'Ilam Persian Melon'	—	—	orange red	—	compact habit
'Ilam Red Velvet'	—	—	deep red	—	petals slightly turned back; Wells Hybrid
'Irene Koster'	7a–9	8 ft. (2.4 m)	white	M	flowers flushed pink, fragrant; Occidentale Hybrid
'Jolie Madam'	5b–8a	—	pink	LM	upright habit; orange yellow blotch; from Holland
'Kathleen'	5a–8a	—	light orange	LM	darker blotch in flower; Exbury Hybrid
'Kilauea'	5a–8a	—	reddish orange	L	compact, dense habit; Knap Hill Hybrid
'King's Red'	—	—	vivid red	M	large ball truss; difficult to root
'Klondyke'	5a–8a	—	strong orange	LM	orange-yellow blotch in flower; Exbury Hybrid
'Koster's Brilliant Red'	5b–8a	—	reddish orange	M	Mollis Hybrid; single flowers
'Lemon Drop'	4a–8a	6 ft. (1.8 m)	vivid yellow	VL	fragrant; Weston Hybrid
'Magnifica'	7a–9a	8 ft. (2.4 m)	purplish red	LM	orange-yellow blotch in flower; Occidentale Hybrid
'Marina'	5a–8a	—	pale yellow	EM	deeper yellow blotch in flower; Exbury Hybrid
'Marion Merriman'	5a–8a	—	brilliant yellow	LM	vivid orange blotch in flower; Knap Hill Hybrid
'Marydel'	—	—	white with purple margins	L	Polly Hill selection from hybrid population of *atlanticum* × *periclymenoides*
'Melford Red Letter'	5b–8a	—	reddish orange	M	Ilam Hybrid
'Mrs Betty Oliver'	5a–8b	—	pastel pink	EM	Occidentale Hybrid; highly scented
'Mt. St. Helens'	—	—	pink	M	yellow and orange blotch in flower; Girard Hybrid
'My Mary'	5b–8a	—	light yellow	EM	fragrant; stoloniferous; Beasley Hybrid
'Nancy Waterer'	5b–8a	6 ft. (1.8 m)	vivid yellow	LM	Ghent Hybrid
'Narcissiflorum'	5b–8a	6 ft. (1.8 m)	light yellow	LM	flowers double; Ghent Hybrid
'Norma'	—	—	reddish orange	LM	flowers edged in deep pink; Rustica Flora Pleno Hybrid

Table A8. Deciduous azalea hybrids (continued)

NAME	USDA HARDINESS ZONES	HEIGHT IN 10 YEARS	FLOWER COLOR	FLOWERING SEASON	COMMENTS
Northern Lights Hybrids	4a–8a	—	—	—	group of very cold hardy hybrids developed at the University of Minnesota
'Old Gold'	5a–8a	—	light orange	LM	flower flushed pink; Exbury Hybrid
'Orangeade'	5a–8a	—	orange	LM	Knap Hill Hybrid
'Orient'	5a–8a	—	reddish orange	LM	orange blotch in flower; Exbury Hybrid
'Oxydol'	—	—	white	—	Exbury Hybrid
'Parade'	5b–8a	6 ft. (1.8 m)	red	L	Weston Hybrid; fragrant
'Peachy Keen' ('Ilam Peachy Keen')	5b–8a	—	light pink	M	Ilam Hybrid
'Persian Melon' ('Ilam Persian Melon')	5a–8a	—	orange-yellow	—	large truss; Ilam Hybrid
'Persil'	5a–8a	—	white	M	pale yellow blotch in flower; Knap Hill Hybrid
'Prince Henri de Pays-Bas'	5a–8a	6–8 ft. (1.8–2.4 m)	strong orange	L	upright grower; Ghent Hybrid
'Princess Royal'	—	—	white with yellow blotch	—	Knap Hill; flowers flushed pink
'Queen Emma' ('Koningin Emma')	—	—	light orange	—	Mollis Hybrid
'Raphael de Smet'	5a–8a	6 ft. (1.8 m)	white with pink edge	LM	upright growth habit; flowers double
'Red Sunset' ('Arneson Red')	—	—	vivid red	ML	
'Renne'	—	—	vivid red	—	Knap Hill Hybrid; flowers suffused yellow
'Royal Command'	5a–8a	6 ft. (1.8 m)	reddish orange	M-L	Knap Hill Hybrid
'Rufus'	—	—	dark red	—	Wells Hybrid; bronzed leaves
'Satan'	—	—	vivid red	L	Knap Hill Hybrid
'Sham's Yellow'	5a–8a	6 ft. (1.8 m)	light yellow	M	Knap Hill– Shammarello Hybrid; scented; mildew resistant
'Snowbird'	—	—	white	M	natural hybrid; scented
'Spek's Orange'	5a–8a	4 ft. (1.2 m)	red, tinged orange	—	orange blotch in flower; Mollis Hybrid
'Strawberry Ice'	5a–8a	—	yellowish pink	—	Exbury Hybrid
'Sun Chariot'	—	—	vivid yellow	L	Knap Hill; First Class Certificate, 1967; Award of Merit, 1963
'Sunte Nectarine'	5a–8a	—	deep orange	M	yellow blotch in flower; Exbury Hybrid

able A8. Deciduous azalea hybrids (continued)

AME	USDA HARDINESS ZONES	HEIGHT IN 10 YEARS	FLOWER COLOR	FLOWERING SEASON	COMMENTS
uperbum'	7a–9	—	dark pink	—	orange blotch in frilled flowers; Occidentale Hybrid
weet Christy'	5a–8a	3 ft. (0.9 m)	yellow	E	mildew resistant; fragrant; frilled; Exbury Hybrid
ylphides'	—	—	purplish pink	—	vivid yellow blotch; Knap Hill Hybrid
oucan'	—	—	pinkish white	LM	upright, open grower; Knap Hill Hybrid
ower Dainty'	5b–8a	—	pale pink	—	fragrant; Ghent Hybrid
unis'	—	—	dark red	—	Knap Hill Hybrid
Jnique'	5b–8a	6 ft. (1.8 m)	orange-yellow	LM	upright grower; Ghent Hybrid
ineland Gold'	—	2.5 ft. (0.8 m) in 5 years	orange yellow	L	
iscosepalum'	—	—	pale cream	—	Ghent Hybrid
Washington State entennial'	6a–8a	5 ft. (1.5 m)	purplish pink	M	fragrant; upper lobe is yellow; Occidentale Hybrid
Weston's Innocence'	—	—	white with a yellow flare	L	Weston Hybrid; mildew resistant; fragrant
Windsor Appleblossom'	—	—	pink and white	—	orange blotch; red autumn leaves
Windsor Buttercup'	—	—	light yellow	—	Windsor Hybrid
ellow Cloud'	5a–8a 0°F (–18°C)	3.5 ft. (1.1 m)	light yellow	—	(Knap Hill) Don Hyatt Hybrid; fragrant

Rhododendrons Tolerant to Drought, Heat, and Sun

Drought-Tolerant Rhododendrons

Symptoms of heat damage and drought stress are often difficult to separate because both climatic conditions often occur simultaneously. Because moisture is necessary for evaporative cooling, which lowers leaf temperature by 10–15°F (6–9°C), drought and the resulting loss of moisture to leaves increases heat damage.

Plants listed in Table B1 were selected based on visible plant response in my garden to the severe drought of 2002. Response was measured by severity of damage observed as number of dead branches. Some branch dieback was due to drying out of roots, in which case most of the plant was affected.

Much of the damage was caused by the fungus *Botryosphaeria* affecting single branches. In general, drought-stressed plants are much more susceptible to disease. Did branches die because of the drought or because of susceptibility to *Botryosphaeria*? Both are probably responsible. Some severely wilted and drought-stressed plants showed no sign of branch dieback, while plants at the same site and equally stressed died back severely. When some plants are stressed they succumb to twig blight, whereas others do not. Plants that did not die back fully recovered after the drought. During the summer of 2003, with above-normal rainfall and cooler temperatures, no *Botryosphaeria* twig blight or any other dead branches were observed in my garden.

Plants evaluated were well established in the landscape and growing in a silt loam soil. Most plants were not irrigated during the drought. Small, recently transplanted plants were watered and some larger, severely damaged plants were watered to save them.

Table B1. Severity of branch dieback in *Rhododendron* species and cultivars during drought

NO DAMAGE	MODERATE DAMAGE (ONE TO THREE BRANCHES)	SEVERE DAMAGE (MORE THAN THREE BRANCHES)
R. degronianum ssp. *yakushimanum* (especially 'Mist Maiden')	'Acclaim'	'Artic Gold'
	'Ann Glass'	'Blue Peter'
R. maximum	'Bellringer'	'Cadis'
R. maximum var. *leachii*	'Besse Howells'	'Dorothy Amateis'
	'Brown Eyes'	'Elsie Straver'
R. minus ssp. *carolinianum*	'Calsap'	'King Tut'
R. minus var. *minus*	'County of York'	'Madras'
'Adele's Yellow'	'Daphne'	'Mrs. P. den Ouden'
'Albert Close'	'David Gable'	'Mrs. T. Lowinsky'
'Alice Swift'	'Dr. Tolstead'	'Mrs. W. R. Coe'
'Alumni Day'	'Earlene'	'Nearing Pink'
'Anita Gehnrich'	'Gigi'	'Nova Zembla'
'Anna H. Hall'	'Gilbert Myers'	'Peter Alan'
'Beaufort'	'Golden Gala'	'Phyllis Korn'
'Boule de Neige'	'Golden Star'	'Scintillation
'Bravo'	'Goldfort'	'Snow's Red'
'Caroline'	'Graf Zeppelin'	'Spellbinder'
'Chionoides'	'Great Smokey'	'Sumatra'
'Crete'	'Hallelujah'	'Wheatley'
'Dora Amateis'	'Hatchfield'	'Yaku Duchess'
'Double Dip'	'Henry Yates'	'Yaku Queen'
'Dr. Percel'	'Ice Cube'	
'English Roseum'	'Ida Bradour'	
'Fantastica'	'Independence Day'	
'Ginny Gee'	'Janet Blair'	
'Golfer'	'Late Beginning'	
'Great Eastern'	'Leah Yates'	
'Holden'	'Leann'	
'James Burchett'	'Lee's Dark Purple'	
'John Walter'	'Lodestar'	
'Judy Spillane'	'Lord Roberts'	
'Katherine Dalton'	'Madame Masson'	
'Malta'	'Mardi Gras'	
'Marchioness of Landsdowne'	'Mary Belle'	
'Marie Fortie'	'Nodding Bells'	
'Mist Maiden'	'Pearce's American Beauty'	
'Molly Fordham'	'Pink Flourish'	
'Mountain Marriage'	'Professor Amateis'	
'Olga Mezitt'	'Red Companion'	
	'Royal Purple'	

Table B1. Severity of branch dieback in *Rhododendron* species and cultivars during drought (continued)

NO DAMAGE	MODERATE DAMAGE (ONE TO THREE BRANCHES)
'Parker's Pink'	'Shaazam'
'Party Pink'	'Spring Parade'
'Pioneer'	'Tom Everett'
P.J.M. Group	'Trude Webster'
'Porzellan'	'Vernus'
'Roseum Pink'	'Wilmer Delp'
'Royal Princess'	'Windbeam'
'Solidarity'	'Wynterset White'
'Tony'	'Yaku Duke'
'Yaku Princess'	'Yaku King'

There is considerable difference between cultivars in drought tolerance and in susceptibility to Botryosphaeria. These observations should be of some value to the gardener, especially for the plants listed under no damage and those under severe damage in Table B1. The moderate damage group may shift either way if all variables in soil moisture were removed, and most are satisfactory plants. The drought conditions under which these observations were made were among the worst ever recorded in most of Maryland and much of the mid-Atlantic and northeastern United States.

Heat-Tolerant Rhododendrons

Studies now show that continued heat into the night tends to weaken rhododendrons and increase the incidence and progression of disease. Plants that are more efficient in evaporative cooling through transpiration of water from leaves are more heat tolerant than other plants. The cooling effect of evaporation of water may lower leaf temperatures 10–15°F (6–9°C) below the ambient air temperature. The gardener can also assist in lowering plant leaf temperature by providing shade and by misting plant leaves.

To maintain evaporative cooling, plants must have a constant source of water. Soil water can be made more plentiful and available to plant roots by incorporating organic matter into the soil and by placing a mulch on the soil surface to help lower soil temperature and decrease moisture loss from the soil. Soil moisture and a vigorous root system are vital to evaporative cooling.

Heat tolerance can be bred into plants. Rhododendron species such as *R. hyperythrum*, well known for its heat tolerance, are available to the hybridizer.

Rhododendrons Tolerant to Drought, Heat, and Sun

The well-known species *R. catawbiense* has two forms: a high-elevation form and the lower-elevation form, *R. catawbiense* f. *insularis*, which grows under higher temperature conditions. It was hoped this form would be a source of heat tolerance for hybridizing. Research has shown no advantage over the high-elevation form, in fact the form *insularis* appears inferior to the mountain form in heat tolerance and overall vigor, perhaps due to inbreeding within a small genetic pool. The following rhododendron species appear to be the most heat tolerant.

R. *dauricum*
R. *degronianum* ssp. *yakushimanum*
R. *hyperythrum*
R. *minus* (Carolinianum Group)
R. *minus* var. *minus*

Dr. Leonard Miller of Grove, Oklahoma, has evaluated rhododendron hybrids for heat tolerance in a location where temperatures often exceed 100°F (38°C); in 2001 temperatures exceeded 100°F (38°C) more than 20 days. Miller's plants are irrigated, so drought stress can be removed from the equation, resulting in a more accurate measure of heat tolerance. Plants are sited under afternoon shade. Only plants listed as top performers were taken from Miller's list.

R. smirnowii × *R. yakushimanum*
'Azurro'
'Besse Howells'
'Blinklicht'
'Bravo'
'Cadis'
'Charles Loomis'
'City Park'
'Consolini's Windmill'
'Dexter's Giant Red'
'English Roseum'
'Fantastica'
'Gigi'
'Gloxineum'
'Goldflimmer'
'Gomer Waterer'
'Governor's Mansion'
'Ingrid Mehlquist'
'Jim Lynch'
'Kalinka'

'King Tut'
'Kokardia'
'Lavender Queen'
'Lisenne Rockefeller'
'Mardi Gras'
'Marlis'
'Maxecat'
'Michel Smith'
'Mikkeli'
'Mist Maiden'
'Mrs. Tom Lowinsky'
'Mrs. W. R. Coe'
'Nova Zembla'
'Peppermint Twist'
'Polaris'
'President Lincoln'
'Roseum Elegans'
'Roseum Pink'
'Russell Harmon'
'Sneezy'

'Solidarity'   'Tom Everett'
'Sonatine'   'Vivacious'
'Supernova'   'Vulcan'
'Tiana'   'Wynterset White'

──────────── Heat-Tolerant Rhododendrons: Central Maryland, ────────────
30–40 days above 90°F (32°C)

R. degronianum ssp. *yakushimanum*   'Holden'
R. hyperythrum   'Ice Cube'
R. minus (Carolinianum Group)   'James Burchett'
R. minus var. *minus*   'Janet Blair'
'Albert Close'   'Mist Maiden'
'Album Elegans'   'Mountain Marriage'
'Alumni Day'   'Mrs. Charles S. Sargent'
'Anah Kruschke'   'Myrtifolium'
'Bellringer'   'Parker's Pink'
'Bravo'   'Pioneer'
'Brown Eyes'   P.J.M. Group
'Cadis'   'Purpureum Elegans'
'Caroline'   'Roseum Elegans'
'Chionoides'   'Roseum Pink'
'Crete'   'Spring Parade'
'David Gable'   'Vernus'
'English Roseum'   'Waltham'
'Fantastica'   'Wynterset White'
'Great Eastern'

Heat-Tolerant Deciduous Azalea Hybrids

Many deciduous azaleas are not heat tolerant. Among others, Dr. Eugene Aromi has hybridized Exbury Hybrid azaleas with native heat-tolerant species to develop new heat-tolerant hybrids. The following have been found to tolerate heat well and grow well in zones 6–9 (Bryan 2003).

'Aromi Sunny Side Up'   'Frontier Gold'
'Aromi Sunrise'   'Pink Carousel'
'Aromi Sunstruck'   'Red Pepper'

Sun-Tolerant Rhododendrons

Damage from the sun is caused primarily by heat buildup in the leaves. Leaf temperatures under full sun can be considerably higher than when plants are in shade. The following rhododendrons are relatively tolerant of sun.

'A. Bedford'
'Aglo'
'Albert Close'
'Album Elegans'
'Album Novum'
'America'
'Anah Kruschke'
'Anna H. Hall'
'Artic Gold'
'Belle Heller'
'Bluenose'
'Blue Peter'
'Boule de Neige'
'Bravo'
'Cadis'
'Calsap'
'Catawbiense Boursault'
'Catawbiense Grandiflora'
'Chapmanii Wonder'
'Chionoides'
'County of York'
'Crete'
'Cunningham's White'
'Daphnoides'
'Dora Amateis'
'Dorothy Amateis'
'Double Dip'
'English Roseum'
'Fantastica'
'Gomer Waterer'

'Graf Zeppelin'
'Helen Everett'
'Ice Cube'
'James Burchett'
'Janet Blair'
'Jean Marie de Montague'
'Lee's Dark Purple'
'Lord Roberts'
'Marchioness of Lansdowne'
'Marie Fortie'
'Mrs. Charles S. Sargent'
'Myrtifolium'
'Olga Mezitt'
'Parker's Pink'
'Party Pink'
'Phyllis Korn'
'Pioneer'
P.J.M. Group
'Professor Amateis'
'Queen Anne's'
'Rocket'
'Roseum Pink'
'Spring Parade'
'Tiana'
'Tony'
'Vernus'
'Vulcan's Flame'
'Waltham'
'Yaku Princess'

Glossary

acclimation physiological adjustment by a plant to the environment

adventitious a type of bud that develops at a place other than the leaf axils

aerated containing air, primarily oxygen; usually used in reference to a soil trait, as plant roots require oxygen

allelopathy the suppression of growth of one plant species by another due to the release of toxic substances

anther the pollen-bearing structure of the flower located at the top of the stamen; common to seed plants

antibiosis antagonistic association between organisms that results in the prevention, inhibition, or destruction of one's life

ARS American Rhododendron Society

asexual a type of propagation other than sexual; for example, vegetative propagation is asexual

azaleadron a plant resulting from cross-pollination between an azalea and a rhododendron

backcrossing a hybridizing method in which a seedling is crossed (back) with one of its parents

bioagent a living organism; in this case, identified as a microorganism beneficial in disease control

biocontrol control of plant diseases by living organisms

cambium a cellular layer found between the xylem (wood) and phloem (bark); the cambium produces new cells

cation exchange capacity (CEC) a measurement used in analyzing soil that indicates the total number of exchangeable cations (positively charged particles); reflects the soil capacity to fix and hold nutrients as cations

chelated a mineral in soluble form

chlorosis a disease condition producing a yellowing of the foliage; leaves fail to develop chlorophyll because of nutrient deficiencies or disease; photosynthesis is reduced, causing a weakening of the plant; in extreme cases plant death occurs

compost plant material and animal manures after partial breakdown by microorganisms; very beneficial to soil and plants when dug into or placed on top of the soil as mulch

corolla the petals of a flower

cultivar a clone or individual plant form identified by a particular name; a contraction of "cultivated variety"

deadheading removal of spent flowers to prevent seed set

deciduous a type of plant that loses its leaves at the end of the growing season

diploid refers to chromosome count; a diploid plant has the normal number of chromosomes, one set from each parent; for *Rhododendron* this is 26 chromosomes

dormancy a state of rest in plants when no visible active growth occurs

elepidote one of two major classifications of rhododendron; describes a type of rhododendron that lacks small scales on the underside of the leaf and usually has large leaves

epiphyte a type of plant that grows on another plant or object but is not parasitic; derives nutrients from air, rainwater, and organic matter without growing in the soil

Ericaceae the family of plants including rhododendrons and azaleas; ericaceous plants grow best in acid soil conditions

flocculation the clumping together of soil particles to form larger masses; soil structure is improved by this process

fritted refers to fertilizers having a protective surface that delays nutrient release into the soil; time-released fertilizer

genus taxonomic classification ranking between the family and the species, comprising structurally or phylogentically related species

glomalin a material of high carbon content formed by mycorrhizae on plant roots; acts as a glue to stick soil particles together and improve soil tilth

gravitational pull the force exerted by gravity on the movement of soil water

hardening off the process of adapting a new, tender plant to environmental differences; involves lowering humidity from 100 percent to levels normally encountered outdoors and gradually introducing wind, sunlight, and temperature variations

heat days days when the ambient temperature reaches 86°F (30°C) or higher; important in determining heat damage to plants

heterogeneous differing in kind and exhibiting pronounced variability

hose-in-hose a flower type with two rows of petals, one appearing inside the other

hybrid a plant that represents the combined characteristics of its two parents; typically heterogeneous

indumentum a hairy or woolly texture exhibited on leaf and bud surfaces

ion electrified particle; *see* cation exchange capacity

leached refers to fertilizer that is diluted and removed from the plant area by rain or irrigation water

lepidote one of two major classifications of rhododendrons; describes a type of rhododendron that has small scales on the underside of the leaf

medium (pl. media) refers to growing mixture or mixtures with or without soil

Microfoam trademarked name for a blanket used to insulate plant material during winter storage

mycorrhizae (pl.) beneficial fungi living on the roots of rhododendrons and other plants

pathogenic refers to any disease-causing agent

petaloid a flower in which some or all stamens have converted to flower petals, resulting in hose-in-hose or double flowers

pH a logarithmic scale used to measure effective hydrogen ions on a scale of 0–14; a rating of 7 is neutral, below 7 is acidic, above 7 is alkaline; used in determining soil acidity or alkalinity

phloem a plant tissue active in the transfer and storage of water and minerals; comprises the outer layer or bark of stems

pistil the flower part including ovary, style, and stigma

pollen sac the pollen-bearing part atop the anther

polyploid a plant having greater than the normal number of chromosomes; *see also* diploid, tetraploid

rhizosphere the soil area that surrounds and is influenced by the roots of a plant

RHS Royal Horticultural Society

scion a section of living material used in grafting to another plant; typically a short piece of detached shoot containing several buds; when grafted to a rootstock, the scion supplies the upper portion to the newly grafted plant

seed leaves the first set of leaves developed by a seedling; *see also* true leaves

sepal a modified leaf at the base of a flower; the outermost floral leaves

species taxonomic classification ranking below a genus

stigma female flower part that becomes receptive to pollen; the outermost portion of the pistil

stoloniferous a type of plant that is capable of reproducing itself by sending stolons out from its base; new plants sprout from nodes or from buds at the stolon tip

style flower part between the ovary and stigma; also called the pollen tube

tetraploid refers to chromosome count; a plant having twice the normal number of chromosomes; *see also* diploid

true leaves the second set of leaves produced by a seedling; usually indicates maturity of the seedling to transplant stage

USDA United States Department of Agriculture

xylem plant tissue located inside the cambium; the woody element of plant stems; used chiefly in conducting water and minerals, yet also serves storage and support functions

Bibliography

Bryan, Frank. 2003. Eugene Aromi, hybridizer. *The Azalean* 25(2): 300.

Chamberlain, D. F., and S. J. Rae. 1990. A revision of rhododendrons, subgenus Tsutsusi. *Edinburgh Journal of Botany* 47(2): 89–200.

Chamberlain, D. F., R. Hyann, G. Argent, G. Fearweather, and K. S. Walter. 1996. *The Genus Rhododendron.* Edinburgh: Royal Botanic Garden.

Clark, Scott. 1992. *Rhododendron Borer.* Ithaca, New York: Cornell Cooperative Extension Service.

Comis, Don. 2002. Glomalin: Hiding place for a third of the world's stored soil carbon. *USDA Agricultural Research Magazine* Sept.: 4–7.

Cox, Peter A., and Kenneth N. E. Cox. 1990. *Cox's Guide to Choosing Rhododendrons.* Portland, Oregon: Timber Press.

Coyier, Duane L., and Martha K. Roane, eds. 1986. *Compendium of Rhododendron and Azalea Diseases.* St. Paul, Minnesota: APS Press.

Davidian, H. H. 1982. *Rhododendron Species.* Vol. I, *Lepidotes.* Portland, Oregon: Timber Press.

Davidian, H. H. 1989. *Rhododendron Species.* Vol. II, *Elepidotes (Arboreum–Lactaeum).* Portland, Oregon: Timber Press.

Davidian, H. H. 1991. *Rhododendron Species.* Vol. III, *Elepidotes (Neriiflorum–Thomsonii).* Portland, Oregon: Timber Press.

Davidian, H. H. 1995. *The Rhododendron Species.* Vol. IV, *Azaleas.* Portland, Oregon: Timber Press.

Doubrasa, Nancy, and James H. Blake. 1999. *Azalea and Rhododendron Diseases.* Clemson, South Carolina: Clemson University Cooperative Extension Service.

Galle, Fred C. 1985. *Azaleas.* Portland, Oregon: Timber Press.

Galle, Fred C. 1987. *Azaleas: Revised and Enlarged Edition.* Portland, Oregon: Timber Press.

Greer, Harold E. 1996. *Greer's Guidebook to Available Rhododendrons.* Rev. ed. Eugene, Oregon: Offshoot Publications.

Harvis, John R. 1976. Root hardiness of woody ornamentals. *HortScience* 11(4): 385–386.

Hoitink, Harry A. J., and M. J. Boehm. 1999. *Biocontrol within the Context of Soil Microbial Communities: A Substrate-Dependent Phenomenon.* Columbus, Ohio: Ohio Research and Development Center, Ohio State University.

Hoitink, Harry, A. J., David Y. Han, Alexander G. Stone, Matthew S. Krause, Weizheng Zhang, and Warren H. Dick. 1997. Natural suppression. *American Nurseryman Magazine* Oct.: 90–97.

Kingdon-Ward, F. 1938. *Plant Hunters' Paradise.* London: Jonathan Cape Ltd.

Kron, Kathleen A. 1993. A revision of *Rhododendron* section *Pentanthera. Edinburgh Journal of Botany* 50(3): 249–362.

Kron, Kathleen A. 1996. Identifying the native azaleas. *The Azalean* 18(4): 72–74.

Kron, Kathleen A., and Mike Creel. 1999. A new species of deciduous azalea from South Carolina. *NOVON* 9: 377–380.

Leach, David G. 1961. *Rhododendrons of the World.* New York: Charles Scribner's Sons.

Livingston, Philip A., ed. 1978. *Hybrids and Hybridizers: Rhododendrons and Azaleas for Eastern North America.* Newtown Square, Pennsylvania: Harrowood Books.

Moorman, Gary W. 1982. *Plant Disease Facts.* University Park: The Pennsylvania State University, Department of Plant Pathology, Cooperative Extension.

Musgrave, Toby, Chris Gardner, and Will Musgrave. 1999. *The Plant Hunters.* London: Ward Lock, Willington House.

Neal, John W., Jr., and Larry W. Douglas. 1984. *Bionomics and Instar Determination of Synanthedon rhododendri (Lepidoptera: Sesiidae) on Rhododendron.* Beltsville, Maryland: USDA Agricultural Research Service.

Neal, John W., Jr., and Larry W. Douglas. 1988. *Development, Oviposition Rate, Longevity, and Voltinism of Stephanitis pyrioides (Heteroptera: Tingidae), an Adventive Pest of Azalea, at Three Temperatures.* Beltsville, Maryland: USDA Agricultural Research Service.

Pscherdt, Jay W., ed. 2002. *Rhododendron Powdery Mildew.* Corvallis, Oregon: Oregon State University Extension.

Robson, Mary. 2000. *Rhododendron Powdery Mildew.* Renton, Washington: Washington State University Cooperative Extension Service.

Salley, Homer E., and Harold E. Greer. 1992. *Rhododendron Hybrids.* 2nd ed. Portland, Oregon: Timber Press.

Shrewsbury, Paula M., and Michael J. Raupp. 2000. *Evaluation of Components of Vegetational Texture for Predicting Azalea Lace Bug, Stephanitis pyrioides (Heteroptera: Tingidae), Abundance in Managed Landscapes.* College Park, Maryland: Department of Entomology, University of Maryland.

Steponkus, Peter L., George L. Good, and Steven C. Wiest. 1976. Root hardiness of woody plants. *American Nurseryman* 144(6): 16.

Tam, Puicheung. 1983. *A Survey of the Genus Rhododendron in South China.* Hong Kong: World-Wide Publications.

Trumble, Robert B., Robert F. Denno, and Michael J. Raupp. 1995. *Management Considerations for the Azalea Lace Bug in Landscape Habitats.* College Park, Maryland: Department of Entomology, University of Maryland.

Van Veen, Ted. 1986. *Rhododendrons in America.* 2nd ed. Portland, Oregon: Binford & Mort.

Index

All plants listed here belong to the genus *Rhododendron*. Cultivars that cannot be assigned to a single species are generic cultivars and stand alone in the list (for example, *Rhododendron* 'A. Bedford'). Cultivars that can be assigned to a single species are listed below the species epithet (*R. aureum* 'Wada'). Letters in parentheses after the plant names represent the following: R, rhododendron; L, lepidote; E, elepidote; AZ, azalea; EV, evergreen; D, deciduous.

271

kiyosumense, 20
'Klondyke' (AZ, D), 51, 52, 54, 57, 58, 60,
  63, 67, 68, 69, 70, 80, 199
Knap Hill Hybrids (AZ, D), 66, 79,
  252–253
'Knap Hill Red' (AZ, D), 199
'Kokardia', 263
'Koromo Shikibu' (AZ, EV), 64
'Koster's Brilliant Red' (AZ, D), 78
Kurume Hybrids, 242–243
'K. Wada'. See *degronianum* 'K. Wada'

lace bug, 138–140, Plate 91, Plate 92
lacteum (R, E), 74
'Lady Chamberlain Apricot' (R, L), 76
'Lady Grey Egerton' (R, E), 78
'Landmark' (R, L), 58, Plate 78
landscaping
  accent plants, 93
  border plantings, 94
  color, 92
  companion plants, 97–99
  container growing, 96–97
  foundation planting, 97–98
  group planting, 93–94
  natural screens, 94–95
  spacing, 93, 94, 96
  specimen plants, 93
  woodland planting, 95–96
'Lanny's Pride' (R, L), 51
'Late Arrival' (R, E), 55
'Late Beginning', 261
'Laurie' (R, L), 58, 59
'Lavender Princess' (R, E), 55
'Lavender Queen', 263
layering, 170–171
Leach Hybrids, 253
leaf miner, 141
'Leah Yates', 261
'Leann', 261
'Leanore' (R, E), 76
'Lee's Dark Purple' (R, E), 55, 261, 265
'Lemon Drop' (AZ, D), 56, 62, 67
'Lemon Ice'. See 'Chionoides'
'Lemon Mist' (R, L), 52, 53
'Lem's Cameo' (R, E), 52, 53, 71
'Lem's Monarch' (R, E), 71
'Lem's Stormcloud' (R, E), Plate 54
'Leonard Frisbee'. See *occidentale* 'Leonard
  Frisbee'
lepidote, 11–12, 50, 122
leucaspis (R, L), 17
light, 22, 35–36

Lights Series, 67
Linwood Hardy Hybrids, 243
'Lisenne Rockefeller', 263
'Little Olga' (R, L), Plate 29
'Llenroc' (R, L), 55, 56, 58, 59, 61
'Loderi King George' (R, E), 53, 75, 76
'Loderi Venus' (R, E), 53
'Loder's White' (R, E), 52, 75, 76
'Lodestar' (R, E), 57, 61, 68, 69, 79, 261
'Lord Roberts', 261, 265
'Lorna' (AZ, EV), 58
'Louise Gable' (AZ, EV), 56, 57, 59, 72,
  78, 199
lutescens (R, L), 73, 74, 77
luteum (AZ, D), 20, 62, 65, 66, 75, 76,
  77, 79

macabeanum (R, E), 17, 76
macranthum. See *indicum*
'Macranthum'. See *indicum*
macrosepalum, 19, 54
'Madame Butterfly' (AZ, EV), 67
'Madame Masson' (R, E), 261
'Madras', 261
'Madrid' (R, E), 60
'Magnifica' (AZ, D), 77
makinoi (R, E), 54, 58, 62, 67, 68, 70, 74
'Malta' (R, L), 57, 79, 261
'Manda Sue' (R, E), 53
'Manitou' (R, L), 63
'Marchioness of Landsdowne', 261, 265
'Marcia' (R, E), 76
'Mardi Gras' (R, E), 63, 76, 261, 263
'Margaret Douglas' (AZ, EV), 51, 52, 62, 64
'Maricee'. See *sargentianum* 'Maricee'
'Marie Fortie', 261, 265
mariesii (AZ, D), 20, 69
'Mariko'. See *nakaharae* 'Mariko'
'Marina' (AZ, D), 66, 70
'Marinus Koster' (R, E), 76
'Marion Lee' (AZ, EV), 64
'Marion Merriman' (AZ, D), 69
'Marjorie Ann' (AZ, EV), 69
'Markeeta's Flame' (R, E), 52, 53
'Markeeta's Prize' (R, E), 53
'Marlis', 263
'Mars' (R, E), 201
'Martha Hitchcock' (AZ, EV), 64, 67, 69,
  199
'Mary Belle' (R, E), 58, 59, 261
'Mary Dalton' (AZ, EV), 59
'Mary Dell' (AZ, D), 70
'Marydel' (AZ, D), 83

weeds, 120, 182
weevil, 143–145, Plate 95, Plate 96
'Westbury' (R, E), 69
Weston Hybrids, 253
'Weston's Aglo' (R, L), 58, 64
'Weston's Innocence' (AZ, D), 70
'Weston's Pink Diamond' (R, L), 58, 59,
  60, 61, 67, 79
weyrichii, 20
'W.F.H.' (R, E), 75
'Wheatley' (R, E), 54, 58, 63, 67, 69, 261
whitefly, 140
'White Lady' (AZ, EV), 76
'White Lights' (AZ, D), 64, 65, 70
'White Pearl' (R, E), 72
'White Peter' (R, E), 55
'White Surprise' (R, L), 69
'Wigeon' (R, L), 65
wightii, 16
'Wilhelmina Vuyk'. See 'Palestrina'
'Willard' (R, E), 69
'Wilmer Delp', 262
'Williamsburg' (AZ, EV), 69
williamsianum (R, E), 16, 53, 65, 73, 77,
  200, 201
'Wilsonii' (R, L), 79
wind, 22, 38–39
'Windbeam' (R, L), 51, 57, 58, 61, 62,
  63, 67, 68, 69, 70, 79, 262, Plate 70,
  Plate 82

windbreak, 39, 109, 186
'Windsor Appleblossom' (AZ, D), 59
'Windsor Buttercup' (AZ, D), 54, 59
'Winsome' (R, E), 75, 77
'Wintergreen' (AZ, EV), 64
'Wojnar's Purple' (R, E), 55
'Wyandanch Pink' (R, E), 55, 63, 79
'Wyanoki' (R, L), 61, 67
'Wynterset White' (R, E), 57, 262, 264

'Yaku Duchess', 261
'Yaku Duke', 262
'Yaku Fairy'. See *keiskei* 'Yaku Fairy'
'Yaku King' (R, E), 262
'Yaku Prince' (R, E), 60, 66
'Yaku Princess', (R, E), 262, 265
'Yaku Queen' (R, E), 60, 261
yakushimanum, (R, E) 113, 136, 172, 200,
  201. See also *degronianum* ssp.
  yakushimanum
'Years of Peace' (R, E), 55
yedoense (AZ, EV), 20, 65
  var. *poukhanense* (AZ, EV), 20, 56, 57,
  58, 60, 62, 63, 69, 78, 79, 132, 199
'Yellow Cloud' (AZ, D), 70
'Yellow Eye' (R, L), 63
'Yellow Hammer' (R, L), 77
'Yomo no haru' (AZ, EV), 67
yungningense (R, L), 65
yunnanense (R, L), 53, 74

For more information and an opportunity to make wonderful friends, we invite you to join the American Rhododendron Society and the Azalea Society of America.

American Rhododendron Society
11 Pinecrest Drive
Fortuna, California 95540
(707) 725-3043
http://www.rhododendron.org

Azalea Society of America
1000 Moody Bridge Road
Cleveland, South Carolina 29635-9789
(800) 446-0428
http://www.azaleas.org